ARMSTRONG WHITWORTH

Order DT51 was for two 1A-Co-2 locomotives for the North Western Railway, India. Given Armstrong Whitworth numbers D44/5 and numbered 332 and 333 by the NWR they were completed in 1935 and No. 332 is seen here complete in Scotswood Works.

Brian Webb collection

Published by LIGHTMOOR PRESS in conjunction with
THE RAILWAY CORRESPONDENCE & TRAVEL SOCIETY
© Lightmoor Press, The Railway Correspondence & Travel Society and Brian Webb, 2010
Designed by Ian Pope
British Library Cataloguing-in-Publication Data. A catalogue record for this book is available from the British Library
ISBN: 9781899889 45 7
All rights reserved. No part of this publication may be reproduced, stored in a retrieval system or transmitted, in any form or by any means, electronic, mechanical, photocopying, recording or otherwise, without the prior written permission of the publisher.

Lightmoor Press is an imprint of
Black Dwarf Lightmoor Publications Limited
144b Lydney Industrial Estate, Harbour Road
Lydney, Gloucestershire, GL15 4EJ

Railway Correspondence & Travel Society
16 Welby Close, Maidenhead, SL6 3PY

Printed in England by Information Press, Eynsham, Oxford
www.informationpress.com

ARMSTRONG WHITWORTH

A Pioneer of World Diesel Traction

Brian Webb

Armstrong Whitworth produced a single part-articulated three-coach train set for the Sao Paulo Railway, Brazil, in 1933 to order number DT19 with the Armstrong Whitworth works number D16. It was designed for service between Santos and Sao Paulo which route included the famous Serra Incline. This was over 6¾ miles in length with several passing loops and had an average gradient of 1 in 12. It was worked by attaching a steam tank locomotive to the train, the locomotive having a gripper device which attached to the continuous rope haulage. The Armstrong Whitworth unit therefore had weight and length constraints, these being discussed in the section on Articulated Train Sets.

Brian Webb collection

CONTENTS

Acknowledgements 5
Foreword 7
Introduction 7
Armstrong Whitworth's First Diesel Railway Work 9
Oil-Electric Traction and the Diesel Traction Department 17
The First Railcars 29
The First Shunters 45
1,700 BHP for South America 55
Railcars for India 67
The Railbuses 85
Main Line Locomotives 93
The 0-4-0 Shunters 113
Articulated Train Sets 131
Large 0-6-0 Shunters 143
The Final Contracts 157
Armstrong Whitworth Diesels in Colour, compiled by David Kelso 169
Proposed Designs and the End 177

ACKNOWLEDGEMENTS

The total lack of surviving documents at those official sources thought most likely to have them has made this study of this subject long and difficult. It would also appear that the work of Armstrong Whitworth so far as diesel traction is concerned went virtually unnoticed by contemporary railway enthusiasts, so much which could have been recorded was lost. The salvation of this study came when it was discovered that in some cases former employees of Armstrong Whitworth saw fit to take away with them various items of records which, when made available to the author, provided a foundation upon which to base future researches.

Many people have assisted in many ways, special thanks are due to Donald C. Plyer, George M. Cowell, Charles R. Parker, William Ormston, and Jim Allison. Also to the following firms and organisations, Vickers Ltd, Sulzer Bros UK Ltd, Laurence, Scott & Electromotors Ltd, GEC Traction Ltd, GEC Diesels Ltd, British Leyland Ltd, RFFSA Brazil, Western Australian Government Railways, Indian Railways, St. Kitts Basseterre Sugar Factory, Thames Board Mills Ltd and Preston Corporation.

The following people have assisted in various ways and with photographs: Allan C. Baker, Mike Satow, Peter Clark, Philip G. Graham, Geoff Horseman, Ken Hoole, Alan Wright, Les Charlton, Harold D. Bowtell, John Benson, P. S. A. Berridge, Trevor Lodge, Les Nixon, George S. Toms, Jorge L. San Martin, Patrick Dollinger, J. W. Armstrong, W. Bryce Greenfield.

Public institutions and railway societies have also played their part and include Glasgow University Archives, National Railway Museum, Industrial Railway Society, The Railway Correspondence & Travel Society, and the Stephenson Locomotive Society. The original manuscript was typed by Deborah L. Scheetz and the publishers would also like to thank Emma Pope who rekeyed the entire manuscript. To all others who have helped, grateful thanks are recorded.

Two examples of Armstrong Whitworth diesel-electric units. *Above* the prototype lightweight railbus, built in 1933 to order DT16, is seen on main line trials on the London & North Eastern Railway. *Below* is the articulated train set supplied to the Buenos Aires Western Railway in 1934 under order DT30.

FOREWORD

The late Brian Webb was a true railway diesel enthusiast. During the late 1970s and early 80s he produced five books covering railway diesel engines and the early locomotives of British Rail, published by David & Charles. He also completed the late David Gordon's manuscript on Lord Carlisle's Railways published by the RCTS in 1978. As a professional interior designer and lecturer at Carlisle Technical College he also was involved in the design of covers for a number of RCTS books and *The Railway Observer*.

Brian was an only child who lived with his parents in Carlisle. His father spent a lifetime in public transport from where, no doubt came Brian's interest in railways. A constant companion for his last 15 years was Miss Sandra Tassle who devoted a tremendous amount of her time in assisting with the preparation of his publications. Regrettably Brian died at the early age of 46 in 1981.

The March 1979 *Railway Observer* carried a report from the Publications Department … 'we have the completed manuscript of Brian Webb's history of the Armstrong Whitworth diesel locomotives which will soon go to the printers.' Unfortunately this did not happen. A number of members have speculated that it was felt there was insufficient interest in diesels at that time coupled with the fact that a large proportion of the output of Armstrong Whitworth went to overseas markets.

Remarkably the complete manuscript with photographs and drawings has survived. Thirty years on the Publications Committee of the RCTS decided that this historical material should be published. Today there is very much more interest in early diesel locomotives. Much of Armstrong Whitworth's pioneering work led to the development of the diesel locomotive we know to-day. Additionally there is greater interest in the UK's industrial history. In his Introduction Brian states that the work at Scotswood has always been shrouded in mystery mainly due to a dearth in published material. This still holds true in the first decade of the 21st century. A search of to-day's Internet and enquiries at the Tyne and Wear Archives will produce very little on the locomotive building activities of the company.

The book represents Brian Webb's manuscript as completed in 1979 together with his selection of photographs and drawings. Apart from a few extra images and captions it has not been updated or edited in any way. Black Dwarf Lightmoor Publications is a highly respected publisher of historical material on all aspects of transport history and The Railway Correspondence and Travel Society is delighted to have worked with Lightmoor to publish this important historical work.

W. Gordon Davies
Chairman,
RCTS Publications Committee 2010.

INTRODUCTION

The choice of one individual locomotive builder for special treatment in the field of British internal combustion rail traction resulted in the selection of Sir W. G. Armstrong, Whitworth & Co. (Engineers) Ltd, who were first in the field in the UK. Armstrong Whitworth with their Diesel Traction Depertment were among the pioneers of diesel electric mainline rail traction, and like Frichs in Denmark they produced in a short period a wide range of vehicles meeting just about all categories of railway requirements.

A lot of railway locomotive students know about the work which went on at Scotswood works, but the work has always been shrouded in mystery due mainly to the dearth of published material over the four decades since the firm ceased to build locomotives.

Although some twenty or so years of intermittent research has gone into this study the author cannot claim that it stands as a complete study. However, at the point at which new information is few and far between it is hoped that readers will find the story of the achievements of Armstrong Whitworth in diesel traction interesting and its publication worthwhile.

Brian Webb
1978

The unsuccessful 1-C-1 diesel hydraulic shunter with Armstrong Whitworth mechanical portion supplied to the Buenos Aires Great Southern Railway in 1929. Fitted with one 600 bhp Sulzer engine and Vickers Williams-Janney transmission.
Sulzer Bros UK Ltd

ARMSTRONG WHITWORTH'S FIRST DIESEL RAILWAY WORK

The birthplace of railways and steam locomotion is usually credited to be the north east of England around the River Tyne. The same may be claimed for internal combustion engined main line locomotives. The former statement has been discussed in detail many times but the second, which really interests us here, has been less so.

During the first decade of the present century the firm of R. & W. Hawthorn, Leslie & Co. Ltd were thinking about alternatives to steam locomotion and, through their association with William Peter Durtnall (1873-1947), were probably the first in the world to offer high-power locomotives with internal combustion engines allied to electrical transmission.

Durtnall already held a firm belief in electrical transmissions when the abortive main line locomotive of Diesel-Sulzer-Klose, incorporating direct drive, was being designed – it was to fail miserably in 1912 when tested. Durtnall had little faith in mechanical, hydraulic, compressed-air, and similar systems, Leslie independently examined the alternatives.

The outbreak of war in 1914 was partly responsible for the failure of a plan to supply ten Hawthorn, Leslie built Durtnall-designed 'Paragon' Thermo-Electric locomotives for service in Australia. These machines were to be 1,000 hp units running on two six-wheel bogies for the Trans-Australian Railway. If this plan had gone through it was hoped to run the locomotive on UK main lines prior to shipment.

Strangely, this advanced thinking was not maintained after hostilities and in 1920 when a prototype twin-bogie Thermo-Electric locomotive was built and tested at Hawthorn, Leslie's works, little attention was attracted and the idea lapsed into obscurity. It must be remembered that little of any worth was being achieved elsewhere with high power main line internal combustion locomotives.

From this point Hawthorn, Leslie did little with such forms of locomotion until their association as mechanical structure supplier to English Electric Co. Ltd, brought them back into electric and then diesel electric traction in 1934.

The first real practical work with large oil-engined locomotives and railcars in the UK was to be undertaken a few miles west of Hawthorn, Leslie's works, again on the banks of the Tyne, at Scotswood. Here was situated one of the most famous engineering works in the world. This gigantic riverside sprawl at Elswick and Scotswood was renowned for its skills, inventive innovation and product quality. The products included some of the most awesome weapons of war and it was largely due to this area of work that the large complex was developed. The works were of course those of Sir W. G. Armstrong, Whitworth & Co. Ltd.

The achievements of this works stemmed from the genius of its founder William George Armstrong, later Lord Armstrong, a pioneer of hydraulic power – notably turbines, shipbuilding, machine tools, aircraft, airships, motor cars, steam and heavy oil marine engines and many others.

Another branch of work was railway locomotives and although this had not reached any importance at all by the end of the 1914-1918 war, it was seen as a possible outlet for the extra workshop capacity and army of skilled engineers which would be difficult to employ with the end of hostilities and decline in armament work. In common with other firms in similar situations, plans were drawn up to convert the shell factories into locomotive shops, work starting immediately after the Armistice in 1918.

The Whitworth armour plate works, an old competitor of Armstrongs was at Openshaw, Manchester. They too were also put on locomotive work but only on overhauling and repairing. No new locomotives were to be built there. On Tyneside, locomotive repair work was carried out in the Elswick shops but Scotswood was to concentrate on 'new' work.

During the middle of the nineteenth century Armstrongs had completed a few locomotive orders in attempts to diversify further and enter a new market but had failed. It was to be sixty years before a serious entry was successfully made.

The first Armstrong Whitworth locomotive order was for fifty North Eastern Railway Class 'T2' 0-8-0 goods locomotives (L&NER Class Q6), the first example being steamed on 12th November 1919. This work was to go from strength to strength so that within twenty years 1,532 steam, electric and diesel locomotives, railcars, etc. had been turned out. Quality was foremost at Scotswood and their work has been acclaimed many times by engineers as being 'second to none'.

In the main, orthodox steam locomotive work was to occupy Scotswood for a dozen or so years but the air of innovation pervading the works found them involved in building the Ramsay 2-6-6-2 steam turbine locomotive in 1922 (works No. 160) and their first non-steam locomotives, two Bo-Bo electrics for South African goldfields in 1924 (works No's 603/4).

Armstrong Whitworth's reputation brought them many overseas orders and into contact with the Russian Railways, first with orthodox steam locomotive spares and boilers but soon in the field of internal combustion rail traction.

The Russian Railways were involved early with oil-engined rail traction through the team which worked with Lomonossoff using mainly the German locomotive industry to construct their locomotives. A varied selection of large bulky multi-axle locomotives resulted, which were employed mostly on slow freight duties.

Armstrong Whitworth were brought into this work when they won a contract to build the power equipment and mechanical portion for a locomotive which was apparently a combination of oil engine, gas turbine and compressed gas powering a reciprocating engine which drove the wheels. The locomotive was based on a proposal by Professor A. N. Schelest of Moscow Technical University, originating from before the First World War. He proposed a highly supercharged diesel engine to supply its exhaust gases into a pressure vessel or receiver via a

compressor. From this the gas was to be fed into a conventional reciprocating engine to drive the wheels.

By 1921 the idea had developed to include a gas turbine driving a reciprocating air-compressor which supplied air to drive the turbine via a combustion chamber. The exhaust from the turbine was once more to be fed into a pressure vessel and again to the reciprocating driving engine, an extremely complex attempt to find a solution to a basic problem.

The Russian government authorised a Schelest locomotive, together with others using electrical and hydraulic transmissions, during 1923. Schelest himself and a technical team worked at Armstrong Whitworths and eventually in late 1926 a gas generator was run suitable for a locomotive of approximately 1,000 hp. The system was evidently proved feasible to Schelest but his work was ended abruptly when the project was stopped by a decree from Moscow which demanded the team and the equipment return to Russia. Nothing more was heard of it in the west.

As can be seen, Armstrong Whitworth were becoming conversant with alternatives to steam locomotion from an early date but it was not to be until 1926 when their chance came by being associated with a challenging order from the Buenos Aires Great Southern Railway of Argentina (BAGSR).

For some time the Chief Mechanical Engineer of the BAGSR, one Pedro C. Saccaggio, had been contemplating diesel traction trials on his railway due to the fact that conventional steam traction could no longer fill the demands being made by the increasing traffic on the suburban services around Buenos Aires.

The obvious choice of straight electric traction was eliminated due to the costs involved in electrification, so Saccaggio decided to use a form of electrical traction without fixed supply systems of overhead wires or third-rails. He chose the travelling powerhouse system involving a vehicle carrying its own generator set which could supply electricity to traction motors distributed throughout the train with which it operated.

Initial studies were directed towards steam power utilising a purpose built/designed water-tube boiler, non-condensing steam turbine and an electric generator. It was revealed by the study that a 2,000 bhp travelling powerhouse of 160 tons weight with a guaranteed thermal-efficiency at the generator terminals of double that obtainable at the drawbar of a contemporary steam locomotive was feasible.

Thinking along the line of development in order to eliminate the costly boiler in steam systems, brought in the idea of some form of internal-combustion prime-mover. This idea appealed greatly to Saccaggio when it became apparent that powerhouses with two eight-cylinder 600 bhp diesel engines driving generators could operate with five-coach train sets and the project was put in hand. At the same time some twin-bogie diesel electric locomotives were acquired for evaluation but these are outside the scope of this work.

Saccaggio visited Europe and the UK in the search for suitable power equipment and found the task difficult in view of the size/weight of available diesel type engines and electrical equipment. An order was placed with Sulzer Bros Ltd of Winterthur, Switzerland, for some 600 bhp engines and also with Oerlikon of Zurich for generators. The traction motors were ordered in the UK from Metropolitan Vickers Ltd and the control gear from the English Electric Co. Ltd. Armstrong Whitworth had supplied numerous steam locomotives to the Argentine and Saccaggio gave them the order for the mechanical portions, these being supplied for finish-erection in the BAGSR workshops.

The task before Armstrong Whitworth was of some magnitude, for they had three units to tackle, two 1,200 bhp twin-engined diesel electric mobile powerhouses under order No. E64, and one diesel hydraulic shunting locomotive, order No. E65.

It must be remembered that at this time there was very little experience to be drawn upon in the UK concerning main line diesel traction (or in Europe for that matter). So with a country of steam-bound locomotive manufacturers (except in one or two instances) and an even more conservative railway system, previous experience upon which to draw was virtually nil. Serious limitations on the design of the mobile powerhouses were set by the size of available power equipment and the integration of European and UK equipment into a workable unit. Moreover, severe axle-loading restrictions and loading-gauge size on the BAGSR called for great ingenuity, time, and energy from the design team. The accommodating of the equipment within what amounted to a very restricted box seemed at times quite insurmountable.

Although the powerhouses were really only a sub-contract job, and at that mechanical portions only, Armstrong Whitworth deserve credit for their courage in tackling the work. The powerhouses had plate frames with a Bissel-truck at each end and four rigid axles in the centre. This gave them a 2-8-2 layout to the observer but with only two axles fitted with traction motors, the layout 1-A2A-1 was more correct.

The superstructure was over-all, having one driving cab, engine room in the centre with engines set side by side and generators towards the cab end. The engines used were Winterthur built Sulzer 8LV28 eight-cylinder units with 280mm x 320mm cylinders. They ran at 700 rpm and gave 600 bhp each. These engines were some of the last of their type built and of mostly cast iron construction. Sulzer fuel-injection equipment was fitted and each cylinder head had a pre-combustion chamber. Each engine drove a massive Oerlikon generator. The power equipment was shipped direct to the Argentine. The weight of an engine and generator was fifteen tons. Metropolitan-Vickers Ltd supplied the traction motors of each powerhouse, these being of 144 bhp each, one being driven by each power unit. The traction motors in the train set totalled ten, five being driven by each power unit with Oerlikon supplying these motors.

The complete powerhouses were variously reported to weigh either 85 or 92 tons. Principle dimensions are given as: overall length 41ft, maximum height over roof 13ft 8in., rigid wheelbase 15ft 2in., total wheelbase 32ft 2in., all wheels were of 3ft 1½in. in diameter.

The design initiative was under the surveillance of Sir Brodie Henderson of Messrs Livesay, Son & Henderson, the consulting engineers.

The mode of operation was to have one powerhouse permanently coupled to its five-coach train set. The coaches were twin-bogie vehicles built by BAGSR, each bogie having one 125 bhp traction motor of axle-hung type. With twelve out

Front and rear three-quarter views of one of the Armstrong Whitworth 1,200 bhp 1-A2A-1 diesel electric mobile powerhouses built for the Buenos Aires Great Southern Railway in 1929. The engine room roof and sides have been removed to show side by side mounted engines and generators. They were built to the BAGSR's gauge of 5ft 6in. which gave the extra width to get the two diesel engines side by side. The powerhouses were assembled at the railway's own works at Remedios de Escalada. *Brian Webb collection*

BAGSR mobile powerhouse UE1 with its full motorised suburban train at Buenos Aires. The five coaches were fitted with traction motors and each of the two sets consisted of three first and two second class coaches. The second class coach nearest the powerhouse also had a luggage compartment.
Jorge L. San Martin collection

The rear view of a BAGSR motorised suburban set UE1 showing the driving cab at the opposite end to the mobile powerhouse.
Jorge L. San Martin collection

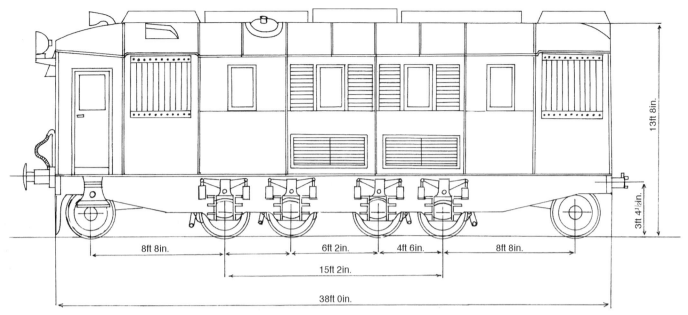

Side elevation of one of the mobile powerhouses reproduced at 4mm to 1 foot scale.

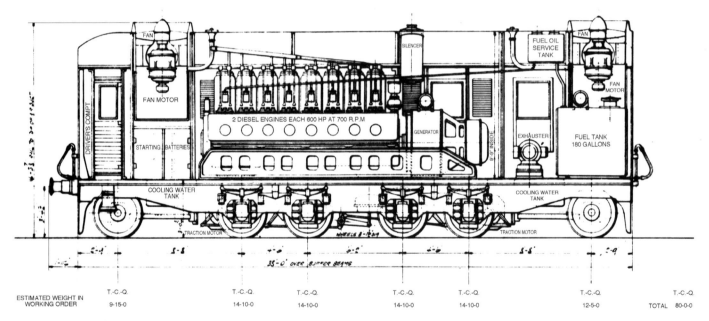

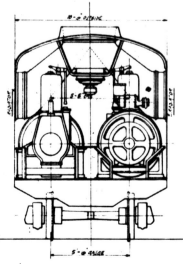

Cut away side elevation and section of the mobile powerhouse units UE1 and UE2 (AW 935/6). These have been reproduced to as close to a scale of 4mm - 1ft as possible, however, it should be noticed that there are some discrepancies in dimensions between the two drawings. Throughout this volume we have endeavoured to reproduce the drawings as accurately as possible to either 4mm or 7mm to 1 foot scales wherever dimensions are known.

Brian Webb & University of Glasgow

UE2 and train at Buenos Aires. *Jorge L. San Martin collection*

The two train sets coupled together making an impressive ensemble. *Jorge L. San Martin collection*

of twenty-six powered axles a high adhesion factor was obtained, giving the trains excellent acceleration and making them ideal for the frequent stops encountered on suburban passenger duties.

The trains were reversible, capable of being driven from either end and both trains could work in multiple if required to form a ten-coach train. Each coach was 85ft long and fitted with centre couplers and shock absorbers and gave a train which seated 554 passengers in three first and two second class coaches, one of the latter having a luggage compartment.

The powerhouses were numbered UE (Usina Electric) 1 and 2 and carried Armstrong Whitworth steam series works numbers 935/6, being built under order E64. Their operation began in 1929 on the suburban shuttle service between Buenos Aires Plaza Constitución Station and Quilmes, a distance of 17.2 kilometres (10.68 miles) each train alternating with the other on duties of eight hours one day, sixteen hours the next, giving 350 km (217.35 miles) daily, seven days a week.

Due to the engines being stopped and started some two hundred times daily there was much trouble with broken joints, pipes, studs etc., so modification was necessary to overcome governor control at engine unloading. A form of automatic load regulator was devised which shut off the fuel prior to taking the load off the engine. Later engines were kept idling at stops.

UE1 and UE2 with mileages of 1,888,450 km/1,795,340 km or 1,172,727/1,114,906 miles were out of use according to Argentine sources by 1954. However, withdrawal is given as April 1963 but this refers to a hybrid rebuild of both units undertaken in 1954 at the works of Fabrica Argentina De Locomotoras at Tolosa. This Bo-2-2-Bo mobile powerhouse was numbered UE6 and had two Paxman 827 bhp engines and did incorporate certain parts from UE1 and UE2.

The diesel hydraulic locomotive was not at all in the tradition of sound thinking usually associated with Saccaggio. This curious 1-C-1 rigid framed unit was described as a shunting locomotive and was powered by the same Sulzer engine as the mobile powerhouses but only a single engine was fitted. The 600 bhp locomotive was equipped with a Vickers built Williams-Janney 'swash plate' type hydraulic transmission which was quite unsuited for traction applications. It is suggested that the transmission which was driven via a reduction gear coupled to the diesel engine, was in fact designed for stationary application in a Merseyside factory.

The locomotive was reputed to weigh 76 tons but opinions vary on this, for final erection was undertaken by the BAGSR. It ran on 4ft 7½in. diameter driving wheels, had an overall length of 42ft 5½in. and rigid wheelbase of 13ft 0in. Total wheelbase was 26ft 9in. The layout of the locomotive was based on the hood type with a single driving cab towards one end. Final drive was by jackshaft at the cab end, and siderods.

Saccaggio is reported to have had little interest in this machine which suggests it was thrust upon the BAGSR by someone else. The machine was thus doomed to failure at the start and it did little running, being extremely troublesome due to transmission overheating, oil pressure variations and leakages. It is recorded to have covered 33,040 km or 20,517 miles as BAGSR No. 501 until withdrawn in October 1940. It was scrapped at Escalade shops in May 1943 although it had probably lain derelict for over a decade. Armstrong Whitworth gave this locomotive works number 937.

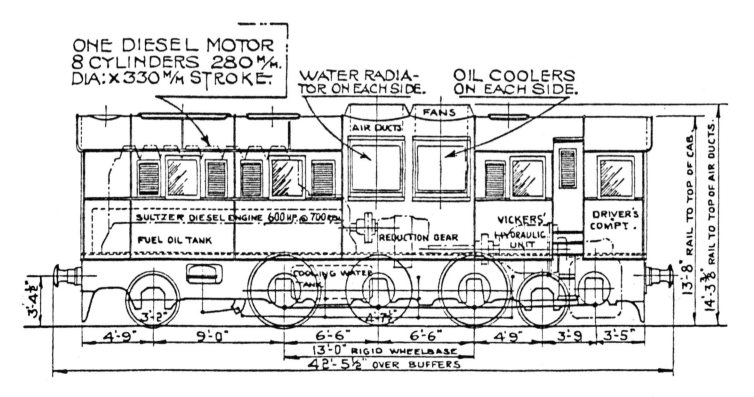

A diagram of the 1-C-1 diesel hydraulic shunter AW937. Scale 4mm - 1ft.   *Jorge L. San Martin collection*

Two views of the 1-C-1 diesel hydraulic shunter No. 501.   *Jorge L. San Martin collection*

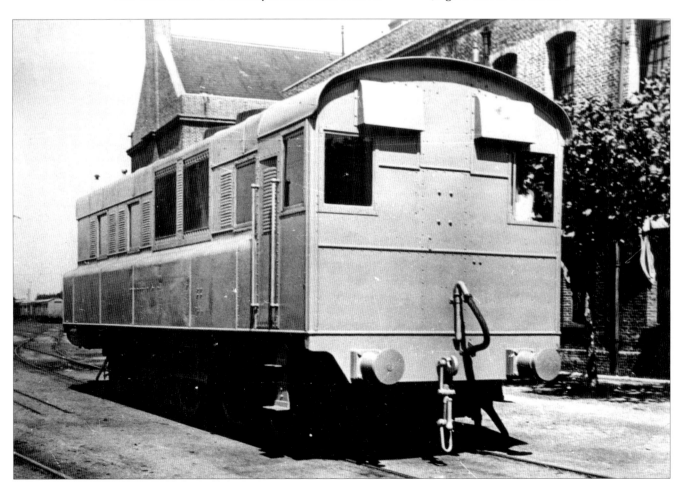

OIL-ELECTRIC TRACTION AND THE DIESEL TRACTION DEPARTMENT

The use of the description 'oil-electric' was a feature of Armstrong Whitworths when referring to their diesel electric locomotives or rail vehicles. Whether this was a rejection on their part of the claim made by Germany that Diesel invented the compression ignition engine in use today, is not known, but it is a possibility.

During the late 1920s Armstrong Whitworth conducted very extensive studies into the relative economics of oil-electric rail traction compared to steam and to electrification. The application of oil-electric traction to the various classes of traffic carried on the British main line railways was studied and it was concluded that at that period it was not possible to compete economically with electrification on very dense suburban work involving high average speeds such as those found on the Metropolitan lines of the London Underground. Steam traction was eliminated from comparison, so the only possible test cases were between oil-electric and electric.

Armstrong Whitworth took the Southern Railway electric suburban service and the study presented the following points to consider:

Scheduled speed	25mph
Length of average section	1.3 miles
Average running time	2 mins 47 secs
Average station stopping time	20 secs
Deceleration	1.75mph per sec
Emergency running time	150 secs

It was found that a SR eight-coach electric train had a continuous hp per ton of 3.38 and weighed 308 tons with passengers. A competitive oil-electric train would comprise two three-coach sets with two trailers in between, or be formed of four-coach sets. Each oil-electric set comprised a power vehicle articulated to a short coach, the prime mover being a 900 bhp unit. The power vehicle would be readily detachable by lifting off the coach from the articulating bogie, thus facilitating dispatch to locomotive or carriage works for attention. The weight of the eight-coach train set, formed of two sets with trailers, was put at 383 tons, giving 4.65 bhp per ton, with a total of 1,780 bhp.

Armstrong Whitworth proposed that auxiliary power, comprising a small high-speed automotive oil engine and generator, be used to supply power for train heating, lighting, braking, etc. in each set to avoid the necessity of running the main engine continuously. Traction motors would be provided on the leading bogie of the power vehicle and outer bogie of its articulated coach portion, variations being possible to suit particular requirements.

Articulation of trains was popular with Armstrong Whitworth for the way in which it kept down train length, weight, overall cost and enabled small engines to be used. In their opinion, these outweighed the disadvantages of articulation with regard to train maintenance. Another point of importance was that reduction in train weight cuts fuel consumption.

In forming assessments of railway electrification costs, Armstrong Whitworth based their calculations on £7,500 to £9,000 per running track mile for a 600 volt DC third rail system, the sum including all associated work such as substations, telegraph, electrification of sidings and depots, special fencing etc. They established the point at which oil-electric traction equalled that of electric and then the points onward where it had a distinct advantage. Some estimates indicated that the SR electric railway system could be better operated by oil-electric:

A. A railway need only purchase sufficient units to meet immediate traffic requirements, further being added as traffic increases. This allows capital expenditure to be spread and thus to be commensurate with revenue. In contrast, electrification requires heavy capital outlay before the service starts, it being in many cases years before receipts reach carrying capacity.
B. Electric rolling stock is restricted to electrified routes, being often idle after peak carrying periods, weekends, and not available for excursion traffic over non-electrified routes, nor for use elsewhere; oil-electric trains are not so restricted.
C. Breakdowns in transmission of current on electrified routes causes suspension of the whole service; oil-electric trains, as with steam, being independent and breakdowns only affecting one unit.

One of Armstrong Whitworth's 'pet promotions' was the mobile powerhouse concept introduced to them by Saccaggio. In their opinion it was possible to use oil-electric traction to build up a suburban system to a point justifying electrification, the acceleration attainable with oil-electric and the higher speed schedules were equal to electric. The progressive build up of traffic, followed by electrification, enabled the displaced oil-electrics to move to other areas to continue the process. By using mobile powerhouses the coaching stock of their trains could easily be converted to straight electric, retaining the same traction motors and thus run over electrified routes as electric trains and use the mobile powerhouses to take the trains beyond the electrified area.

It was, of course, common practice to run steam-hauled trains over electrified sections to serve areas outside the electric system, a disadvantageous method, opined Armstong Whitworth. Steam trains were slow, impeded traffic; but through running was necessary to avoid passengers having to change trains. Mobile powerhouses would solve this problem.

For lines of secondary character other than suburban but including stopping, express, and branch line trains of short distances, the oil-electric motor-coach train was envisaged to replace steam. By using these motor-coaches or railcars

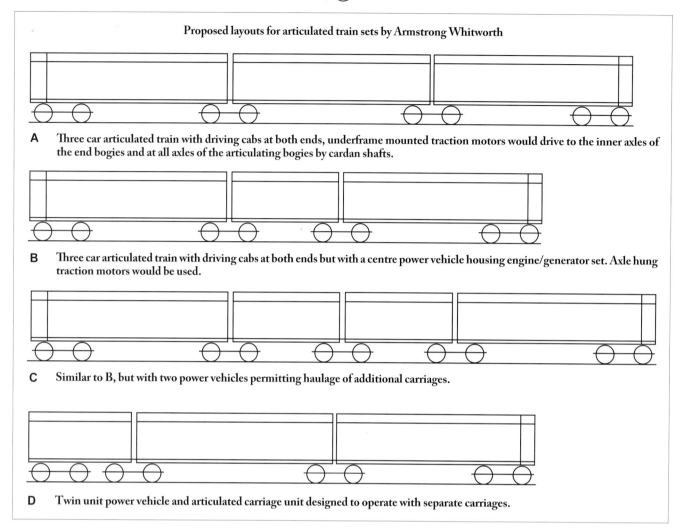

Proposed layouts for articulated train sets by Armstrong Whitworth

A Three car articulated train with driving cabs at both ends, underframe mounted traction motors would drive to the inner axles of the end bogies and at all axles of the articulating bogies by cardan shafts.

B Three car articulated train with driving cabs at both ends but with a centre power vehicle housing engine/generator set. Axle hung traction motors would be used.

C Similar to B, but with two power vehicles permitting haulage of additional carriages.

D Twin unit power vehicle and articulated carriage unit designed to operate with separate carriages.

in multiple-unit to suit traffic demands they could be much cheaper than steam, saving in labour by eliminating firemen and reducing drivers and only consuming fuel when in operation.

Main line passenger and freight duties offered opportunities for the oil-electric. Standby time was important on this type of work, so a unit which could be shut-down – consuming no fuel – was an obvious requirement. The inability of steam to maintain power and speed when climbing heavy gradients, the necessity to double-head heavier loads – requiring with steam two crews – not to mention frequent attention at running sheds, were great disadvantages.

Armstrong Whitworth were protagonists of the practice of converting the gear ratios of oil-electric locomotives to suit freight – that is high tractive effort, slower speed; or lower tractive effort, high speed for passenger duty. They estimated that a 1,200 bhp 100 tons oil-electric locomotive comprising a twin articulated layout could be adapted as standard by a railway and be used for any traffic with the appropriate gearing. It was stated that one such locomotive could replace an L&NER 119 ton 2-8-0 of Class 'O2' or the GWR 122 ton 2-8-0 of '4700' Class on freight or mixed traffic work respectively.

By providing two sets of gears with each locomotive, an oil-electric would be available to suit seasonal traffic demands; mineral traffic in winter, increased passenger traffic in summer.

Light branch line services were to be covered by using light-weight single-unit vehicles which could haul a light trailer if required. The competition of road motor buses could, Armstrong Whitworth, said, be met by such vehicles with high acceleration and high speed, in spite of frequent stops. The aim was to provide superior accommodation in a sixty seat vehicle about 60 feet long, weighing 40-45 tons, powered by a 200/250 bhp engine. Double-ended control would permit rapid turnaround at terminals, and trailer cars would have a driving position at the outer end. It would be possible to operate two such vehicles in multiple unit, or in cases of heavier traffic, provide an articulated twin-unit.

At the time of these proposals the 'Sentinel' and other makes of lightweight, modern geared steam railcars were becoming popular, but as Armstrong Whitworth pointed out, the perennial steam problems with boilers was inherent, and thus their downfall. Armstrong Whitworth said that evidence available to them showed that the cost of operating a light oil-electric railcar was not more than half that of steam, and was often considerably less.

For shunting work the oil-electric locomotive was already being adopted in the United States of America, where quite large twin-bogie locomotives in the 300-800 bhp range were in operation. Elsewhere the shunter in this form was mostly a

small, low-power unit, allied to mechanical transmission.

Armstrong Whitworth saw the future of oil-electric shunting, even in low-power locomotives, while USA experiences proved that oil-electric shunters could work up to 20% more traffic than steam and operate twenty-four hours per day. It was also capable of displacing more than one steam shunter.

With steam locomotive work in decline due to the 1930s slump in the engineering industry, to which Armstrong Whitworth were as susceptible as anyone else, thought was directed towards diesel traction as a possibility for providing new work in a field in which competitors showed little interest. Obviously work was needed to keep the locomotive section in business when the remaining orders for locomotives were completed. 1930/31 saw ten L&NER 2-6-0s of Class 'K3' and twenty-five 0-6-0PTs of GWR '5700' Class finished, it not being until 1934 when steam locomotives were again under construction.

Scotswood Works included a fine locomotive erecting shop, having three longitudinal rail tracks and pits, the centre track being multiple gauge. The impression has been given from various published photographs of the building of diesel vehicles at Scotswood that a separate erecting shop existed for diesel work. This was not the case, but the dearth of steam work

Inside the locomotive erecting shop at Scotswood Works in 1932. Under construction are twin-unit 1,700 bhp mobile powerhouses and a 1,700 bhp locomotive for the Buenos Aires Great Southern Railway. Also present are two DT1 railcars and the 90 bhp 0-4-0 DE shunter of order DT11.
Brian Webb collection

Another view inside the erecting shop on the same occasion. The overhead crane is apparent as is the mixed gauge middle road. *Brian Webb collection*

certainly implied the suggestion to the observer.

Overhead cranes of 70 tons and 80 tons capacity were installed on the top gantry, with two five-ton cranes running on the lower gantry. In addition was the adjoining marine-engine building shop with similar lifting gear; this shop was used for locomotive work as occasion demanded.

Armstrong Whitworth Board's decision to make a definitive move into diesel traction was indeed a great one, made with considerable hope: the hope being that once the advantages and success of diesel power were demonstrated the project would go from strength to strength and enable a new market to be opened up with both home and overseas potential. It was a gamble in a steam-minded country.

Armstrong Whitworth were very well qualified for their move into diesel traction for not only were they extremely versatile in skills, their experience with producing marine oil-engines and transmissions gave them an advantage over traditional locomotive builders in that it was possible to manufacture power equipment indigenously, rather than to rely on specialist outside suppliers.

It has been proved many times since, that the locomotive builder most likely to succeed in advanced railway motive power, other than steam, was that which could build its own engines, etc., or that which was allied financially to a group capable of supplying sophisticated equipment outside the normal realm of steam locomotives. Independence from other industries

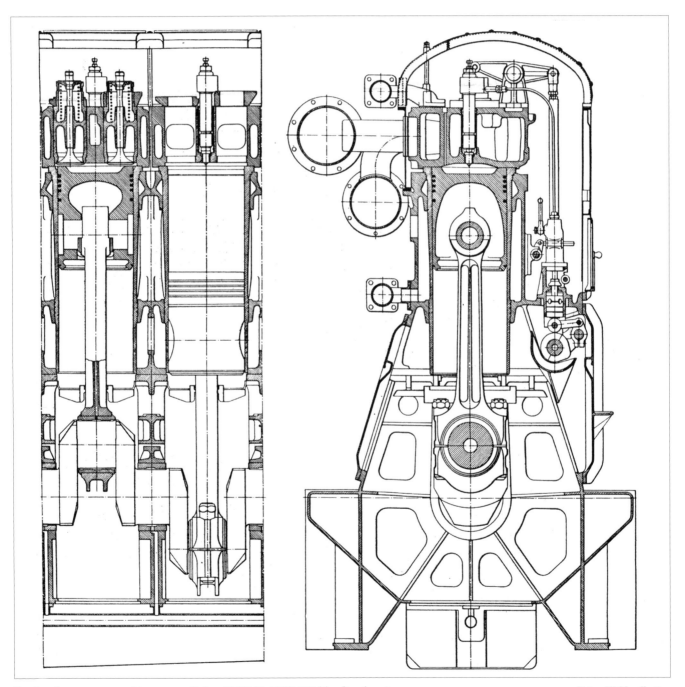

Sectional arrangement of Armstrong Sulzer 8LD34 1,000/1,260 bhp diesel engine. *Brian Webb collection*

was achieved well by Armstrong Whitworth, although the recruitment of specialist staff on the diesel and electrical design sides was necessary.

The link between Armstrong Whitworth and Sulzer Bros through marine work was seen as a line of development, so that a licence was taken up which enabled Scotswood Works to build the Sulzer range of rail-traction diesel engines. At the end of the 1920s the Sulzer rail traction diesel engine was of cast iron construction, each cylinder head and the crankcase being individual castings; the pistons too were cast iron. Sulzer fuel injection pumps and nozzles were used and the cylinder heads had pre-combustion chambers.

Before diesel traction got underway at Scotswood the Sulzer range had been extended to about a dozen models of 180-1,200 bhp, all classed within the LV range. Cylinder dimensions varied between 220mm x 280mm in the LV22 size giving 250 bhp at 775 rpm from six cylinders, to the LV34 eight-cylinder unit measuring 340mm x 400mm and putting out 850 bhp at 550 rpm. The LV range had monobloc cast-steel crankcases with separate iron castings for each cylinder and cylinder head. By 1933 the cast steel construction had given way to the welded frame construction. By the time Scotswood was tooled to produce these engines, the benefit of the redesign work and development undertaken at both Winterthur and St. Denis had resulted in a much more modern design.

To start with, Armstrong Whitworth shipped eight 8LV34 engines from Sulzer Bros' Winterthur works for use in the four Buenos Aires Great Southern Railway twin-units of 1,700 bhp, but apart from this instance, all the future engines to be installed in the products of the diesel traction department were built at Scotswood. The initial batch was six 6LV22 units of 250 bhp for railcar and shunting locomotive use.

Subsequently the engine shop built the 800 bhp 8LD28 unit, the 6LD22 and the 6LD25 of 350/400 bhp and 450/600 bhp respectively. The largest engines built were the two 8LD34 units for Indian locomotives, which, as it turned out, did very little traction work. There was a brief excursion into the Sulzer LF engine range in 1937 with the 6LF19 275 bhp units for use in a subcontract for railcar power-bogie power units. The latter is interesting in being the only order for mechanical transmission units built at Scotswood, although some proposed designs had such transmissions.

The production of the Armstrong-Saurer engine under license from Adolph Saurer of Arbon, Switzerland since 1931 by Armstrong-Saurer Commercial Vehicles Ltd, an Armstrong Whitworth subsidiary also operating at Scotswood, gave the diesel traction department access to another engine range. The value of the small automotive type engine for use in low-powered rail vehicles and for locomotive auxiliary purposes was taken full advantage of – but its original and principle use did still remain in the chassis of the Armstrong-Saurer truck range produced at Scotswood.

Full engine testing rigs were provided at Scotswood and the dynamometer was constantly employed during the peak of diesel engine production.

Armstrong Whitworth chose electric transmissions for its rail traction work which was in contrast to other locomotive manufacturers' thinking. A small list of specialist electrical manufacturers was used by Armstrong Whitworth. These were, in the majority of cases, Laurence, Scott & Electromotors Ltd of Norwich, who built many of the generators and frame-mounted traction motors. Compton Parkinson Ltd of Chelmsford supplied most of the axle-hung traction motors and some generators, their experience in the former giving them an advantage over the Norwich firm. Other contractors favoured included GEC Ltd, English Electric Co. Ltd and the European firm of Brown Boveri.

In the case of a vehicle with frame-mounted traction motors the final drive was always by cardan-shaft to a worm gearbox carried on the axle. Craven-Guest hollow face worm and worm wheel gears were employed, the latter being gripped between two cast-steel spiders keyed to the splines on the axle.

Most of the diesel vehicles built were fitted with British-Isothermos axleboxes, manufactured at Scotswood under licence from Societe Internationale Isothermos of Geneva by The British Isothermos Co. Ltd, an Armstrong Whitworth subsidiary.

The non-roller-bearing Isothermos axleboxes were noted for their reputation of reducing tractive resistance and economising in oil consumption. In principle, mechanical oil circulation was involved which ensured that a large quantity of oil was supplied to the axle journal and bush. At low speed oil was reduced to a drip but at high speeds the oil was flung by centrifugal force to the roof of the axlebox and led by channels to the journal and bush; an efficient oil sealing ring prevented oil leakage along the axle.

The axlebox only carried a small quantity of oil as it was apparently only necessary to top up the oil every 100,000 miles, while oil delivery rates – depending on rotational speeds – were put at up to 80-100 lbs per hour. This gave …copious lubrication, negligible wear and cool bearings'.

Armstrong Whitworth had various patents and ideas on diesel electric traction and auxiliary equipment used. One of the most publicised patents was the ABE (Armstrong Beckett Electrical) transmission. As stated previously Armstrong Whitworth thought it quite normal to apply electrical transmission to all types and sizes of rail vehicles with diesel prime movers. Their competitors dismissed entirely the diesel-electric system for anything except large work, considering it far too complex and costly for mundane applications on light railways and shunting locomotives.

In an attempt to simplify and make more acceptable electrical transmissions to prospective customers, the ABE transmission was used. This was virtually a generator and a traction motor, but the former also charged the battery – so producing a system which, Armstrong Whitworth said, could be built at a fraction of the cost of orthodox equipment. The simplification, it was claimed, decreased its likelihood to give much trouble and allowed that which did occur to be entrusted to normal railway maintenance staff, unskilled in electrical work. The ABE transmission was costed at only ten per cent more than a system employing a well-designed mechanical transmission and fluid couplings, etc.

An innovation devised and patented by Armstrong Whitworth was an auxiliary generator and radiator fan driven from the diesel

Taken from the *Armstrong Whitworth Record*, the company's in-house journal, for autumn 1931 this view is of Armstrong-Sulzer engines for oil-electric locomotives and railcars in course of erection in the new diesel traction shops at Scotswood Road Works.
John Horne collection

Diesel engine test bed at Scotswood Works showing engines of Armstrong-Sulzer type for order DT63 on test. This order was for ten 0-6-0 shunting locomotives for the London, Midland & Scottish Railway.
Brian Webb collection

engine by a free-wheel, allowing it to operate off the battery for short periods and thus provide more power for traction purposes. It was tried on a number of 250 bhp vehicles with poor results and was removed in some cases.

The use of an auxiliary Armstrong-Saurer engine and generator set in some of the larger vehicles proved a mixed blessing. It did, however, enable the main engine to be devoted entirely to traction purposes, as all auxiliaries were driven off the auxiliary set. At starting the main engine electrically, power was drawn from the auxiliary set, which was started by a starter motor on the auxiliary generator. Such equipment was installed in vehicles of orders DT8, DT19, DT23, and DT51, effectively raising the available bhp of the six units concerned. The additional complexity introduced by the auxiliary set was harshly criticised by the users of the vehicles concerned who doubted its value.

Vehicles having no auxiliary set had their engines started by motoring the main generator and driving this by fitting a larger battery of twenty-four cells or more (48 volts). Later work changed to virtually road vehicle starting techniques, using a 24 volt generator and starter – order DT71 being an example.

Some 250 bhp installations without an auxiliary set had an auxiliary generator fitted whose field strength varied according to engine rotation speed. This gave in practice somewhat haphazard battery charging, being before the days of automatic voltage regulators. Battery charging on vehicles of under 200 bhp was by the main generator during idling periods, a relay being provided to stop the battery contactor closing whilst the volts were too high. During engine traction periods, the self-excited field current gave a small charge, and except on top notch this was augmented by a current through a charging resistance.

Armstrong Whitworth's use of a load regulator coincided with the development of similar equipment by Sulzers in Switzerland. The idea was basically a rheostat driven by an oil motor and controlled by the governor. All the Armstrong-Sulzer engined vehicles had load regulators which worked well, but some variations were used in some rail vehicles to obtain improved part-load performances. Force-ventilation was used by Armstrong Whitworth in their 250/350 bhp shunting locomotives for frame-mounted traction motors. This was achieved by a small blower motor which ensured that cooling was effective at all speeds and times. This was the main reason for their advantage over a competitor's diesel electric shunter on

the LMS which was prone to traction motor overheating at low speeds.

The staffing of the Diesel Traction Department was to include names which proved of inestimable value to British Railway engineering in later years when cessation of railway work at Scotswood compelled them to seek fresh employment. In 1932 the Diesel Traction Department had three areas of work: electrical, diesel, and mechanical.

D. J. Watkins was Chief Electrical Engineer, with F. Turner on control gear, and D. C. Plyer dealing with the generators and traction motors. Diesel engines had A. Orton as Chief Engineer, with Messrs Williams and Latham as draughtsmen and technical men. Mechanical design staff shared with steam work, had C. D. Hanna as Chief Engineer and G. McArd as Chief Draughtsman. The testing facilities for diesel engines were under Seal, with vehicle testing/demonstration under Powell. Included amongst sales, technical, and export representatives were Messrs Beckett, Gregson, Parker, and Rudd.

Some reorganisation in 1934 saw Watkins became Scotswood Contracts Manager in addition to his electrical section post, although with J. H. A. Spaink, D. C. Plyer, F. Turner and H. K. Whitehorn on contracts.

The man responsible for harmonising all the work, and indeed much of the publicity for the diesel work, was Charles Joseph Hyde-Trutch. The usual problems of division between drawing office disciplines was broken down by a course arranged at Rutherford Technical College in Newcastle upon Tyne under T. Matthewson-Dick of the L&NER, at which the mechanical draughtsmen studied electrical traction.

Finally, mention must be made of the dispatch arrangements concerning export orders when direct sea voyages from the Tyne were called for. The river at Scotswood was not capable of taking large ships, so Armstrong Whitworth made use of the nearest deep water quay at the adjoining works of Vickers, Armstrong Ltd, Elswick. The Elswick quay, with its giant hydraulic crane, would be hired for the occasion and the ship berthed there.

The procedure adopted was for the locomotive or railcar to be taken down to Scotswood Jetty. This tidal jetty had a 100-ton capacity crane which ran on a substructure extending over the river, under which barges or pontoons were positioned at high tide by tugs. The crane with a lifting beam would load its cargo on to the pontoon, which would have rails laid on it, two locomotives being accommodated side by side. The loaded pontoon was then taken by tugs of the Foster Bros fleet, often *Manxman* or *Highgarth*, to Elswick, where the crane would lift the locomotive on to the waiting ship as deck or hold cargo, as required.

A carriage body of Sao Paulo trainset DT19 being lowered onto a pontoon at Scotswood Jetty for movement to Elswick Wharf where it will be loaded aboard an ocean-going vessel together with the rest of the order for shipment to Brazil. *Brian Webb collection*

Table 1
Power Equipment Fitted to Armstrong Whitworth Diesel Rail Vehicles

Vehicle Order Number	Engine Make	No. of Cylinders	BHP	RPM	De-Rating bhp	Main Generator Make	Auxiliary Engine Make/bhp/rpm	Traction motor make No. & type	Notes
DT1	Sulzer 6LD22	6	250	775	---	LS	---	GEC 2 AH NS FV	twin engine
DT3	Sulzer 8LV34	8	850	550	---	BB	---	EE 10 AH NS FV	twin engine
DT4	Sulzer 8LV34	8	805	550	---	BB	---	EE 6 AH NS FV	
DT7	Sulzer 6LD22	6	250	775	---	LS	---	LS 1 FM – FV	
DT8	Sulzer 8LD28	8	800	700	---	LS	Saurer 6BLD 6-cyl 75 hp 1,600 rpm	CP 3 AH NS FV	ABE
DT11	Saurer 6BLD	6	95	2,000	---	LS	---	LS 1 FM – FV	ABE
DT12	Saurer 6BLD	6	100	2,000	---	LS	---	LS 1 FM – FV	ABE
DT16	Saurer 6BLD	6	95	2,000	---	LS	---	LS 1 FM – FV	
DT19	Sulzer 6LD25	6	450	700	382	LS	Saurer 4BOD 4-cyl 50 hp 1,600 rpm	CP 4 AH NS FV	
DT20	Sulzer 6LD22	6	250	775	---	LS	---	LS 1 FM – FV	
DT22	Saurer 6BLD	6	85	1,700	---	LS	---	LS 1 FM – FV	ABE
DT23	Sulzer 8LD28	8	800	700	---	LS	Saurer 6BLD 6-cyl 75 hp 1,600 rpm	CP 3 AH NS FV	
DT30	Sulzer 6LD25	6	450	750	350	LS		CP 2 AH NS FV	
DT31	Saurer 6BXD	6	122	1,400	95	LS		CP 2 AH NS FV	ABE
DT34	Saurer 6BXD	6	122	1,400	90/85	LS		LS 1 FM – FV	ABE
DT36	Saurer 6BLD	6	85	1,700	78	LS		LS 1 FM – FV	ABE
DT41	Saurer 6BLD	6	122	1,400	103	LS		LS 1 FM – FV	ABE
DT43	Saurer 6BXD	6	140	1,400	121	LS		LS 1 FM – FV	ABE
DT44	Saurer 6BXD	6	122	1,400	116	LS		LS 1 FM – FV	ABE
DT51	Sulzer 8LD34	8	1200	630	984	LS	Saurer 6BLD 6-cyl 75 hp 1,600 rpm	CP 4 AH NS FV	ABE
DT60	Saurer 6BLD	6	100	1,700	92	LS		LS 1 FM – FV	ABE
DT61	Saurer 4BOD	4	60	1,700	58	LS		LS 1 FM – FV	ABE
DT63	Sulzer 6LTD22	6	400	1,000	350	CP		CP 1 FM – FV	
DT68	Sulzer 6LTD22	6	400	1,000	340	CP		CP 1 FM – FV	ABE
DT71	Saurer 6BXD	6	140	1,500	---	LS		LS 1 FM – FV	supercharged engine
DT73	Sulzer 6LD25	6	600	750	---	EE		EE 3 FM – FV	

Table 2
Diesel Traction Department Order Numbers
See Table 7 for details of orders for vehicles
(Items not traced were not new locomotive orders)

DT1	Vehicles D1-D3, built new
DT2	not traced
DT3	Vehicles D4-D6, built new
DT4	Vehicle D7, built new
DT5	not traced
DT6	not traced
DT7	Vehicle D8, built new
DT8	Vehicle D9, built new
DT9	not traced
DT10	not traced
DT11	Vehicle D10, built new
DT12	Vehicles D11-D14, built new
DT13	Two Armstrong-Sulzer 8LDA28 Engine/Generator Sets. One for DT8, one for DT23
DT14	Two Armstrong-Sulzer 8LDA25 Engine/Generator Sets. One for DT19
DT15	Five Armstrong-Saurer 6BXD Engine/Generator Sets. One for DT11, four for DT12
DT16	Vehicle D15, built new
DT17	Vehicle D1. Sold to L&NER
DT18	Twenty-five Armstrong-Saurer 6BXD Engines for Railcars. One each for DT31, 34, 41, 44 (order book states twenty transferred to DT52)
DT19	Vehicles D16-D19, built new
DT20	Vehicle D20, built new
DT21	Vehicle D10. Demonstrated at Frodingham Iron & Steel Co.
DT22	Vehicles D21-D26, built new
DT23	Vehicles D27 and D28, built new
DT24	Two Armstrong-Sulzer 8LDA28 Engine/Generator Sets. For DT23 (order book states one transferred to DT13)
DT25	Vehicle D10. Demonstrated at J. Lyons & Co., Greenford
DT26	Vehicle D8. Demonstrated on Southern Railway
DT27	not traced
DT28	not traced
DT29	not traced
DT30	Vehicles D35 and D36, built new
DT31	Vehicle D37, built new
DT32	One shunting locomotive with hydraulic transmission for stock. (Order cancelled)
DT33	not traced
DT34	Vehicle D39, built new
DT35	Vehicle D15. Demonstrated on L&NER
DT36	Vehicle D40, built new
DT37	Vehicle D10. Demonstrated at North Eastern Electric Supply Co.
DT38	Vehicle D10. Demonstrated on L&NER at York
DT39	Vehicle D10. Demonstrated at Rowntree & Co., York
DT40	Vehicle D10. Demonstrated on North Sunderland Railway
DT41	Vehicle D41, built new
DT42	Vehicle D25. Sold to North Sunderland Railway
DT43	Vehicles D46-D51, built new
DT44	Vehicle D43, built new
DT45	Vehicle D21. Sold to North Eastern Electric Supply Co., Dunston
DT46	Vehicle D9. Demonstrated on L&NER
DT47	Vehicle D8. Demonstrated on Hartley Main Colliery Railway
DT48	Vehicle D29. Demonstrated at W.D. R.E. Shoeburyness
DT49	Vehicle D24. Demonstrated at Bass Ratcliff & Gretton, Burton-upon-Trent
DT50	Vehicle D22. Demonstrated at Dorman Long & Co., Middlesbrough 3/1934 [?]
DT51	Vehicles D44 and D45, built new
DT52	Ten Armstrong-Saurer 6BXD Engines for DT43
DT53	Vehicles D2 and D3. Sold to L&NER
DT54	Vehicle D22. Demonstrated at Warner & Co., Cargo Fleet
DT55	Vehicle D24. Demonstrated at ICI Metals Ltd, Kynoch Works, Witton
DT56	Three 25-ton 0-4-0 DE Shunting Locomotives for stock. Twin engined. (Order cancelled)
DT57	Vehicle D23. Demonstrated at Gas Light & Coke Co. Beckton
DT58	Vehicle D15. Sold to L&NER
DT59	Vehicles D27 and D28. Demonstrated on Ceylon Govt Railways
DT60	Vehicle D52, built new
DT61	Vehicle D53, built new
DT62	not traced
DT63	Vehicles D54-D63, built new
DT64	Vehicle D8. Demonstrated and sold to Ribble Navigation, Preston
DT65	Vehicle D23. Sold to Admiralty, R.N. Dockyard, Chatham
DT66	Ten Armstrong-Sulzer 6LTD22 engines for DT63
DT67	Eight Armstrong-Sulzer 6LF19 engines and mechanical transmissions for use in power bogies of Birmingham Carriage & Wagon Co. built Central Argentine Railway railcars. Built new
DT68	Vehicle D64, built new
DT69	Vehicles D35 and D36. Sold to Buenos Aires Western Railway
DT70	Vehicle D37. Sold to Buenos Aires Western Railway
DT71	Vehicles D65-D70, built new
DT72	Ten Armstrong-Saurer BXD engines of modified design for stock
DT73	Vehicles D71 and D72, built new
DT74	Vehicles D27 and D28. Reconditioning after trials in Ceylon
DT75	Vehicles D27 and D28. Sold to Buenos Aires Great Southern Railway 1/1937
DT76	Vehicle D24. Sold to Thames Board Mills Ltd, Warrington 2/1937
DT77	Vehicle D22. Sold to A. Reyrolle & Co. Ltd, Hebburn 3/1937
DT78	Vehicle D26. Sold to Magnesium Elektron Ltd, Manchester 4/1937
DL1	Vehicle D24. Demonstrated at Austin Motor Co., Birmingham
DL2	Vehicle D23. Demonstrated at Admiralty, Chatham
DL3	Vehicle D24. Demonstrated at Dunlop Rubber Co., Birmingham
DL4	Vehicle D8. Demonstrated at Lever Bros Ltd, Port Sunlight
DL5	Vehicle D24. Demonstrated at Newills Dock Co.
DL6	Vehicle D24. Demonstrated at Bede Metal & Chemical Co., Hebburn

Probably the first of the railcars approaching completion in the autumn of 1931 in another view from the *Armstrong Whitworth Record*.

John Horne collection

THE FIRST RAILCARS

The initial venture of the Diesel Traction Department was an order for three identical diesel electric railcars for demonstration on British main line railways. Built under order No. DT1 and carrying works numbers D1 to D3, they were designed to meet the requirements of all four railways and it was hoped to demonstrate them widely to show their effective uses.

It was intended that for the majority of purposes the vehicles would work as single units, or with a 30 ton driving trailer, but they were to be capable of operation in multiple with others of the same type, or as part of a train set of such cars and trailers.

Their flexibility of operation was set out thus:

A. As a two-coach train, formed of two railcars
B. As a two-coach train, formed of a railcar and trailer
C. As four- or six-coach sets, two railcars and four or six trailers
D. As a six-coach train, three railcars and three trailers

These railcars had sufficient power to haul trailers and maintain high-speed schedules under most conditions. At first sight, a single vehicle with its own diesel-electric equipment of 250 bhp seems unduly costly but in the eyes of Armstrong Whitworth it was justifiable.

These cars were built in the tender shop at Scotswood, the first chassis being completed during late summer 1931, with its body fitted by October. The railcars were of all steel construction, the underframe consisting of two main solebars of rolled steel channel running full length between the headstocks. Bracing was by longitudinal and cross-members, also of rolled steel, securely riveted. Headstocks, braced by diagonals, were stiffened by reinforcing plates running full width both top and bottom. Additional strengthening was provided under the power unit. The standard buffing and drawgear was lightweight in design. Mild steel plates and sections were used for the bogie frames, stiffened with blocked angles and braced against lateral distortion. The bolster was supported on two nests of

The first Armstrong Whitworth railcar *Tyneside Venturer* on a test run on the L&NER Newcastle-Carlisle line when new.

University of Glasgow

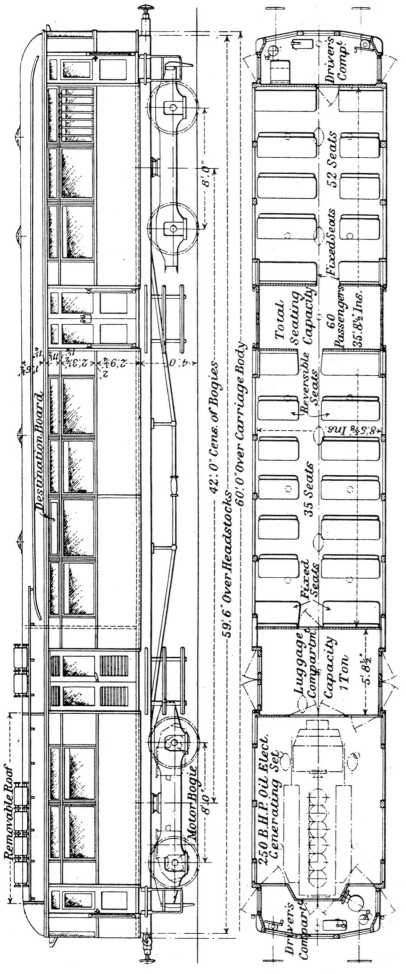

Diagram of DT1 type railcar. Scale 4mm - 1ft.
Brian Webb collection

Opposite: The engine being craned in to one of the railcar units at the Scotswood Works. The Sulzer diesel unit appears to have the generator attached and all is sat on a bedplate. The ease of its removal whilst in service is therefore apparent and could be carried out at any reasonably equipped repair facility. *Brian Webb collection*

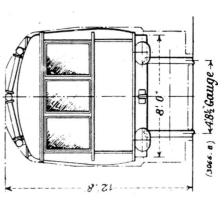

spiral springs carried on a channel spring plank slung from the bogie frame by adjustable swing links. The laminated bearing springs had rubber auxiliary springs and the axleboxes were of Isothermos type. Consolidated Brake Co. Ltd vacuum braking was fitted, with a handbrake wheel in each cab. The sanding was foot operated.

The all-steel body was built on to the railcar underframe by Cravens Ltd of Sheffield and consisted of rolled steel sections riveted and well braced to the underframe. The body sides and roof were of steel sheet, riveted and weatherproofed at the joints. The roof over the power equipment compartment had the radiators mounted on it and was removable to allow access to engine and generator from above and, if need be, lifting out.

There was accommodation for sixty passengers in reversible upholstered seats covered in moquette with leather facings. Lighting was electric and all metal fittings were chromium plated. The passenger compartment sides and partitions were lined with mahogany-faced plywood panels, while the floor was of deal covered with felt and a heavy linoleum. The ceiling was in finished and moulded Sundeala panels.

Each car had five distinct compartments, starting with a driving cab at each end. Next to No. 1 cab was the engine room, being followed by the guard's and luggage compartment with a capacity of one ton, and the passenger area. The windows were of frameless balanced drop type. The cars were fitted for multiple-unit operation with the appropriate lighting, braking, and power-control jumper cables at each end.

The engine used came from the initial batch of Scotswood-built Armstrong-Sulzer engines of type 6LV22, a six-cylinder vertical unit rated at 250 bhp at 775 rpm. Laurence Scott & Electromotors Ltd supplied the main generator of the self-ventilated, part decompounded type, being of lightweight, but rigid, construction. An auxiliary generator of the same make was fitted to supply excitation, control current, and charge the battery; this was mounted on top of the main generator. Traction motors by GEC Ltd were self-ventilating axle-hung units – one to each axle of the bogie at the engine room end. They had Spencer-Moulton rubber nose-suspension springs. The usual fuses, contactors and reverser were fitted for the motors: in a case slung under the railcar. The generator control cubicle was in the engine room and housed automatic field rheostat (to control tractive effort), ammeter, voltmeter, etc. The driving cabs contained the driving controls and instruments – master controller, engine start buttons, driver's brake valve, vacuum gauge, sanding pedal, lighting switches, warning horn lever and dead man's handle.

The roof-mounted engine coolant radiators had thermostatic control for circulation. When the car was coasting or standing at stations with its engine shut down, the water pump was driven from the battery, as was the vacuum exhauster. The usual engine safety devices were fitted and were automatic in operation.

Following completion and trials of the first railcar at Scotswood Works in October/November 1931 it was made available for inspection by railway officials of the L&NER, including H. N. Gresley their CME on 23rd November. This was followed by a trial run over the L&NER, on the Newcastle-Blackhill route under the supervision of Gresley and Col. P. D. Ionides of Armstrong Whitworth.

Tyneside Venturer in its blue and cream livery during its demonstration period.　　　　　　　　　　　　　　　　　　　*Brian Webb collection*

Tyneside Venturer leaving Newcastle Central whilst on trials. *Colling Turner, John Alsop collection*

Tyneside Venturer running in multiple with one of the other railcars, probably *Northumbrian* painted in undercoat only, at an unidentified location. *John Alsop collection*

Tyneside Venturer seemingly on shed at an unknown location. *Brian Webb collection*

Tyneside Venturer together with a trailer car running into Scarborough from Pickering on the 29th July 1933.
Dr J. R. Hollick, John Alsop collection

The second Armstrong Whitworth railcar *Lady Hamilton* in the yard at Scotswood Works.　　　　*Brian Webb collection*

On the outward run nine stops were made, as on a typical service over the route, and 6½ minutes were gained on the schedule of 45 minutes set by the L&NER. The return journey was via Lanchester, Durham and Birtley and being non-stop enabled a top speed of 64 mph to be attained. Gresley was said to have been impressed by the railcar and to have described the trial as 'extremely successful'. The outcome was that the L&NER decided to permit further trials on various parts of its network.

Tests carried out over the York-Malton-Whitby-Scarborough route on 21st-22nd January 1932 with the first car now called *Tyneside Venturer*, proved its ability to cope with various duties with complete ease. On the run from York to Malton speeds over 60 mph were attained, while on the Malton-Whitby line, with gradients of 1 in 49 to 1 in 75 between Levisham and Goathland, it exceeded 40 mph.

The coastal section from Whitby to Scarborough, with the notorious bank of 1 in 39/43 between Whitby West Cliff and Hawsker followed by the 1 in 39 to Ravenscar, was negotiated very well. The former bank was climbed at an average of 25 mph, while the latter, following a stop at Fyling Hall, saw the three miles to and through Ravenscar Tunnel covered at 23 mph. The whole of the run to Scarborough was with the engine unit to the rear.

The railcar was turned on Scarborough turntable before setting off for York. It stopped en route at Ganton and Knapton to permit acceleration tests, during which it was recorded that the car could achieve 20 mph in 26 seconds, 30 mph in 46 seconds and 40 mph in 82 seconds. Fuel consumption worked out at one gallon for five miles, with averages of four mpg on gradients and six mpg on the level.

On 16th February 1932, Armstrong Whitworth carried out another trial and demonstration run for the benefit of railway officials from home and overseas; this time between Newcastle and Hexham. By this time the second railcar was available to operate in multiple with the blue and cream painted *Tyneside Venturer*.

The westbound run to Hexham, 20¾ miles, was carried out reaching a maximum of 60 mph. It was noted that the vehicles were operating so evenly that the couplings between them were floating most of the time. On the return trip the official party visited Scotswood Works to see work in progress on the third railcar, 1,700 bhp twin-units for the Argentine, 15- and 40-ton shunting locomotives, narrow gauge railcars for India, and the prototype 800 bhp mainline locomotive for British trials.

At a luncheon held at the central Station Hotel, Newcastle, much hope was expressed by those present that the work underway at Scotswood would revive the hopes of the British locomotive industry and bring an upsurge in work to Tyneside.

The second railcar was subsequently named *Lady Hamilton* in connection with some 'hoped for' trials on the Southern Railway and the fact that they had a locomotive named *Lord Nelson*! This car was noteworthy in pre-dating the much publicised mainline running of the 'Armstrong-Shell Express' by being run to London King's Cross from Newcastle on the East Coast route on 7th July 1932. The car stayed in London for a week, carrying out demonstration runs between King's Cross and Hertford North.

The return northbound run saw the car following the 13.40 express, taking 5 hours 58 minutes for the run to Newcastle at an average speed of 47.6 mph. Although this was not a fast average, it must be remembered that it compared well with the five hours allowed for a typical London-Newcastle express of the period.

The railcar was stopped twelve times and suffered nine signal checks, all of which combined to reduce accelerating times and retard running, while the car had a top maximum speed of 65 mph. Fuel consumption for the run was 42.8 gallons, giving 6.27 mpg, at a cost of $^{1}/_{2}$d per mile.

The actual running times recorded by Armstrong Whitworth are as follows:

	Arrive	Depart	Stopping Time/Reason
Finsbury Park	--	13.50	--
Grantham Station	15.49$^{1}/_{2}$	15.52	2$^{1}/_{2}$
Retford (Grove Road Box)	16.31	16.38	7
Doncaster (South Box)	16.59$^{1}/_{2}$	17.02	2$^{1}/_{2}$
Doncaster Station	17.03	17.07	4
York Station	17.51	17.56	5
York-Northallerton section			4/signal checks
Castle Hill	18.38	18.46$^{1}/_{2}$	8$^{1}/_{2}$
Wiske Moor	18.48	19.08	20/defective signals
Wiske Moor-Newcastle section	19.24	19.27	
	19.57	19.58	6$^{1}/_{2}$/signal checks
	20.03	20.05	
Newcastle Station	20.28		

Totals, London Newcastle: 6 hours 38 minutes, including 1 hour stopping time

London Newcastle: 5 hours 38 minutes running time

Mileage: 268
Fuel cost: 42.8 gallons;
6.2 mpg or 11s 8d for journey

During December 1933 the Southern Railway Locomotive Committee enquired of Armstrong Whitworth for information on diesel railcars and details were sent to them for a railcar of 41 tons 17 cwt in working order. This seated sixty passengers and was evidently powered by a 100 bhp engine, a cost of £3,485 was quoted. It would appear that one of the DT1 railcars was sent to the Southern Railway for trials in April 1934. But, apart from it catching fire at New Cross shed on 28th April 1933 due to steam locomotive sparks, little is known, or has yet been discovered, to enable its identity or its performance to be established. It may have been *Lady Hamilton* which was involved.

On 18th June 1934 *Lady Hamilton* began fast cross-country services between Hull, York, Selby and Pontefract, giving a weekly mileage of 2,380 in summer and 1,626 in winter.

The third of the railcars, *Northumbrian*, was used by Armstrong Whitworth, Shell-Mex, and BP Ltd to provide a special demonstration service between London Euston and Castle Bromwich to convey specially invited guests attending the British Industries Fair in February/March 1933. It was an express luxury service and, prior to final planning arrangements, *Northumbrian* worked a trial run over the route to prove proposed schedules on 16th February 1933.

Once these were established, the railcar was taken into the LMS carriage works and fitted out as a luxury private saloon with accommodation for twelve people, a completely equipped kitchen, as well as wardrobe and toilet accommodation. The internal decor was redesigned to achieve a luxurious effect with carpets, curtains, separate arm chairs and tables in carefully chosen colours.

One saloon seated eight, the other four; mahogany panelling was used with a cream painted ceiling and subdued lighting

Lady Hamilton in multiple with *Northumbrian* just west of Hexham on a trial run on the Newcastle-Carlisle line. *Brian Webb collection*

Northumbrian, in its temporary guise as the Armstrong-Shell Express, pulls out of Euston in February/March 1933 while working a special in connection with the British Industries Fair at Castle Bromwich over LMS metals. *Brian Webb collection*

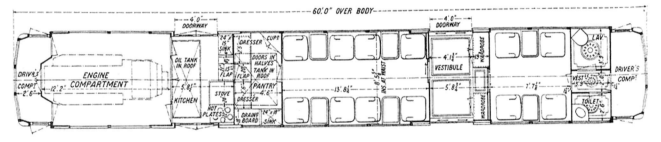

The interior layout of the Armstrong-Shell Express showing the kitchen, wardrobe and extra toilet facilities that were fitted. *Brian Webb Collection*

effects, strip lighting behind translucent pelmets was fitted to the sides. The carpets had thick pile and the chairs and tables were provided by the Pullman Car Co. Ltd. Coloured table covers and oiled silk window curtains completed the interior.

Recording instruments mounted in a panel in each compartment provided a new source of interest and information for passengers. These instruments included clock, speedometer, fuel gauge and animated route chart to show the car's progress on the journey. The service operated Monday-Friday from 20th February to 3rd March 1933 between Euston and Castle Bromwich, a special station being built at the latter for this purpose. Painted blue and cream, and temporarily renamed 'The Armstrong-Shell Express', the car set out to emulate daily its test run when it had covered the 113 miles run in 2 hours 7 minutes.

The schedules were as follows:

Euston, depart 11.35	Castle Bromwich, depart 16.43
Birmingham, arrive 13.41	Birmingham, arrive 16.58
Birmingham, depart 13.47	Birmingham, depart 17.03
Castle Bromwich, arrive 14.03	Euston, arrive 19.15

The average fuel consumption for the 113 miles trip was 22.5 gallons at 3½d per gallon, a total of 6s 7d. Speeds of 70 mph were recorded. The timings needed an average speed of 53.4 mph and were adhered to, except when two snowstorms caused signal checks and loss of time.

The car covered 2,420 miles and used 427 gallons of fuel. The catering service was undertaken by the LMS Hotels Department under the direction of the Royal Train Chef. After the end of its

Northumbrian in service with a trailer consisting of an ex NER clerestory.

John Alsop collection

One of the railcars running in undercoat on a trial run with a trailer car passing the birthplace of George Stephenson at Wylam.
Brian Webb collection

The third DT1 railcar *Northumbrian* passes Wiske Moor troughs on the L&NER main line in 1934 on an Up run.
J. W. Armstrong

Tyneside Venturer photographed at Middlesbrough shed on the 7th June 1933, still in Armstrong Whitworth colours some six months after its purchase by the L&NER.
J. W. Armstrong, Brian Webb collection

duty the car re-entered Wolverton to be restored to its original form as *Northumbrian*.

Tyneside Venturer in the meanwhile, had been put into regular service on the L&NER in the Newcastle and Middlesbrough areas from the 11th April 1932, continuing until 12th December, a thirty-five week service period. In the Newcastle area the car started work at 06.55 Monday and finished at 00.03 Friday, being in service 17 hours 8 minutes daily. Running service was nine hours eight minutes, with eight hours idle at stations etc., building up a daily mileage of over 207 miles. The car worked Newcastle-Hexham, on the line to Blackhill to Rowlands Gill and Lintz Green, and also on the North Wylam line.

On Teeside the car worked Monday-Friday from 05.04 to 21.43, putting in 16 hours 39 minutes and 7½ hours running. Idle time amounted to 9 hours 9 minutes and the daily mileage was 162 miles. On Saturdays the service was from 05.04 to 23.32, putting in 18 hours 28 minutes and 9 hours 14 minutes running. Idle time was 9 hours 14 minutes and daily mileage, 206. The car worked Middlesbrough-Guisborough and a few trips to Loftus and Saltburn.

The railcar achieved 100 per cent availability for thirty-five weeks, building up a mileage of 34,146 miles which, on an annual basis, gave it some 50,000 miles per year. The car's average fuel consumption was 4.82 mpg. A pool of twelve L&NER drivers were used for the car and they drove under the watchful eye of the maker's representative.

Upon inspection of the vehicle and equipment after thirty-five weeks it was found that the engine was in excellent condition, only slight re-grinding of exhaust-valve seats being needed, the valves themselves having been replaced at twenty-eight weeks due to slight pitting. Cylinder liners, although slightly worn at the top, were in good condition. However, the intention to replace mild steel liners with nitricast iron liners was carried out to gain operating experience. Some remetalling of connecting rod white metal bearings, due to poor adhesion and cracking, was carried out, as was also done to two of the main crankshaft bearings. Fuel injection valves had only slight carbon deposits and had been changed monthly. The electrical equipment was entirely satisfactory and, apart from some attention to fuses and a reversing finger due to bad contact, only cleaning was needed.

Trials of Railcar *Tyneside Venturer* – extract from official Armstrong Whitworth report dated 11th March 1937.

Date Started Service	Service Worked	Miles Weekly	Days Weekly	Fuel mpg
11.04.1932	Newcastle-Hexham	978	5	5-5½
09.05.1932	Newcastle-Hexham	1045	5	5-5½
18.10.1932	Middlesbrough-Guisborough	1035	6	4½
20.02.1933	Saltburn-Scarborough	1112	6	3½
01.05.1933	Middlesbrough-Guisborough	1280	6	4
17.07.1933	Scarborough 'Round the Moors'	350	5	3½-4

> Copy of Confidential Report on the Three Railcars of Order DT1 and their performance during 1934/35
>
> | | *Tyneside Venturer* | | *Northumbrian* | | *Lady Hamilton* | |
> |---|---|---|---|---|---|---|
> | miles run per year | 22551 | 45612 | 33088 | 47414 | 44525 | 60799 |
> | miles per day in service | 158 | 185 | 286 | 263 | 361 | 383 |
> | availability (per cent) | 45 | 77 | 68 | 53 | 73 | 50 |
> | fuel, mpg | 3.85 | 3.51 | 5.00 | 5.33 | 4.70 | 4.92 |
> | lubricating oil (per cent) | 1.90 | 1.16 | 2.20 | 1.98 | 1.48 | 1.04 |
> | fuel cost (pence per mile) | 1.08 | 1.05 | 0.78 | 0.56 | 0.83 | 0.60 |
> | lubricating and stores per mile | 0.33 | 0.18 | 0.31 | 0.19 | 0.23 | 0.15 |
> | total including wages and maintenance (pence per mile) | 10.50 | 5.30 | 5.18 | 4.94 | 4.87 | 5.60 |
> | total including coachwork, interest, depreciation (pence per mile) | 20.45 | 9.10 | 7.22 | 8.08 | 6.18 | 8.13 |
>
> As can be seen, the availability was not all it should have been, but the report stated 'The L&NER are trying to improve their availability'.

Following this inspection the car was handed over to the L&NER for service between Saltburn and Scarborough. The L&NER purchased *Tyneside Venturer* on 24th November 1932 at a price of £7,500; it became No. 25 and retained its name.

In L&NER service during winter the car worked between Middlesbrough and Scarborough and in summer took the 'Round the Moors Tour from Scarborough'. This tour departed Scarborough at 10.00, arriving at Whitby for lunch via Malton and Pickering, and the car hauled a trailer coach.

For a short period in 1935 the railcar was used in the Bradford/Keighley area.

Tyneside Venturer received works visits in September 1934, April 1936 & October 1937, generally spending eight to twelve weeks in works. It was taken out of service during April 1939 after sustaining minor collision damage at Middlesbrough. Repairs were not forthcoming, having completed just in excess of 250,000 miles running. It was then taken to Darlington Works where it was stored out of use.

Tyneside Venturer **now in L&NER livery of green and cream with that company's style of lettering for the name and numbered 25.**
Brian Webb collection

What looks to be *Northumbrian* in service with a trailer car during a station stop. *Brian Webb collection*

The L&NER purchased the other two cars on 26th April 1934 at £5,500 each; *Lady Hamilton* became car No. 224 and *Northumbrian* No. 232.

Lady Hamilton appears to have clocked up considerably less miles than *Tyneside Venturer* being plagued by many reliability issues. It was in for repair in January-February 1935 and for general repairs in December. During 1936 it received attention in June, August and October and again in January and May 1937. The last problem appears major as *Lady Hamilton* was still in works in December 1938. A further visit to works was undertaken in April 1939 with electrical problems. At this time it may have been working in the Hull area from where it was withdrawn in December 1939. It had also spent a period in the London area although no details are known. Despite its problems *Lady Hamilton* was the last of the railcars in use.

After purchase by the L&NER *Northumbrian* was set to work between York, Harrogate and Leeds with a weekly mileage of 1,670 to 1,740 miles. Towards the end of October 1935 it was at Darlington Works for major repairs to the power unit which required its removal to Armstrong Whitworth for attention. *Northumbrian* returned to service at Neville Hill Shed, Leeds. A further engine failure occurred in July 1936 leaving *Northumbrian* out of service for twelve months. Like *Lady Hamilton* it returned to service in the Hull area in July 1937. There followed a slight problem with a traction motor but thereafter it was not in need of general repairs until May 1939. It was during 1938 that *Northumbrian* could often be found deputising for the bedeviled *Lady Hamilton*.

Having gone in for repair these were not forthcoming and Northumbrian was put in store with Tyneside Venturer at Darlington Works where in August 1944 all three railcars could be found awaiting scrapping.

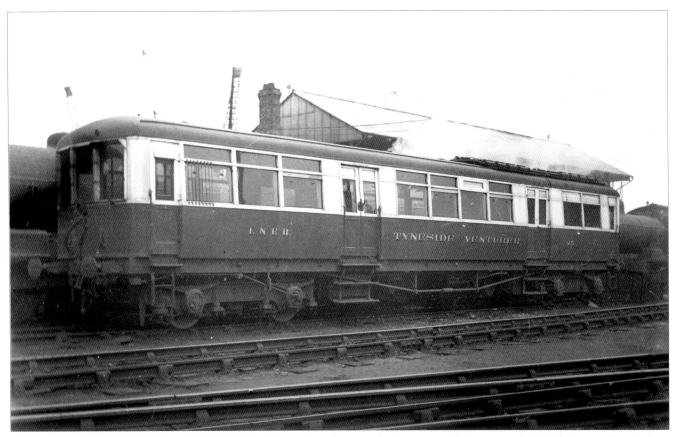

Tyneside Venturer is seen again at Middlesbrough, probably towards the end of its service life bearing its L&NER livery, albeit looking somewhat shabby.
J. W. Armstrong, Brian Webb collection

Carrying L&NER livery and its number of 232, *Northumbrian* is seen in works with a ladder resting up against the far end. Notice the wire mesh grill over the end windows.
Brian Webb collection

This striking image was originally entitled 'A Railway Colossus' with the addition of 'with an ordinary steam locomotive'. Taken somewhere on the L&NER during trials D8 looks well used and not spruced-up for the obvious publicity shot. It was obviously hoped that this was to be the new order.
Brian Webb collection

AW D8/32, the prototype 0-6-0 DE shunter of 250 bhp at work on the L&NER.   *Brian Webb collection*

THE FIRST SHUNTERS

During 1932 Armstrong Whitworth put in hand two prototype oil-electric shunting locomotives under orders DT7 and DT11. The first of these, order DT7, was a milestone in UK shunting development and represented the first attempt by a British locomotive manufacturer to enter the field of highpower, mainline standard, shunting locomotives. It was completed at Scotswood in late spring 1932, carrying works No. D8, and was to set the standard for all 250-400 bhp 0-6-0 shunters for the next decade or so.

The mechanical portion followed locomotive practice with plate frames but welding was extensively used in its fabrication: including cross-stretchers and racking plates to carry the jackshaft unit, and bufferbeams, the latter carrying standard buffing and drawgear. Axleboxes, guides, and bearing springs were of the usual type, except the attachment flanges of the axlebox guides to the frame were larger to provide a larger bearing area on the frame plates and to combine the brackets for spring link connections. Compensated springing was provided between first and second axles. The jackshaft drive unit, placed between the centre and rear axles, was carried in bearings lubricated on the isothermos principle, fitted into openings in the frame, and with definite location in all directions.

The engine bonnet housing was of conventional construction, based on a rolled-steel framework covered with sheet steel and holding the engine/generator set, auxiliary generator, fuel tank and silencer; the radiator was at the front end. The bonnet top had sliding and removable access sections; full height bonnet side doors were provided along each side of the bonnet. The driver's cab at the rear end had side doors and windows, giving limited forward vision alongside the sloping bonnet side, but the rearward vision was excellent over the low height rear battery box which resembled the coal bunker of a steam tank engine to the traditionalist.

Braking was by two vacuum cylinders, sited under the battery box at both sides of the rear underframing, operating through a shaft and rigging to brake blocks on all wheels. The brake hangers for the centre axle were arranged to allow for the $1^{1}/_{2}$ inch side movement allowed with this axle. Hand sanding gear was fitted.

The control gear, in a cubicle in the cab, was designed for the work of the locomotive – namely shunting at low speeds. Simplicity of control was obtained by using one power handle and a reverse-forward gear handle. All controls were duplicated, allowing for operation from both sides of the cab. A time-lag deadman's pedal was fitted. The driver had no need to watch the controls, for it was impossible to overload the engine; this enabled him to give his full attention to the shunting work.

An Armstrong-Sulzer type 6LV22 vertical engine with six cylinders, exactly similar to that of the railcars, was fitted, but a 6LD22 engine could be fitted if required. Electrical equipment was by Laurence, Scott and Electromotors Ltd, comprising a directly coupled main generator and one frame mounted traction motor mounted directly above the final drive unit, a forced ventilation machine. Final drive was by jackshaft and siderods.

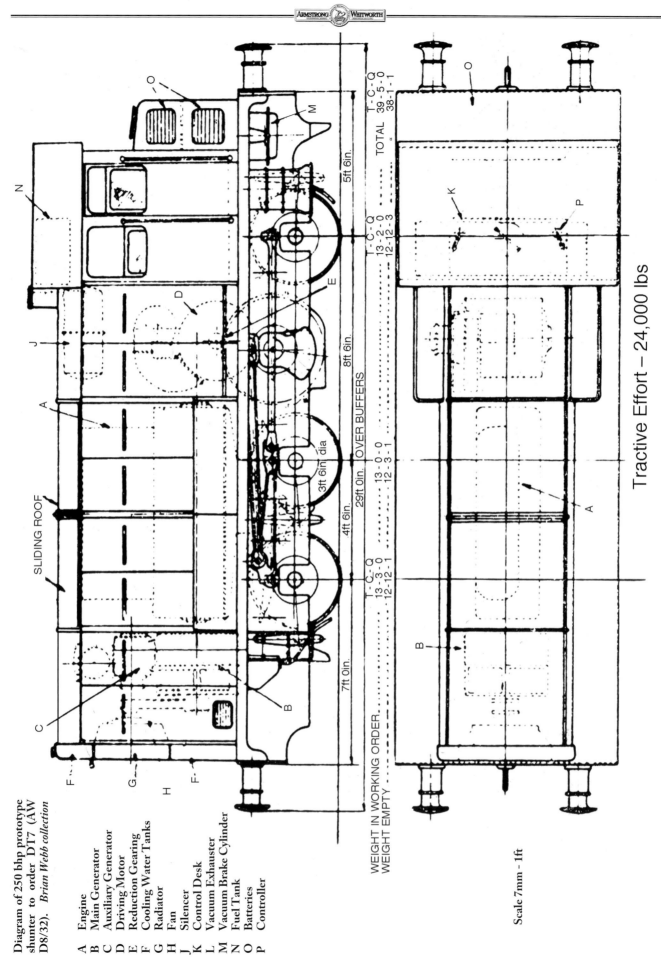

Diagram of 250 bhp prototype shunter to order DT7 (AW D8/32). *Brian Webb collection*

A   Engine
B   Main Generator
C   Auxiliary Generator
D   Driving Motor
E   Reduction Gearing
F   Cooling Water Tanks
G   Radiator
H   Fan
J   Silencer
K   Control Desk
L   Vacuum Exhauster
M   Vacuum Brake Cylinder
N   Fuel Tank
O   Batteries
P   Controller

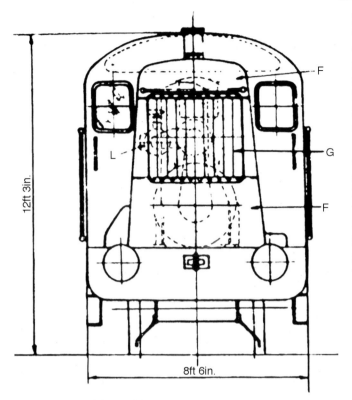

End elevation of the 250 bhp prototype. *Brian Webb collection*

Engine starting was by motoring the main generator from the battery, which was kept charged by the auxiliary generator – automatically controlled to give its correct charging current at both engine speeds. Full protective devices provided the safety equipment for the engine and electrical equipment.

Following extensive works tests and trials, the shunter was officially unveiled for trials on the L&NER on 10th June 1932 and taken to the Forth goods yard where it demonstrated its prowess. It successfully hauled, stopped, and started, a 550 ton freight train on a 1 in 200 gradient, then undertook shunting and remarshalling work. The activity was keenly watched by a party of Armstrong Whitworth and L&NER officials: it was actually driven for a period by H. N. Gresley, the L&NER CME, who was impressed by the locomotive's capabilities. An agreement was reached with the L&NER to enable the locomotive to do yard shunting in railway goods depots on Tyneside, taking effect from 11th July.

It was first sent to Blaydon shed for work in Forth and Blaydon yards, being employed normally on three shifts of eight hours per day, six days each week, commencing at 06.00 Monday and operating continuously until 06.00 on Sunday. The only exceptions being August Bank Holiday Monday, when it was not on duty, and one week when it only worked two eight hour shifts per day. At Forth yard it shunted miscellaneous traffic, but at Blaydon, mostly heavy goods and mineral traffic. From 22nd August it moved to Heaton South and North sidings, continuing there until 30th October when the trials ceased.

The locomotive was handled throughout by L&NER drivers, one per shift, under the supervision of an Armstrong Whitworth representative, a total of twenty-seven drivers handling the locomotive during its sixteen weeks' trial: one hour's tuition was sufficient for each driver. The locomotive performed satisfactorily, the only troubles being with a derailment in the fourth week at Blaydon yard, a blown fuse, blocked sanding gear, leaking radiator elements, and lubrication problems with the jackshaft bearings. Availability was assessed as follows:

Total Hrs Scheduled for Duty	Total Hrs on Duty	Hrs Oil Engine Working	Oil Engine Failures	Availability (percent)
2,233	2,193	1,505	none	98.5

The difference of 1.5% was due to the derailment and some persistent troubles with the vacuum brake. The oil engine itself was available 100%.

An interesting fact emerged from the trials: the locomotive's engine running hours, as checked by the recorder, amounted to 1,505 hours or 68.7% of the actual time the locomotive was on duty. This meant that for just over 7.5 hours in a twenty-four hour duty the locomotive was standing by and consuming no fuel. The total time spent standing by during its sixteen weeks trial period was a remarkable total of five weeks: The superiority over steam traction in this aspect alone was made the most of by Armstrong Whitworth. During sixteen weeks of 2,193 service hours the locomotive consumed 5,628 gallons of fuel, or 21.8 lbs per hour.

Trials and demonstrations were also undertaken at the following locations:

1. SR at Bricklayers Arms, Eastleigh and Norwood yards.
2. Industrial service with Hartley Main Colliery.
3. Industrial service with Lever Bros Ltd, Port Sunlight.
4. Industrial service with Ribble Navigation, Preston Docks.

LIST OF TRIALS UNDERTAKEN BY 250 BHP 0-6-0 DE

Location	Service Days	Service Hours	Locomotive Hours	Fuel (gallons)	Lub. Oil (gallons)	Maintenance (man hours)	Load Factor (per cent)
L&NER	87	2,765¼	2,764¼	7,379	41¾	181¼	21.6
1.	58	1,185¼	654½	2,948	23	105¼	20.2
2.	16	270½	246½	915	17	65	27.4
3.	28	252	231	800	8	50	25.7
4.	13	106¼	104¼	322	4	6½	24.6
Totals	202	4,579¼	4,000½	12,364	93¾	453	21.8

PARTICULARS OF 250 BHP 0-6-0 DE SHUNTER ON TRIAL ON THE L&NER IN 1932

Yard	1. Forth	2. Blaydon No. 3 pilot	3. Blaydon No. 2 pilot	4. Heaton No. 2 pilot South	5. Heaton North
Date	11/7/32 to 24/7/32	25/7/32 to 31/7/32	2/8/32 to 21/8/32	22/8/32 to 16/10/32	17/10/32 to 30/10/32
Service (day)	3 shifts of 8 hrs	2 shifts of 8 hrs	3 shifts of 8 hrs	3 shifts of 8 hrs	3 shifts of 8 hrs
Service (week)	6 days or 144 hrs	6 days or 96 hrs	6 days or 144 hrs	6 days or 144 hrs	6 days or 144 hrs
Ave. load	200 tons	180 tons	180 tons	400 tons	300 tons
Max. load	600 tons	200 tons	200 tons	815 tons	——
Ave. no. of wagons per day	600	350	520	1000	1000
Length of haul	300 yds	120 yds	120 yds	360 yds	415 yds
Ave. no. of kicking off shunts per day	150	175	260	500	500
Ave. length of kicking off shunt	15 yds	8 yds	60 yds	10 yds	15 yds
Incline	1 in 200	1 in 198	1 in 198	1 in 143 1 in 204	level 1 in 732

Notes: At 1 the locomotive was mainly used in making up trains. At 2, 3, 4 the work was heavy, but medium at 1 and 5.

At Hartley Main it worked on trip duties to the coal staith on the Tyne, although its cooling system was not designed for such lengthy duties. The trials at this location terminated when a runaway wagon of ballast travelling at high speed hit the locomotive at the rear, almost totally destroying the cab, but fortunately without injury to the crew. The accident happened at the staith. The locomotive returned to Scotswood Works for repairs.

The prototype on trials at Hartley Main Colliery.
Brian Webb collection

During trials at Preston Docks the locomotive hauled and pushed a load of 981 tons on a level curved track.

After being frequently exhibited at Scotswood Works it was sold under order DT64 in March 1935 to Ribble Navigation, who gave it the name *Duchess* and used it alongside their steam shunters until it and they were replaced by new Sentinel diesels in early 1969.

Its thirty-four years at Preston were dogged by long and frequent periods in the workshops, their engineer expressing the comment that, in spite of the locomotive being an historic landmark in British railway history it was so 'at a cost which wasn't forseen when purchased'.

The main problem was with the drive, taken from the engine via a free wheel to operate the auxiliary generator and radiator cooling fan. This chain driven device was used by Armstrong Whitworth in orders DT1 (the three railcars) and DT7, proved most troublesome in service, and was not repeated in other locomotives or cars. The Preston shunter was many times failed due to a flat battery caused by haphazard charging by the auxiliary generator.

The prototype was sold to Ribble Navigation - Preston Docks and there was named *Duchess*. *Brian Webb collection*

Duchess remained in service at Preston until 1969 and is seen here at work in July 1967. *Allan C. Baker*

D10 was lent to the North Sunderland Railway and is here seen on a light passenger train at Chathill on the L&NER main line. Note that the locomotive did not have any provision for train braking!
Brian Webb collection

Order DT11 was for the small shunter completed in late 1932, carrying works No. D10. This prototype for demonstration was a fifteen ton unit of 0-4-0 layout, employing, of course, oil-electric transmission.

Its mechanical structure incorporated an all-welded plate frame base, rigidly braced and strengthened to support the power unit, reduction gear and jackshaft units. Horn blocks and brake hanger brackets were bolted on to facilitate renewal. The superstructure was simple, comprising a bonnet and open cab with roof, side running boards were fitted to enable the locomotive to be driven in shunting tractor fashion from a position outside the cab in addition to inside.

The engine used was the Armstrong-Saurer type 6BXD six-cylinder engine of 95 bhp at 2,000 rpm directly coupled to a Laurence, Scott and Electromotors generator. These items were resiliently mounted transversely across the front end of the locomotive on three rubber bushed bearings fixed to the underframe. Behind the power unit in the centre of the locomotive was a Laurence, Scott traction motor also transversely set above the reduction box and scotch-yoke type final drive within the wheelbase.

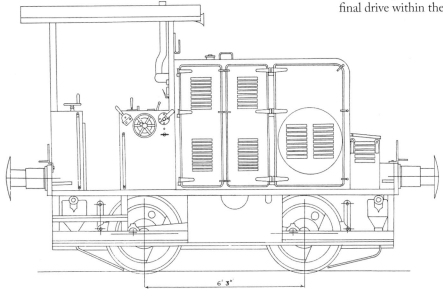

Side elevation of AW D10/32, the 15-ton 95 bhp 0-4-0 DE built under order DT11. Scale 7mm - 1ft. *Brian Webb*

The light shunting loco/tractor AW D10/32 being driven from the running board as it shunts in Scotswood Works yard. *Brian Webb*

Although AW D10 was never sold it was demonstrated widely, here with an unusually heavy train for its 95 bhp. It is seen at Scunthorpe while working at the Appleby-Frodingham steelworks. *Brian Webb collection*

The transmission was of the ABE type incorporating a self-excited generator and traction motor. Engine starting was by means of a winding on the generator excited from the battery, which also provided current for control, as well as lighting, and was charged by the engine when idling. The generator was arranged to take the full engine bhp throughout its speed range, so any tractive effort could be obtained simply by opening or closing the engine throttle.

The locomotive was available as a 'running-board' or cab type: in the former case the driver stood on the running-board and drove via the throttle-switch handle on each side of the locomotive. A special coupling and uncoupling device could be fitted.

It is recorded that the locomotive started shunting at Scotswood Works on 3rd December 1932; after three months it was sent out on demonstration. It was tried at Scunthorpe at the Appleby-Frodingham steelworks where, in spite of its low power, it completed its work successfully, shunting loads of coal, iron ore and scrap.

Following this it moved to the Lyons factory at Greenford, Middlesex, returning northwards to trials at Dunston Power Station on the south side of the Tyne – almost opposite Scotswood Works. D10 visited York where it was demonstrated on the L&NER and at Rowntree's chocolate factory on their internal rail system. Trials were carried out on the North Sunderland Railway on mixed traffic duties, even though the locomotive did not have equipment for train braking.

In September 1933 the locomotive was exhibited on the Armstrong Whitworth stand at the Shipping, Engineering and Machinery Exhibition at Olympia demonstrated on a 150 foot length of track.

While working on the North Sunderland Railway the locomotive did some 6,000 miles in five months, on trains of one or two coaches and wagons, weighing up to 90 tons, on the $4^{1}/_{4}$ mile line between Chathill on L&NER main line, and Seahouses on the coast. It could shunt up to 200 tons with ease and put in a weekly mileage of approximately 280, consuming about sixty-six gallons of fuel oil and two pints of lubricating oil. Each week 6-8 hours maintenance/preparation time was needed on the locomotive. The only replacements carried out were new brake blocks, two new pistons, and one cylinder head. In these instances it must be remembered that the locomotive had done a considerable amount of heavy industrial work prior to its NSR duties.

The locomotive returned to its shunting work at Scotswood on 4th August 1934. A surviving summary of running records relating to this locomotive, dated 23rd January 1937, stated the following:

1. Demonstrated at various industrial works and light railways, 1933/4.

Approx. time in service:	9½ months
Service hours:	2,340 (246 hrs/month)
Engine hours:	1,225 (129 hrs/month)
Locomotive hours:	1,050 (110 hrs/month)
Fuel consumption, total fuel consumed:	2,123 gallons

Fuel, gallons per service hour:	0.91
Fuel, gallons per engine hour:	1.74
Fuel, gallons per locomotive hour:	2.23

2. Lubricating oil consumption for period of service on the North Sunderland Light Railway:

Period:	6¾ months
Service hours:	1,675½ hours
Engine hours:	694 hours
Locomotive hours:	604 hours
Mileage:	6,594 miles
Total oil used:	46 gallons

3. Yard service at Scotswood Works. Three months 1932/3, twenty-nine months 1934-7. Approx. time in service – thirty-two months.

Service hours:	6,700 (209 hrs/month)
Engine hours:	6,125 (191 hrs/month)
Locomotive hours:	N. A.
Fuel, total consumed:	3,975 gallons
Fuel, per service hour:	0.59 gallons
Fuel, per engine hour:	0.65 gallons

On 23rd February 1937 it was reported that the locomotive had put in 6,261½ service hours, 5,706 engine hours and used 3,623 gallons of fuel.

The locomotive remained in use at Scotswood for many years, but no more were built to this design. It was withdrawn for scrapping in 1953 and cut up by Shaw & Co., Dunston in January 1954.

An interesting range of shunters were on offer by Armstrong Whitworth in 1933. Although this was subject to some revision as reported later, it is interesting to consider the earlier range at this point. Single and twin-engined 0-4-0 DE shunters were envisaged in the 15-30 tons range. These comprised the 15-ton shunting tractor just mentioned; a 15-and 20-ton conventional design with tractive efforts of 8,400 and 11,200 lbs and fitted with Armstrong-Saurer BLD and BXD engines, respectively. These will be covered later. The twin-engined unit comprised 25-and 30-ton locomotives of identical mechanical design powered by BLD or BXD Armstrong-Saurer engines, each engine having its own generator, but supplying current to one frame-mounted traction motor located transversely above the jackshaft final drive unit behind the cab. The engines were located longitudinally side by side in a wide bonnet with two front radiators.

The following brief table gives the characteristics of this interesting proposed design:

Locomotive type	Speed mph	Tractive effort lbs	Maximum tractive effort (lbs)
25 ton	4	9,750	
	6	7,600	
	8	6,000	
	10	4,900	
	12	4,200	14,000
30 ton	4	14,700	
	6	11,000	
	8	8,750	
	10	7,250	
	12	6,200	16,800

At 4 mph the 25 tons and 30 tons locomotives could haul 500 tons and 600 tons respectively on level track.

Both designs would have used the ABE transmission, but if required the frame-mounted traction motor and jackshaft drive could be replaced by two axle-hung traction motors, thus permitting a shorter wheelbase version. Multiple-unit control was available for tandem working.

A low-level view of one of the 0-4-0 shunters designed to give the impression of power and undoubtedly used for advertising purposes.
Brian Webb collection

A post-war shot of CM210 at work. Note the fold-back buffers locked back towards the centre.

GEC Traction Ltd

1,700 BHP FOR SOUTH AMERICA

Reports of the work underway at Scotswood Works on four large oil-electric twin-units of 1,700 bhp culminated in an exhibition at the works on Monday, 21st November 1932. Mr Walter Runciman, MP, President of the Board of Trade, and a party of railway officials and engineers were conveyed there from Newcastle Central. The party travelled in two railcars – *Lady Hamilton* and *Northumbrian* (*Tyneside Venturer* was in regular service on the L&NER at that date). On show were the 1,700 bhp mobile powerhouses of the Buenos Aires Great Southern Railway (BAGSR), one of which was run in the works yard on a short length of 5ft 6in. gauge track.

The party saw three powerhouses and one locomotive of similar design at the works, together with the 250 bhp shunter, the 95 bhp shunting tractor, and the engine building and testing rigs. Major-General Guy Dawnay, Chairman of Armstrong Whitworth, presided at the luncheon which followed at the Central Hotel in Newcastle. Here, Mr Runciman said that the British Government had great interest in the work of Armstrong Whitworth's diesel department, and that they thought it had good prospects for the future.

To deal first with the mobile powerhouses: these were ordered in 1931 to the requirements of P. C. Saccaggio, CME of the railway, following his experience with the 1929 1,200 bhp powerhouses and with the desire to extend their use. Built under the supervision of the consulting engineers Messrs Livesey, Son & Henderson, they were completed under order DT3 with works numbers D4-D6, and were shipped fully erected in November and December 1932.

Each powerhouse comprised two vehicles permanently coupled together, and each vehicle housed one engine/generator set and its auxiliaries. The leading unit contained the driver's compartment, and the trailing unit the rotary vacuum pump and spare lubricating oil tank. Both vehicles were mounted on two four-wheel bogies: one on each vehicle having two traction motors. They were designed to work with eight-coach suburban train sets which the BAGSR built themselves.

As the powerhouse driving cab was at the outer end, the units were always permanently coupled to their train set, operation in a reverse direction being controlled from a driving compartment in the end carriage. In addition to the powerhouses own powered bogies, power was applied uniformly throughout the train set traction motors, two to one bogie of each carriage, with a total number of twenty motors to the complete powerhouse and its train set. Each set weighed 406 tons and seated 916 passengers.

The mechanical structure of the powerhouses comprised an underframe of four main rolled steel longitudinals: the inner was of 'H' section beams, carrying the engine/generator and the outer of channel section beams. Strong cross braces gave rigidity, and the outer ends carried buffing and drawgear. The two halves of each powerhouse were coupled by central adjustable tie rods, pivoted near the bogie centres, and passing through buffing blocks on the inner ends of the frames. The superstructure embodied a framework of welded rolled steel sections covered with aluminium sheeting attached by rivets.

The two powerhouse units to order DT3 for the Buenos Aires Great Southern Railway under construction in Scotswood Works.
Brian Webb collection

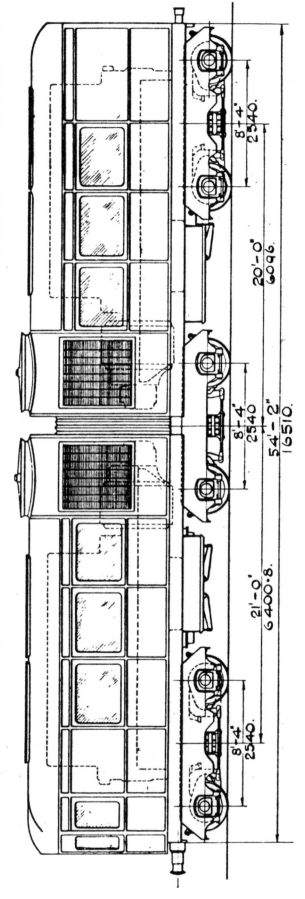

The first proposal for the BAGSR 1,700 bhp mobile powerhouse units was for an articulated twin unit as illustrated here. Scale 4mm = 1ft.

Brian Webb collection

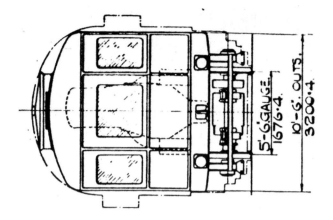

Additional strength, to carry such items as corridor connections, was obtained by using steel sheeting for critical areas.

Ample window space and air ducting for the oil and water cooling radiators were provided in the bodysides; air flow was controlled by a central roof mounted fan unit.

The bogies were a development of the BAGSR Saccaggio type enclosing the laminated axlebox springs and permitting the anti-twist property of central loading. Spacing and rigidity of the side plates was obtained by channel sections. The outer bogies of each powerhouse, on which were mounted the four traction motors, had swing-link bolsters with laminated and helical springs; while the inner bogies had fixed bolsters without springs.

Auxiliary bearing springs on the motor bogies were of rubber and helical types on the carrying bogies. Roller bearing axleboxes by J. Stone & Co. were used throughout the powerhouse and their train sets.

Braking was by blocks on all wheels, activated by vacuum gear and driven by an exhauster driven by a motor installed at the inner end of each powerhouse. This provided vacuum for the single-pipe train braking system: one brake cylinder for each bogie operated four blocks, one for each wheel, via the usual brake rigging.

No sanding gear was fitted, as the adhesive weight of the powerhouse and train set was ample for the severe acceleration of the service operated.

The driver's cabs contained brake valves, horns, and emergency valves, the latter being controlled by the deadman's button and driver's controllers in such a manner that in case of a mishap to the driver or train the brakes were automatically applied and all power cut off.

The two engines installed in each powerhouse were Sulzer type 8LV34 eight-cylinder, in-line, four-stroke unit with 340mm diameter x 400mm stroke cylinders giving 850 bhp at 550 rpm. They had Bosch pumps and injection valves, pre-combustion cylinder heads, and cast-steel crankcases. They were imported complete from Sulzer Bros, Winterthur.

Brown-Bolveri main generators were directly coupled to the engines, having a rating of 570 KW dc and being separately excited. Traction motors were of English Electric manufacture

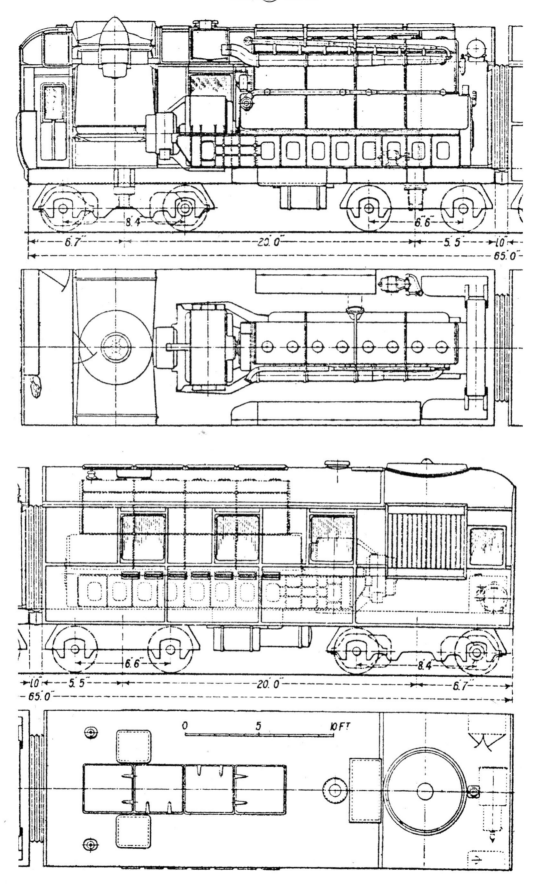

Order DT3 AW D4-6 were BAGSR mobile powerhouses UE3-5. This diagram shows the layout of these twin 850 bhp Sulzer engines. Reproduced at 4mm - 1ft.
Brian Webb collection

This page & opposite top: The Sulzer 850 bhp diesel engine/generator set being lowered into one half of a BAGSR mobile powerhouse in Scotswood Works.
Sulzer Bros UK Ltd

One of the units on a short length of 5ft 6in. gauge track laid in the yard at Scotswood.

and of axle-hung, nose-suspended, self-ventilated type. Each engine/generator set supplied current to eight motors on the train and two on the powerhouse, giving a total of twenty per train set. It was possible to operate on half the engine power – that is, with one power unit closed down.

The starting tractive effort of these trains was over 60,000 lbs, allowing for initial acceleration of 1 mph per second up to the maximum speed of 70 mph, and they put in some remarkable performances. The trains were similar to the 1929 sets, and used the Saccaggio patent coupling between the carriages and powerhouses. These took the form of tie-bars between the bogies of each carriage, attached to the bogie centres, and allowed a lightweight design of underframe for the 80ft carriages. The uniform power distribution throughout the train sets enabled buffing stresses to be kept low, again allowing further lightening of the rolling stock.

The vehicles were painted in crimson lake livery with aluminium painted roof and gold lettering. On the BAGSR they were numbered UE3-5.

The then president of the Argentine Republic, General Agustin P. Justo, together with other government ministers, was present on the inaugural run of these trains.

Following trials and training runs the sets started work on the Buenos Aires suburban main line between Plaza Constitucion and Glew, calling at intermediate stations. One set was occupied for two turns of about eight hours duration daily, running a total of 550 kms (341.55 miles). A second set was used on a 'semi-accelerated' service on the same route, again in two eight hour shifts, running some 488 kms (303 miles) per day. The third set was on stand-by. Together they ran a total of 44 local trains per day.

In mid-1934 Sir Follet Holt, chairman of the BAGSR, said that results from oil-electric traction showed that the railway should adopt this form of traction as soon as possible, to replace steam.

Armstrong Whitworth reports on these units indicate that, in spite of engine crankshaft failings, the units worked well. The first crankshaft troubles occurred on the same day when, after some eight months service, units UE3 and UE5 failed at 73,000 and 63,800 kms (45,333 and 39,619 m) respectively. The causes of failure in these Sulzer-built engines were not satisfactorily settled, but redesigned crankshafts were fitted which was a four month task, the new shafts coming from Sulzers. These cut down the vibrations which, it was opined, might have caused failure. In due course all the powerhouse engines received them, together with new cylinder blocks in some cases. By 1943 no further problems with Sulzer crankshafts had occurred, but some of another make again fractured.

The Armstrong Whitworth report on BAGSR mobile powerhouses between June 1933 and the end of 1935 stated that they had an aggregate mileage of 485,000 miles. In February 1937 the following figures were recorded:

Vehicle No.	Date of first trial	Date into traffic	Total mileage	Fuel mpg 6-7 months	Normal weight of train (incl. powerhouse)
UE3	27/4/33	12/6/33	251,121	0.72	541.3 tons
UE4	20/6/33	12/7/33	221,887	0.77	528.9 tons
UE5 *	31/7/33	31/7/33	187,554	0.75	528.9 tons

* Up to end of October 1936

BAGSR 1,700 bhp Bo-2+2-Bo DE mobile powerhouse at work with its motorised train set on a Buenos Aires suburban service.

Sulzer Bros UK Ltd

A posed publicity view of the two units with their trains.   *Brian Webb collection*

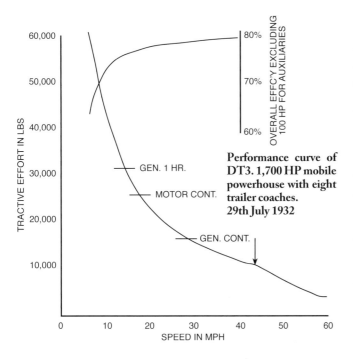
Performance curve of DT3. 1,700 HP mobile powerhouse with eight trailer coaches. 29th July 1932

Apart from the aforementioned accelerated services, the units also worked to existing steam diagrams. Running costs were put at 1s 0d per mile, the powerhouses averaging 66,000 miles each per year. Up to the end of May 1952 UE3 and UE4 had achieved mileages of 1,280,000 and 1,250,000 miles respectively. By this time they had been fitted with new Paxman RPHXL-II 800 bhp engines and Metropolitan Vickers generators.

UE3/4/5 were withdrawn during the 1959-61 period although the official date quoted is April 1963, and scrapping date December 1963. Their respective mileages were given as 2,592,883/2,389,515/2,528,344 km or 1,610,180/1,483,888 /1,570,101 miles.

The BAGSR 1,700 bhp locomotive was built simultaneously with the powerhouses, and was generally similar mechanically and in power equipment. It was built under order DT4, and carried works number D7.

The locomotive was of twin-unit layout, permanently coupled, with a driving compartment at each outer end. Each half of the locomotive contained the following items: half the 88 cell 450 amp/hour battery in ventilated boxes at the sides of the engine room; engine cooling system – a 15/30 hp vertical fan motor with air ducts, side panel, twenty section radiators (eight for oil and twelve for water cooling); two main cooling water tanks on floor level plus a high level auxiliary tank; Reavell rotary vacuum brake exhauster with a 6/12 hp motor, in one unit only, balanced in the other half by a 2½ hp Westinghouse air compressor motor. In addition, of course, there was the engine/generator set, which was similar to that used in the three powerhouses, except that they had fabricated crankcases.

The locomotive power units were reversed, in other words, the generators faced the inner end of the locomotive body and the cooling units were thus at the outer ends, immediately after the driving cabs, this being the chief clue of identity to the casual observer.

Each body unit was built upon an underframe of 'I' section steel longitudinals and solebars with a steel floor. This comprised

The 1,700 bhp mainline diesel electric locomotive CM210 for BAGSR built under order DT4, AW D7 of 1933.   *Brian Webb collection*

two main units 15in. deep and 12in. deep solebars with cross staying. The floor was of ¼in. thick plate, riveted to the frame, with welded joints. The body was entirely of 14 w.g. Aluminium sheeting on a rolled steel section frame.

Bogies of Saccaggio design were fitted, these having swing bolsters and Stone's self-aligning roller bearing axleboxes. The outer bogies had one axle-hung traction motor on the inner axles; the two inner bogies had all axles motored: giving an axle layout of 1A-Bo+Bo-A1. The engine was the Winterthur-built Sulzer 8LV34 unit used on the powerhouses, driving a Brown-Boveri 570 KW generator of dc type with an overhung exciter of 62.5KW. All were mounted on a common bedplate.

The six traction motors were axle-hung, nose-suspended machines by English Electric with a continuous rating of 230 hp, one hour rating being 310 hp. They were self-ventilated. Two sets of gears were provided with the locomotive, one for passenger and the other for freight.

Upon completion, it was claimed to be the second largest diesel electric locomotive in the world, indeed it was the first successful one in all aspects. Its competitor was the Canadian National twin unit of 2,660 bhp with a pair of Glasgow designed and built Beardmore engines, so at that time both honours went to British work. The BAGSR locomotive was shipped fully erected in December 1932, and given running number CM210.

CM210 was put into regular service on 1st October 1933. According to official reports, during its first seven months it covered some 57,000 miles and between 4th December 1933 and 19th December 1935 it had a yearly average of 70,000 miles. Armstrong Whitworth made much publicity out of the feats of this locomotive, which was without doubt an unquestioned success.

After running in on local service, CM210 was put on the Bahia Blanca night trains between Buenos Aires and Olavarria (332 kms, 206.17 m). The train left Buenos Aires in the evening and reached Olavarria in six to seven hours, depending on the number of stops en route. With only 15 minutes turn round, many times, the locomotive would return with the incoming train to Buenos Aires, arriving about 09.45. Train weights varied between 450 and 650 tons on these services. This service was maintained for thirty-two consecutive nights, a distance of 22,000 kms (13,662 m).

During this time no repairs or adjustments to the Sulzer engines were needed: the service ended temporarily when the driver reversed the locomotive accidentally while running and burned out all the traction motors. Following nine days out of service the locomotive recommenced work and did a further thirty-four round trips, covering some 23,300 kms (14,469 m) more. The locomotive had therefore covered around 45,000 kms (27,945 m) in seventy-five days, including the time out of use for repairs to the traction motors. On the whole a good standard of performance was achieved, reaching a mechanical efficiency of 61 per cent and a thermal efficiency of 20 per cent.

As a test of the locomotive's capacity for freight work, it was put on a 3,150 tons train, which was hauled from the yard at Las Flores; starting on level track, a drawbar pull of 57,000 lbs was exerted, as recorded in the dynamometer car. The train was started without any sense of 'snatch', but by a rising pull until the load was in motion; the pull lessened as the locomotive gathered speed. The train was hauled 170 kms (105½ miles) in six hours at an average speed of 28.3 km/hr (17.57 mph).

In 1938 a special tourist train was run to Mar Del Plata (404 kms, 250 m), non-stop. The 730 ton train suffered from signal checks and traffic delays, reducing the average speed of the run to Dolores (203 kms, 126 m) to 53 km/hr (33 mph). From thence the train had a clear track, to reach a speed of 92 km/hr (57.13 mph), with an average of 83.5 km/hr (51.85 mph) for the 201 kms (124.82 m) to Mar Del Plata.

From 1934 the locomotive ran with intermediate gears which gave it a top speed of 100 kms/hr (62.1 mph). On one occasion CM210 took a 973 ton train from Bahia Blanca to Buenos Aires, and ran it to time in spite of a 70 minutes late start.

CM210 in service photographed at Remedios de Escalade Shops of the Buenos Aires Great Southern Railway. *Brian Webb collection*

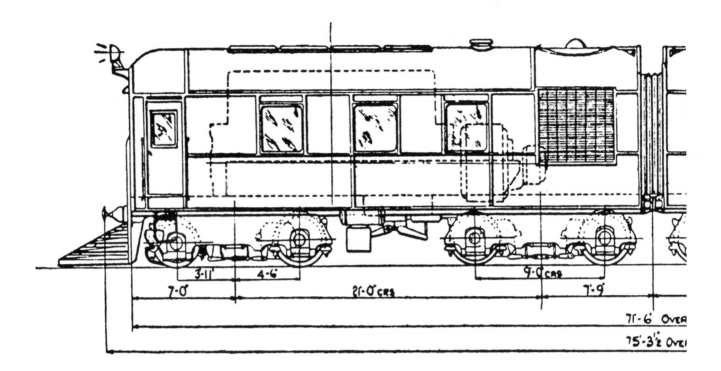

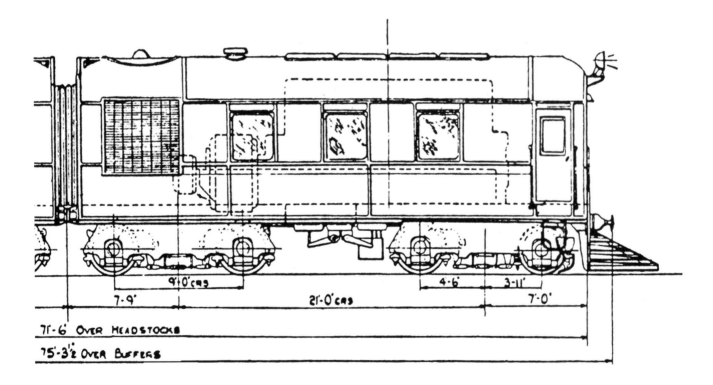

Side elevation of 1,700 bhp BAGSR locomotive No. CM210. This locomotive had an axle layout of 1A-Bo+Bo-A1. The drawing is reproduced at a scale of 4mm - 1ft.
Brian Webb collection

CM210 on a train. *Sulzer Bros UK Ltd*

An official survey of services between 1933 and 1938 gave the following facts:

Year	Mileage run	Notes
1933	15,700 kms / 9749.7 m	Tests, trials, etc., running in on local service to and from Canuelas, 155 kms (96.2 m) per day, trains of 350 tons approx.
1933/4	45,000 kms / 37,945.5 m	Reliability test. Night train to and from Olavarria, 688 kms (427.24 m) per day, seven days per week, train weights of 450-650 tons.
1934/5	145,000 kms / 90,045 m	Night trains to and from Olavarria 686 kms (426.6 m) per day, six days per week, train weight 400-700 tons.
1935	17,000 kms / 10,557 m	Night train to and from Bahia Blanca (via La Madrid), 700 kms (434.7 m) per day, six days per week, ruling gradient 1 in 178, train weight 400-600 tons.
1935-38	*	Night train to and from Bahia Blanca (via Pringles) ruling gradient 1 in 185, 685 kms (425.38 m) per day, six days per week, train weight 400-850 tons.

* The locomotive continued this until well into the Second World War period.

Failures in traffic with CM210 proved remarkably few. Experience gained and modifications made stopped these occurring again, and brought results which were quite miraculous, considering the experience of the BAGSR with their other types of early diesel electric locomotives.

In the following list of failures, a failure is classed as a defect which prevented the locomotive from completing a duty unaided:

Year	Mileage	Failure	Cause
1933	24,219	Traction motors burnt out.	Driver reversed master controller accidentally.
1934	60,237	Engines failed to start.	Driver failed to close main switch.
1936	152,145	Traction motor gear split.	Cotter failed in quill drive.
1936	178,518	One engine stopped.	Broken crankshaft.
1937	240,761	Axlebox roller bearing failed.	Inner ball race split by overtightening.
1938	381,101	One engine stopped.	Threads of waste in fuel transfer pump.

By 1943 it was reported that this locomotive had run 1,286,348 kms (798,822 m) and had only experienced fourteen

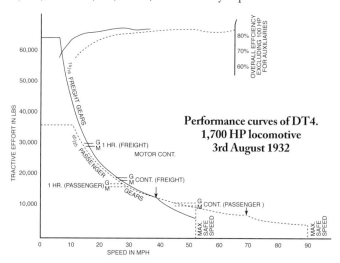

Performance curves of DT4. 1,700 HP locomotive 3rd August 1932

total failures and twenty-eight partial failures, the latter causing delays, but not preventing completion of duty.

What was not mentioned in official reports was the fact that an Armstrong Whitworth engineer handled most of, or supervised carefully, the maintenance work to keep this locomotive at its peak. After every round trip, for example, the engine crankcase doors were removed to look for traces of white metal from the bearings, as warnings of impending crankshaft failure.

The observations of the BAGSR after experience with this locomotive are interesting:

1. The use of bogies rather than plate frames for the 1,700 bhp powerhouses and locomotives was due to the experience gained with the 1929 1,200 bhp plate-frame rigid-wheelbase powerhouses, which suffered seriously from the effects of vibration transmitted from the rail via the mechanical structure to the equipment of the vehicle. Saccaggio wanted to overcome vibratory damage and obtain a smooth level engine room floor, while at the same time gain maintenance advantages by having traction motors mounted on bogies which were easier to work on and remove than wheelsets from plate-frame units.
2. The traction motor gearing of passenger and freight, obtained by changing the gears in the workshop, posed severe problems in flexibility. The locomotive was not a mixed traffic locomotive, in the full sense of the term, since, when this operation was carried out it was still only really suitable for either passenger or freight. This limitation was overcome by fitting a set of intermediate gears, which proved adequate for all the locomotive's duties.
3. Traction motor overheating at low speeds when the locomotive was hauling heavy trains, plus the problem of dirt ingress, was blamed on the inadequacy of self-ventilation of the motors. Troubles resulting from this – such as flashovers and arcing – would have been eliminated by using force-ventilation.
4. The bodywork came in for serious criticism because it soon became apparent that aluminium was not suited for railway work, due to its tendency to bulge and warp and, in the case of air-ducting, crack due to vibration.
5. Ventilation was not adequate for the engine room, and the slight vacuum effect in this area allowed the intake of fine dust which upset the power and auxiliary equipment. New air intake scoops above the driving cab windows were provided at each end.
6. Water and fuel tanks were found to be too flimsy and were prone to leakage, needing to be much stronger. Underfloor fuel pipes were also, it was opined, a serious fire risk.

Mr Gregson, the Armstrong Whitworth South American representative, agreed on the above points, and presented further ones in his report.

On engine crankshaft failures, with the locomotive at 170,700 kms (106,004 m) and 184,000 kms (114,264 m), Gregson said the greater mileage obtained in comparison to the powerhouses was due to the locomotive's less arduous work. Electrical modifications recommended included the use of porcelain rather than 'Bakelite' for insulation on traction motor brush gear to overcome dust accumulations which caused burning. Cablework sagged through being too heavy where clipped suspension was used, so steel troughs and lighter cabling was suggested.

The engines were causing vibrations due to their being mounted directly on the underframe, upsetting instrumentation and control gear. The bodywork Gregson agreed as unsatisfactory and in addition suggested that the cabs have two doors and resiliently bedded windows to overcome vibration problems.

It was found that the engine rooms were too hot to work inside, even in so-called 'cool periods' and windows could not always be opened due to wind borne dust, or to rain.

For many years CM210 worked on the night train, often composed of only four-axle vehicles, with weights of up to 700-900 tons, between Buenos Aires and Bahia Blanca, alternate nights in each direction. With only one man on the footplate, CM210 ran with utmost reliability over the single line route through open country with ungated level crossings. Mileages recorded were equivalent to twenty trips per month.

CM210 was still on the Bahia Blanca run until well after the nationalisation of the BAGSR in 1948, being finally taken out of service on the General Roca Railway in 1960 due more to the shortage of spares rather than run-down condition. With a mileage of 2,912,375 km or 1,808,584 miles it was officially withdrawn in December 1963.

The outstanding achievements of the BAGSR in world diesel traction are due to Pedro C. Saccaggio and his personal assistant Hugh M. Macintyre, each of whom deserves a niche in the history of railways.

CM210 in the livery of the General Roca Railway and photographed after 1948. *Jorge L. San Martin collection*

Kalka-Simla railcar No. 14 seen in service on the 2ft 6in. gauge line in North-West India. The 96km (60 miles) long railway running through the foothills of the Himalayas opened in 1903. Its route twisted through the hills rising some 4,600 feet at a ruling gradient of 1 in 33 crossing over 800 bridges and passing through over 100 tunnels. The introduction of railcars reduced the journey time to under three hours but the fare was almost double the usual First Class rate for the privilege.

P. S. A. Berrige

RAILCARS FOR INDIA

The very first export order to be completed and shipped by the Diesel Traction Department was for four light locomotive railcar chassis of 2ft 6in. gauge for the Gaekwars Baroda State Railways section of the Bombay, Baroda and Central India Railway. The cars were one of four railcar orders executed for India by Armstrong Whitworth. They were completed under order DT12 during midsummer 1932 and shipped during September.

Described as locomotive-railcars, or perhaps railcar-tractors due to the fact that in addition to carrying passengers they were also to haul trains of light trailers, they had an unusual wheel layout: a forward four-wheel carrying bogie under the power unit, and a fixed single axle at the rear end. This was the only driven axle.

Intended to provide an economical means of transport to compete with road services, these low-cost vehicles had to be simple to maintain and operate by local labour, yet at the same time give reliability and low running costs.

The maximum permitted speed of the lines they were intended for was 30 mph so rapid acceleration was of optimum importance, to give an average speed of 20 mph with a 30 ton tail load of three trailer cars over gradients of up to 1 in 100.

Mechanically the vehicles embodied interesting features for the period of their construction, including a quite heavy fabricated underframe built up solely by electric welding. It consisted of two outer solebars with inner members to take coupling loadings, support the power unit, axlebox guides, bogie, and body. The use of a bogie when a four-wheel or two-axle layout might have been thought more appropriate was due to the desire to give easy and safe riding on indifferent track, abounding in curves, a bogie providing the required guidance in this case.

The bogie took the weight on side bearings, carried on spiral springs on the bogie transom, the bogie pivot being free to rise and fall in the spherical bearing and act only as a centring device. Bogie side frames were built up from steel plate on each side of top and bottom channels, providing a very rigid unit enabling the laminated axle-box springs to be placed (and held) centrally over the boxes, and eliminating twisting distortional forces. The bogies were also largely of welded construction.

Braking on the cars was by screw-down hand brakes to each wheel, but one was also given straight air-braking, using air compressed by a unit electrically operated and slung from the underframe.

The engine was an Armstrong-Saurer type 6BLD six-cylinder unit with a continuous rating of 80 bhp at 1600 rpm, but capable of 95 bhp at 2,000 rpm. Laurence, Scott & Electromotors Ltd supplied the generators and traction motors for these vehicles. The transmission was of the ABE type, comprising main generator mounted directly on the engine – the whole unit being mounted transversely across the front of the railcar, with the generator to the right of the driver and the radiator to the left. This supplied current to one traction motor mounted longitudinally and centrally on the underside of the underframe.

Drive was via a cardan shaft and universal coupling to a worm reduction gearbox mounted on the rear rigid axle. The gearbox was built by Armstrong Whitworth, and incorporated Craven-Guest hollowface worm and worm wheel. The latter was gripped between two cast-steel spiders splined on to the axle.

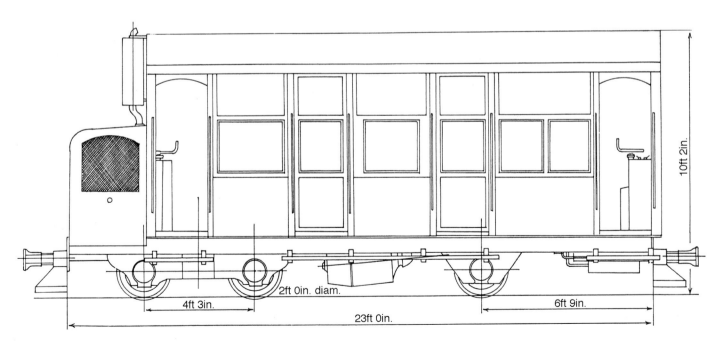

Side elevation of Armstrong Whitworth's first diesel traction export order was DT12 for a railcar chassis delivered in September 1932 to the Gaekwars Baroda State Railways. Reproduced at 7mm - 1ft.
Brian Webb

Above: **One of the chassis of order DT12 with its transverse mounted Armstrong-Saurer diesel engine and generator set in the erecting shop at Scotswood Works in 1932.** *Brian Webb collection*

Right: **Rear view of DT12 chassis showing underframe and frame mounted traction motor. Note control units for both driving positions.** *University of Glasgow*

The railcar carrying/guiding bogie was built up by electric welding and, together with the driven axle, ran in British-Isothermos axleboxes. Rolled-steel disc type driving wheels with cone seating were fitted, arranged to permit ease of removal of the worm wheel or bearings. Roller bearings were used on the worm shaft and axle. As usual, a torque rod attached to the underframe took up the torque reaction of the gearbox. Cowcatchers were fitted at both ends, and the cars also had a rear driving position.

Great interest was caused during the third week of July 1932 when one chassis was, by permission of the LMS, tested and demonstrated on the Leek & Manifold Valley Light Railway the only suitable 2ft 6in. gauge line meeting the requirements of Armstrong Whitworth. The trials were witnessed by Mr Rao Saheb Ram Kishen, the Engineer in Chief of the Gaekwars Baroda State Railway, and by the inspecting engineers, Messrs Rendel, Palmer, and Tritton, together with railway officials from home and overseas. During the trial the railcar hauled a 30 ton L&MV Railway bogie carriage, and managed to maintain 20 mph on the sinuous line – with gradients of up to 1 in 50 – at an average fuel consumption rate of 8 mpg.

Upon their arrival in India they were taken to the Goya Gate workshops where wooden bodies were built and fitted, and sets

In July 1932 one DT12 chassis underwent trials on the 2ft 6in. gauge Leek & Manifold Valley Light Railway in Staffordshire. In these vehicles only the fixed rear axle was driven, giving a wheel/axle layout of 4-2-0/2-A. The drawgear is a temporary fitting to match with Manifold stock.
both Brian Webb collection

The bodies for DT12 and their trailer carriages were built at Goya Gate works in India. A typical train formation is seen here.
Brian Webb collection

of lightweight trailer carriages provided. They were set to work, each with three twin-bogie trailers, on 14th February 1933. The service was inaugurated by H. H. the Gaekwar of Baroda, who was presented with a framed coloured photograph of the first unit by Armstrong Whitworth. The Gaekwar turned a silver master key in the cab, which made the train ready for running, and then fixed a nameplate lettered Economy to the side of the unit. After a special meal the train was run to Padra, seven miles from Baroda.

Each train set seated 106 passengers and provided accommodation for three tons of luggage. The power car itself seated only two first and four second class passengers, the balance of 100 third class seats being provided in the trailers.

Initially, troubles were experienced with engine cooling and frequent loss of service resulted. The engine/generator sets had to be frequently changed; this was facilitated by a spare set supplied with the railcars, and the operation could be carried out in 2½ hours.

By the end of July 1933 a mileage of 58,573 had been covered, giving an average of 94 miles per day. They worked in Baroda area, on the extensive 2ft 6in. gauge network from Goya Gate: to Timba Road, Chhota Udaipur, Padra, and on the Moji Koral to Chandod line. Fuel consumption at this time worked out at 6.7 mpg per 100 tons miles in traffic.

In September 1935 the engines were all modified to direct fuel injection, and the cars operated more successfully.

On 1st February 1936 their performances were given as follows:

Car No.	Miles
101	90,487
102	73,995
103	79,562
104	68,191
Total	312,235

By March 1936 they were averaging 26,000 miles each per year. One year later, in February 1937, the total mileage for the four railcars was 105,000 for the twelve month period.

The popularity with tourists of the Punjab town of Simla, high in the Himalayas, prompted the early use of internal combustion railcars by the Kalka-Simla section of the North Western Railway of India. The Kalka-Simla Railway connected Simla, 6,840 feet above sea level, to Kalka, 2,143 feet above sea level, where it made a junction with the 5ft 6in. gauge main line.

The railway was 60 miles in length, of 2ft 6in. gauge, with a ruling gradient of 3 per cent, combined with severe curves – constant throughout its route, the minimum radius being 90ft. The temperature variations were considerable: running from 110°F in the shade in hot weather at Kalka to only 55°F minimum at Simla on the same day.

At the time the railway was considering diesel traction the line was being operated by a small fleet of petrol mechanical railcars, built by Baguley's of Burton-on-Trent for the Drewry Car Co. Ltd. These handled the majority of the first class traffic, but were aided by steam trains also. The cost of operating sixteen seat petrol railcars over the line made competition with road services difficult, so the decision to try a diesel unit was prompted by economy.

Ordered in August 1933, the railcar was completed at Scotswood by Armstrong Whitworth under order No. DT34 and carried works No. D39. It was delivered during July 1934. Painted in white livery with gold lettering, it became No. 14 railmotor in the Railway's stock list.

It was an unusual twin-bogie vehicle: seating sixteen passengers and being arranged with a side driving compartment at one end only, which was separated from the passenger saloon by a glazed screen. At the opposite end was the engine/generator set, placed on top of the frame in the transverse position. The complete unit was separated in its own compartment by a narrow vestibule which gave adequate insulation from noise and smell to passengers.

An Armstrong-Saurer 6BXD six-cylinder engine, giving 90 bhp at 5,020 feet and 85 bhp at 6,870 feet altitude, was fitted – driving directly to a Laurence, Scott & Electromotors main generator of 350 V, 310 A. The single traction motor, by LSE, was hung longitudinally from the vehicle underframe and drove via a cardan shaft to a worm reduction gear on the inner axle of the bogie, located under the rear engine compartment. Both bogie axles were coupled by coupling rods.

The driving controls were simple; consisting of a tramway type controller and deadman's handle. The positions on the controller

Railmotor No. 14 in its white livery photographed in the yard at Scotswood Works. *Brian Webb collection*

were idling, zero, and three different speed notches. No. 1 notch caused the engine to rev up to idling speed, No. 2 gave normal running speed, and No. 3 was a special notch giving increased power; the alternative engine outputs of 90 or 85 bhp were obtained by a lever key in the engine compartment. Braking was by screw-down hand brake, foot brake, and compressed air.

Ancillary equipment was located as follows: engine room – air compressor (belt driven from the engine), fan and motor duct, oil and water cooling unit; in rear of car – water tank and fuel tank; the battery box was placed alongside the driver's cab; attached to the underframe were belt driven air compressor from the traction motor and lighting dynamo, similarly driven. Swivelling and fixed electric headlights and cowcatchers were fitted. The swivelling light was interesting in that it was operated by a system of rodding connected to the leading bogie and lit up the track ahead no matter whether the railcar was travelling on straight or curved track.

The body was built entirely at the Gloucester works of the Gloucester Railway Carriage & Wagon Co. Ltd, being fitted to the chassis at Scotswood.

The railcar was put into service on 13th August 1934, providing an immediate success on the difficult route. It worked one return trip daily of 120 miles, using 18 gallons of fuel per trip, per day. This compared well with the petrol railcars which used 10-15 per cent more of the five times as costly fuel.

Right: The open door to the rear engine compartment reveals the 90 bhp Armstrong-Saurer engine. *Brian Webb collection*

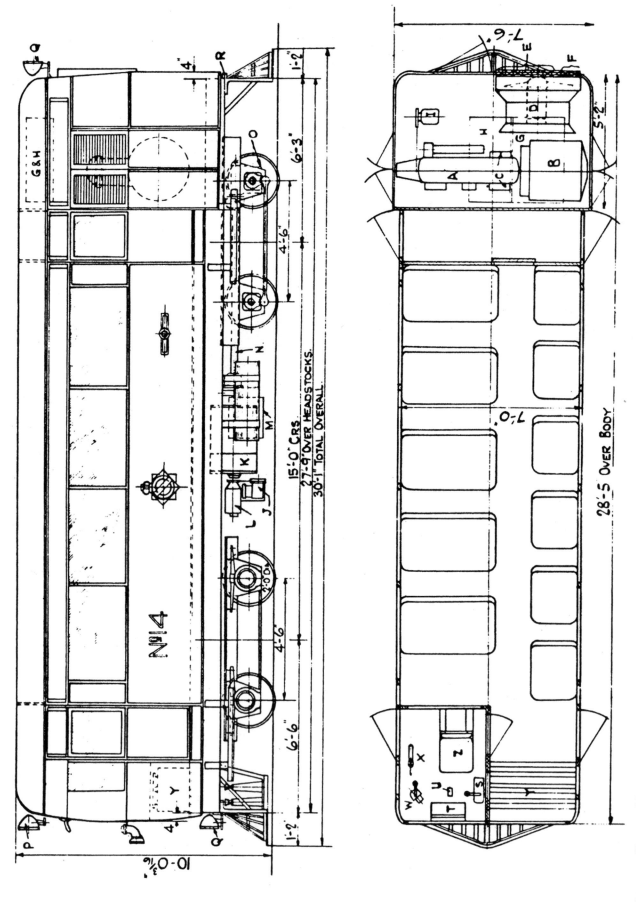

Diagram of layout of Armstrong Whitworth DT34, a twin bogie railcar for the Kalka-Simla section of the North Western Railway of India, AWD39/34. 7mm – 1ft. *Brian Webb collection*

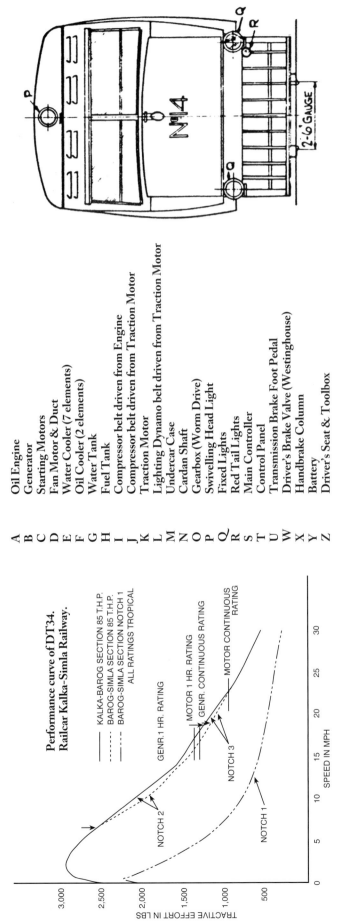

A	Oil Engine
B	Generator
C	Starting Motors
D	Fan Motor & Duct
E	Water Cooler (7 elements)
F	Oil Cooler (2 elements)
G	Water Tank
H	Fuel Tank
I	Compressor belt driven from Engine
J	Compressor belt driven from Traction Motor
K	Traction Motor
L	Lighting Dynamo belt driven from Traction Motor
M	Undercar Case
N	Cardan Shaft
O	Gearbox (Worm Drive)
P	Swivelling Head Light
Q	Fixed Lights
R	Red Tail Lights
S	Main Controller
T	Control Panel
U	Transmission Brake Foot Pedal
W	Driver's Brake Valve (Westinghouse)
X	Handbrake Column
Y	Battery
Z	Driver's Seat & Toolbox

Performance curve of DT34.
Railcar Kalka-Simla Railway.

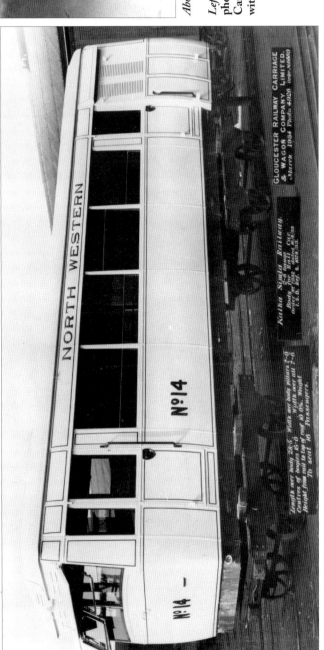

Above: The worksplate at affixed to railcar No. 14.

Left: The bodywork for the Kalka-Simla railcar photographed at the works of the Gloucester Railway Carriage & Wagon Co. before despatch and fitting with underframe, engine etc. *GRC&WCo.*

The interior of the railcar looking towards the driver's position. *GRC&WCo.*

Rear view of the Kalka-Simla railcar at Sinl Station. *P. S. A. Berridge*

Above: Another view of No. 14 in action on the Kalka-Simla route.
P. S. A. Berridge

Right: The engine and ancilliaries in the rear compartment.
M. G. Satow

Although not able to operate at its 25 mph maximum – the car being limited by the tortuous route to an 18 mph limit. It ran very well indeed, but was found too powerful at its 120 bhp delivered engine rating. De-rating to 95 bhp made the vehicle more easily driven and more economic in fuel consumption.

The eight hour trip on 3 per cent gradients was only operated in the Simla season – between 25th April and 25th October each year, so the railcar had a relatively low annual mileage of about 9,000 miles. The railcar cost £3,338 new and by 30th September 1943 it had covered 163,992 miles.

On 20th June 1942 the vehicle was attacked on its down trip after being stopped by boulders placed on the line; its collision with these did not derail it, thanks to the cowcatchers. Two armed men immediately opened fire, killing five passengers and wounding two others and killing the driver. There were thirteen passengers on at the time. The remaining passengers were robbed prior to the gang making off.

The railcar was still in existence in 1978, and in spite of a one time threat to fit an Indian-built Cummins diesel engine, it still had its Armstrong Whitworth equipment. It was still in working order and was due to find a place in the Indian Railways collection for preservation.

This page and opposite top: Due to the railcar being single-ended it was always necessary to turn the car at the end of a run. In the upper view the car is being turned at Simla.
all P. S. A. Berridge

DT34 was still in working order when photographed at Dharm Pur Hmachal in February 1978. It is now preserved in the Indian National Railway Museum.
M. G. Satow

Order DT41 was the chassis for a 2ft 6in. gauge railcar for Central Provinces Railway, India. The unit is seen here on test at Scotswood in 1934. It bore Armstrong Whitworth number D41. *Brian Webb collection*

The Indian railways' use of Armstrong Whitworth railcars was continued in 1934 by the construction, under order DT 41, of one twin-bogie, 2ft 6in. gauge unit for use on the Central Provinces Section of the Great Indian Peninsula Railway. Carrying maker's No. D41, the order was for the complete chassis powered by an Armstrong-Saurer type 6BXD six-cylinder engine running at 140 bhp, but set to operate at 103 bhp with possible de-ratings to 95 bhp.

Electrical equipment was by Laurence, Scott and Electromotors Ltd, and comprised a main generator directly coupled to the engine – the whole being mounted transversely on a three point suspension in a subframe behind the leading driving compartment. The power unit was capable of being run out sideways onto a ramp to facilitate overnight engine replacement, ensuring a high rate of availability for the vehicle.

The single traction motor was mounted under the underframe and drove via a cardan shaft to a worm reduction gear on the inner axle of the bogie at the engine end of the railcar. The bogies followed usual Armstrong Whitworth practice, being of the fabricated, fully-welded type, both bogies having twin-plate side frames and Isothermos axleboxes.

The body was built at the Mutunga workshops of the railway, and seated 58 passengers (third class only). Twin driving cabs, one at each end, were provided. The power unit was housed in its own compartment, together with water and oil tanks, roof mounted silencer, side mounted radiator and fan, control cabinet, and air compressor for braking and starting systems. The battery box, brake cylinder and reservoir were hung from the underframe.

A special double wall sound insulating partition was fitted between the engine room and passenger saloon.

The railcar was ready for service at the end of October 1934 and was probably in regular service during November. It was expected to haul an 11 ton twin-bogie trailer car at speeds up to 40 mph. Its work was restricted to the Pulgaon-Avri branch, doing initially three round trips per day, giving a mileage of 132, but soon altered to four trips daily, increasing the daily mileage to 176.

By 26th May 1936 it was officially recorded as having covered 76,000 miles. And in the twelve months ending February 1936 it put in 59,032 miles. These high mileage figures were attained by using the spare power unit supplied with the vehicle: the unit exchange principle allowing overnight changing and facilitating the high availability. This system was very necessary, for the main workshops were 130 miles away from the railcar's sphere of work.

Armstrong Whitworth reported that the engine changing process developed to a high degree of efficiency. The engine and generator were mounted on combinations of laminated and India-rubber springs in their own subframe. The subframe was on rollers and could be quickly run out of the railcar on to a platform in the workshop. The subframe was a good protection to the power unit during handling and subsequent transportation. With this railcar, overhauled engines were sent up by train and changed overnight by local maintenance staff – namely two steam fitters and an electrician assisted by labourers.

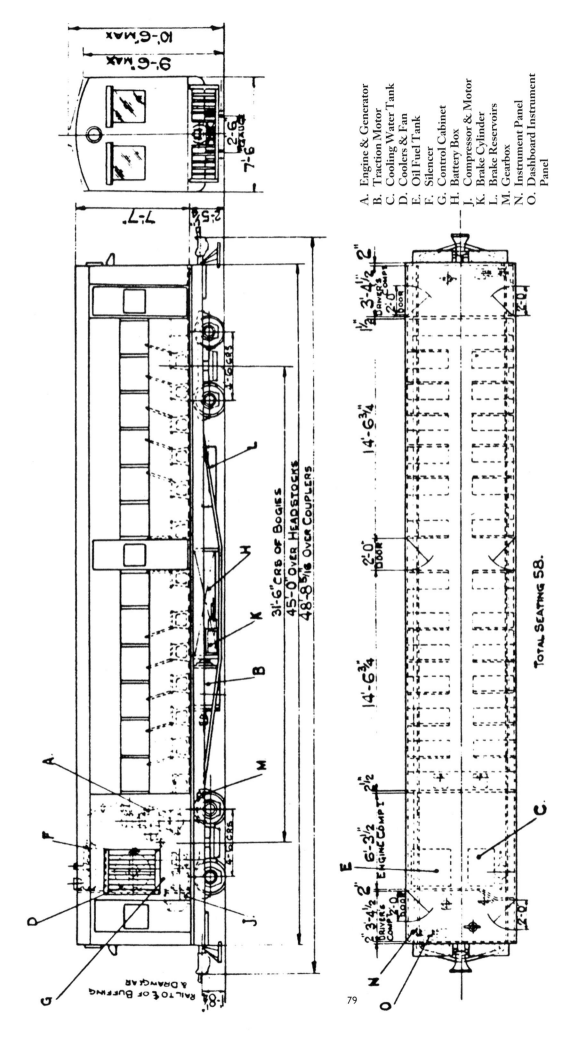

A. Engine & Generator
B. Traction Motor
C. Cooling Water Tank
D. Coolers & Fan
E. Oil Fuel Tank
F. Silencer
G. Control Cabinet
H. Battery Box
J. Compressor & Motor
K. Brake Cylinder
L. Brake Reservoirs
M. Gearbox
N. Instrument Panel
O. Dashboard Instrument Panel

Layout diagram for DT41. The body was to be built in India. 4mm - 1ft.

Brian Webb collection

General view of the rather austere railcar of order DT41. *Brian Webb collection*

The costs of diesel working on the Pulgaon-Avri line were set out as follows:

Item	d per mile
Wages, including guard and allowances for leave, pensions, etc.	3.189
Fuel	.600
Lubricants	.328
Repairs and stores (engine)	.494
Supervision	.103
Overhaul – engine	.218
Overhaul – coachwork	.120
Interest – engine	.885
Interest – coachwork	.163
Depreciation – engine	.983
Depreciation – coachwork	.181
Total	7.264

Comparison for steam traction was put at 29.78d per mile.

Originally numbered 31 in the railway's lists, it was running later as No. 598. At the end of its career, in 1969, the railcar was still on the Pulgaon-Avri section, doing only one round trip per day. It was withdrawn in January of that year when the engine was found beyond economical repair. The railcar was subsequently converted into a second class luggage and guard's carriage.

The largest Indian railcar order – Armstrong Whitworth's largest order to date – was that placed in 1934 by the Madras & Southern Mahratta Railway. The order, No. DT43, was for six 5ft 6in. gauge diesel electric chassis, which were of interest due to the number of Scotswood design and constructional innovations they incorporated.

Carrying works numbers D46-51, the railcars were ordered by the M&SMR with a view to reducing operating costs on branch lines and producing vehicles capable of competing with road transport. The vehicles were to be of low initial cost, and it was desired that some of the construction work be undertaken in the railway's own shops. They were twin-bogie units with a seating capacity for 110 passengers, and were arranged to work in pairs.

The chassis weight was kept to a minimum by Armstrong Whitworth. Twin driving positions were provided and the mechanical structure of the chassis was based on the maker's lattice-girder design, using the principles originated in 1933 for the first Sao Paulo railway motor train set, and welded throughout.

The underframe had excellent vertical rigidity with strong transverse bracing using diagonal strips with a gusset in the middle. Light cowcatchers and bumpers were fitted, and the drawgear was in the form of a tubular strut pin connected at both ends of the chassis to buffer beam sockets, with knuckle joints to allow for vertical displacement.

Box-frame bogies with spring bolsters supported on helical springs were used, having excellent lateral stiffness and rigidity, and the added advantage of having – in common with most Armstrong Whitworth bogie work – frames, axleboxes and laminated spring bearings all on the same centre line.

In these vehicles the weight of the underframe was borne on spring-supported side bearers, located on spherical self-aligning seats. As usual, the centre pivot was non-loadbearing, enabling lightweight pressed bolsters to be employed.

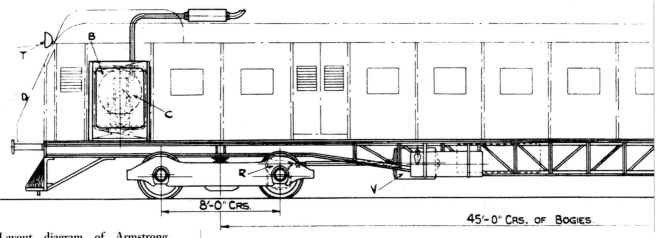

Layout diagram of Armstrong Whitworth's largest Indian railcar contract for six chassis for the Madras & Southern Mahratta Railway. They carried Armstrong Whitworth numbers D46-51 to order DT43. Scale 4mm - 1ft.
Brian Webb collection

A. Engine & Generator
B. Coolers
C. Fan
D. Main Fuel Tank
E. Fuel Service Tank
F. Fuse & Relay Cabinet
G. Starting Contactors
H. Main Contactors

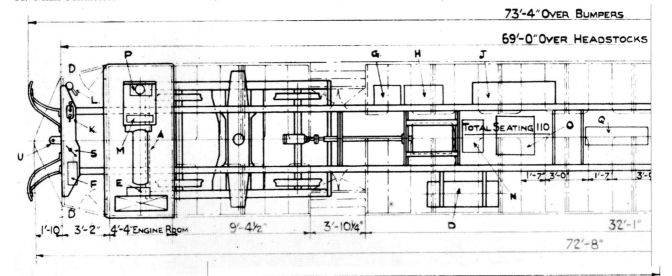

J. Batteries
K. Master Controller
L. Brake Valve
M. Fuel Control Solenoids
N. Battery Charge Resistors
O. General Field Resistors
P. Air Compressor
Q. Air Reservoirs
R. Gearbox
S. Handbrake
T. Headlamps etc.
U. Crawbar etc.
V. Traction Motor

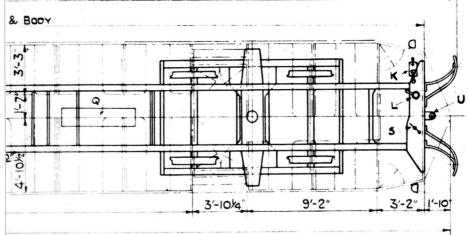

One of the 5ft 6in. bogies for DT43. This shows the standard box frame construction and prominent isothermos axleboxes. This bogie has disc brakes.
Brian Webb collection

The engine was the Armstrong-Saurer 6BXD model with six cylinders, putting out 121 bhp in this application by de-rating. The electrical equipment was by Laurence, Scott and Electromotors, comprising a main generator and a single traction motor.

The engine/generator set was mounted in a subframe placed transversely across the main frame in a compartment behind the leading driving cab. It has the usual sliding out arrangement facilitating engine changing. The radiator, water tank, fuel tank could also be moved en-bloc.

The traction motor was mounted on the underframe and drive was via a Hardy Spicer cardan shaft to a worm gearbox on the inner axle of the bogie at the engine end of the railcar. The driving axle was splined to take the worm wheel, and the gear case ran on deep-groove ball bearings. Large cooling fans were fitted and the oil capacity was quite large. Torque reaction was taken up by radius links and lugs on top of the gearcase.

Both automatic and straight Westinghouse air braking were fitted, with a separate cylinder for each bogie applying two brake blocks to each wheel. One chassis had drum type brakes similar to those used on the light railbus of order DT16. Hand brakes and air-sanding were fitted. The controls were on the ABE system. The Armstrong Whitworth portion of the contract was under the supervision of Messrs Rendel, Palmer, and Tritton, the M&SMR consulting engineers.

The engine incorporated the latest type of dual-turbulence cylinder head which, it was claimed, gave considerable reduction in fuel consumption. Four valves were provided with each cylinder, two inlet and two exhaust, central injection being employed through CAV-Bosch pumps.

The futuristic bodywork was designed under the direction of the M&SMR Chief Mechanical Engineer, Mr R. Lean, and employed a body and roof framing of standard sections with a waist and cant rails of flat mild steel bar. All the joints were arc welded and the roof sheets were welded to the combined tee stanchions and arch rails. All the internal body framing was of $1\frac{1}{4}$ inch bore piping. A floor of teak board was supported by cross-member beams of 'T'-section and by longitudinal tees. Rubber blocks were fitted between these members and the underframe. External roof and body panelling was of aluminium faced three-ply wood with an inside lining of Sundeala and a suitable space for insulation. Two twin-entry side doors were fitted on each side. The bodies were 69ft long by 10ft wide, built in two halves for handling and fixing to chassis purposes. The seating was of wood, and a completed body only weighed $6\frac{3}{4}$ tons.

The chassis arrived at Madras in early February 1935. The first car was put into service on 5th April of that year at Madras, a second followed on the 19th. The two vehicles worked in multiple. Four railcars went to Cocanada on 26th May, followed by the final pair on 1st August. All six cars were based at the same depot to gain the most from them. They worked an aggregate daily mileage of 836. It was usual to keep one car as spare, and they operated in multiples or singly, but were not used with trailer cars.

Some fuel problems reduced mileages until a change to a different make improved the situation. At the beginning of January 1937 their daily service was given as 863 miles, and increasing.

An official Armstrong Whitworth table dated 22nd February 1937 gave the following data:

Car No.	Daily mileage from 4th November 1935	Total mileage
1	164	65,240
2	161	41,386
3	161	55,399
4	178	67,852
5	142	55,889
6	123	22,221
Totals	930	307,987

Four DT43 railcars in India. The unusually modern Indian built bodywork is depicted clearly in this illustration taken at Nayudupeta.
University of Glasgow

The cars were put into use on branch lines to meet competition from road services by giving a more attractive, economical, and speedy service than that given by steam trains.

Interesting insights gained by their use are typified in the operations on the Cocanada-Somagundum branch. In this instance the steam schedule of 99 minutes was cut to 87 minutes on the 29 mile service – with fourteen stops as opposed to the seven intermediate stops of the longer steam schedule. This particular branch was selected due to its operation at a continual loss since 1929 – the date it was opened. It was almost wholly a passenger line with very little freight traffic revenue.

In 1930 the traffic on the line was put at 200,000 per mile per year, but was falling away rapidly due to the competition of road services – having reached around 90,000 by the time the railcars were placed in service. After some experience in operation, the economies of the railcars allowed fare reductions, and passenger traffic increased by 40 per cent.

Maintenance and inspections took six hours per week; urgent work was carried out as required between rosters. Engines were examined at two or three week intervals and overhauled at 20,000-25,000 mile intervals.

Whilst being a modern-looking unit this close-up of the driving end shows the bodywork to be quiet angular.
University of Glasgow

A railcar built in 1934 for the Buenos Aires Western Railway seen in Scotswood Works yard. *Brian Webb collection*

The lightweight prototype railbus of advanced concept built by Armstrong Whitworth for British trials in 1933 under order DT16. Carrying Armstrong Whitworth number D15 it is seen here in the yard at Scotswood Works. *Brian Webb collection*

THE RAILBUSES

Armstrong Whitworth built two vehicles which came under the description of lightweight railcars or railbuses. Both were quite large twin bogie units, but quite dissimilar in design and construction – and for different rail gauges.

The first of these was completed in the spring of 1933 under order No. DT16, being a prototype for demonstration in the UK. This unit was claimed to be the lightest British-built 60 seat railcar then built, weighing only $17\frac{1}{2}$ tons in working order. Its seating capacity could be between 57 and 71, according to whether a luggage compartment was provided.

Armstrong Whitworth claimed that this type of railbus compared well in first cost with a diesel road bus, and was designed for frequent high-speed local services: competing with road services over local branch lines and on feeder services to main lines.

The mechanical design incorporated lightweight, but conventional, bogies with swing bolsters. The rigid design, of welded construction, was built up from flanged plates and pressed channel sections to form bogie frames of box girder form. Isothermos axleboxes with laminated axlebox springs were carried on hangers with Silentbloc rubber bushes. Spiral bolster springs were employed, and the hemispherical side bearings supported the vehicle underframe through rubber pads, the centre guiding pivot being non-loadbearing.

The wheels were 2ft 9in. in diameter, having Lang wooden centres with steel tyres bonded to the axles to allow track circuit operation. An underframe of two pressed-steel flanged plates was fish-bellied to allow the elimination of unnecessary weight. Pressed-steel stretchers were provided at intervals between the longitudinals, these being used to support engine/generator set, traction motor, etc. Normal buffing and drawgear was not fitted, but lightweight bumpers were installed at the ends of the underframe, and a removable towing link was carried in the tool box for use in emergency.

The twin-cab body was built by Park Royal Coachworks Ltd, London, to the design of Armstrong Whitworth. The vehicle was streamlined at the ends and sides, being scientifically proportioned to reduce air resistance. A deep skirting surrounded the vehicle to reduce air resistance at the underframe and bogie area, but was easily removable to permit undergear maintenance. The body was virtually an adaptation of road vehicle techniques to meet rigorous railway requirements, and was built up from two deep pressed steel underframe members, centrally placed, instead of the usual channel solebar construction used in rail vehicles.

Floor framing was of oak flitched with mild steel plate to the pillars, which, with the rails and other items of framing of oak and ash, were also flitched at all important joints with steel plate. The roof was of silver spruce board, supported on ash hoopsticks strengthened with mild steel carlines. The roof was covered with waterproof canvas coated with white lead. Exterior side panelling was of aluminium sheet, and the ends of hand beaten steel sheet.

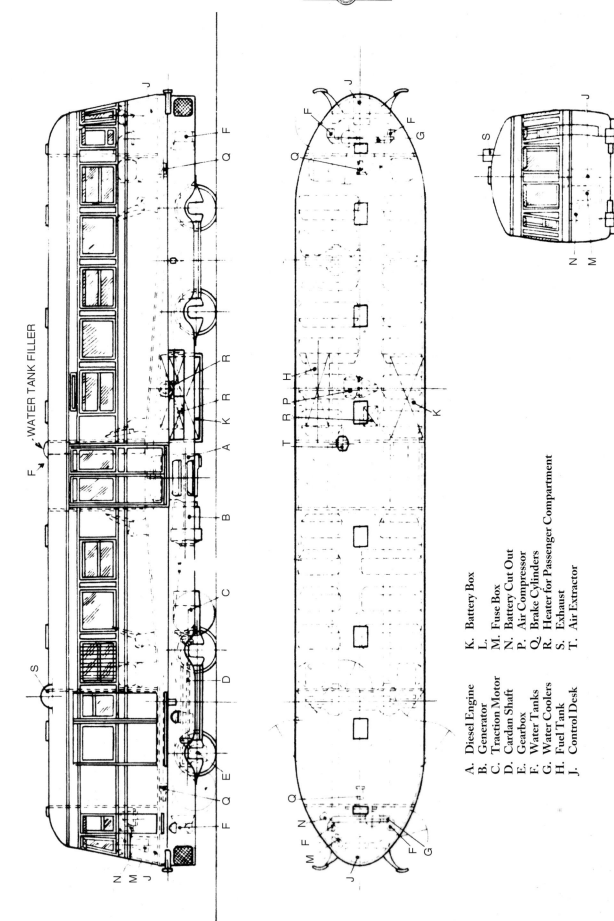

Layout diagram of DT16. Scale approx. 4mm – 1ft as no dimensions on original drawing.

A. Diesel Engine
B. Generator
C. Traction Motor
D. Cardan Shaft
E. Gearbox
F. Water Tanks
G. Water Coolers
H. Fuel Tank
J. Control Desk
K. Battery Box
L. Fuse Box
M. Battery Cut Out
N. Air Compressor
P. Brake Cylinders
Q. Heater for Passenger Compartment
R. Exhaust
S. Air Extractor
T.

Brian Webb collection

The railbus on the L&NER. *Brian Webb collection*

The passenger saloons were very attractive, being finished in Rexine cloth and mahogany mouldings. The floor was sound insulated with Insulwood and covered with a cork floor covering. Seating was of Park Royal 'Tub' type with back and seat cushions of latex rubber upholstered in moquette with leather ends.

Heating was by passing engine coolant water through a small radiator, the heat being pushed by a belt driven fan through ducting at skirting level between the body side panels, louvres admitting the heat into the compartment. The louvres were adjustable by the passengers.

The engine was the Armstrong-Saurer 6BLD model with six cylinders giving 95 bhp at 2,000 rpm. This drove a main generator which was suspended with the engine as a single unit by three resilient points from the underframe. The single traction motor, too, was suspended similarly from the underframe – driving via a cardan shaft to a worm drive axle-mounted gearbox by Craven-Guest on the leading axle of the powered bogie. The generator and motor were by Laurence, Scott & Electromotors. The control and transmission were of the ABE type and incorporated a deadman device.

Engine cooling was by radiators at both ends of the car beneath the underframe. The engine exhaust was passed through a silencer under the engine and out through the vehicle roof. Braking was by an internal expanding brake using Ferodo-lined shoes upon steel drums secured to the wheel bosses. Air for the braking came from a Westinghouse compressor mounted in the underframe. Hand braking was provided and operable from each driving cab.

After initial tests and trials at Scotswood, the 'bus' was run in on the L&NER in the Tyneside area during the early summer. On its early trials the railbus was found excessively noisy. In order to reduce this it was decided that the underfloor engine must be shielded. It was returned to Scotswood, where a wooden frame was built around the engine. Upon this was mounted panels of what would be, it was hoped, suitable soundproofing material. The railbus resumed trials and set off from Newcastle Central for a trip on the Newcastle-Carlisle line. It had only reached Elswick when the 'soundproofing' caught fire and all the passengers, including L&NER officials, left the bus whilst the fire was put out!

The railbus ran from Newcastle to Kings Cross on 30th July 1933 in 5 hours 48 minutes. It had 8 stops and signal checks en route, and maintained an average speed of 46.15 mph, using 35 gallons of fuel, or 7.65 mpg. Whilst in London the vehicle was demonstrated between Kings Cross and Hertford to British and foreign railway officials, including the fast running of 2nd August 1933 – stopping for 2 minutes at Bayford, and 1½ minutes at Belle Isle box on the return run. Hertford is 19½ miles from Kings Cross, and a top speed of 58 mph was recorded on the outward trip, bettered by 60 mph on the inward run. Fuel consumption varied between 9.3 and 7.15 mpg.

On its northbound return run to Newcastle the 268 miles

consumed 35 gallons of fuel, costing 13s 2d (66p). Armstrong Whitworth claimed that the lightweight design and streamlining enabled them to install only a 95 bhp engine – a 30 per cent reduction compared to a vehicle of conventional construction.

Following the trials from Kings Cross it was widely reported that two more vehicles were ordered by a South American railway, but in fact none were built and the car remained the sole example.

The railbus was put into regular service on the western branches from Newcastle on 25th September 1933, running for eleven weeks and covering 137.5 miles per day with a fuel consumption of 8.15 mpg. On 11th December 1933 it commenced more intensive duties involving 223 miles per day on round trips to Morpeth, Blackhill, and Hexham.

The vehicle was purchased by the L&NER on 28th June 1934, becoming 294 in their fleet, at a cost of £2,500. Its original cost was said to be £4,370.

Following service at Scarborough, on 16th September 1934, it began two weeks work replacing *Lady Hamilton* on the Hull-York-Selby-Pontefract service, which it operated at a fuel consumption of 11.4 mpg with an average speed of 47½ mph. On 13th October 1934 the vehicle had its engine converted to direct fuel injection and dual turbulence cylinder heads. Returned to service at Newcastle, the fuel consumption improved from 8.9 mpg to 11.6 mpg on a weekly mileage of 1500-1800 miles.

Armstrong Whitworth recorded the railbus as having accomplished the following:

Year	Miles	Traffic hours	Fuel
1934	17,737	921	9.63 mpg
1935	44,049	2,701	9.62

The railbus was scrapped at Darlington in 1939, and late spring found two other railcars out of use at Darlington works.

The second railbus turned out by Armstrong Whitworth was for the Buenos Aires Western Railway under order No. DT31. Designed in conjunction with Messrs Livesey, Son, & Henderson, the BAWR consulting engineers, it was quite different from the aforementioned unit.

Mechanically it followed usual Armstrong Whitworth constructional techniques, was light, but strong, and involved fabrication by welding. It was a twin-bogie unit with a body built in London by Park Royal Vehicles Ltd, and taken to Scotswood for mounting on the chassis. The body provided seating for sixteen first class and thirty-two second class passengers. It was built mostly of steel, though following road-bus techniques in that its frame was built on to the floor bearers, which were then bolted to the underframe – just as a bus body is attached to its chassis. In contrast to the British railbus, it was capable of hauling goods vans or light coaches (up to 40 tons), if necessary. Driving cabs were provided at both ends.

The engine was an Armstrong-Saurer type 6BXD six-cylinder unit, nominally rated at 140 bhp, but de-rated to 122 bhp at 1,400 rpm. The complete engine/generator set was mounted transversely on top of the underframe behind the driving cab at the leading end, being set in its own subframe. As was usual, engine changing was easily carried out by sliding the whole unit out sideways. The main generator was by Laurence, Scott & Electromotors, but the traction motors were by Crompton Parkinson. Here it is interesting to record the principal difference from the preceding railbus: it had axle-hung, nose-suspended traction motors in contrast to the frame-mounted type. Previous to this vehicle only the three railcars of DT1 had used this type of motor in a single-unit railcar. Both motors were mounted on the axles of the leading bogie under the engine compartment.

Really intended for outer suburban duties, it was put into service on 26th November 1934, replacing the BAWR Armstrong Whitworth motor-train of DT30 which was due for engine examination. It later went into temporary service between Luten and Moreno.

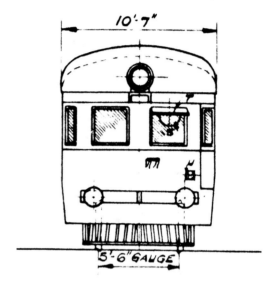

Above and opposite: Layout diagram of DT31, built in 1934 for the Buenos Aires Western Railway. Scale 4mm - 1ft.
Brian Webb collection

A. Oil Engine
B. Generator
C. Exhauster
D. Water Cooling Elements
E. Oil Cooling Elements
F. Air Heating Ducts
G. Heating Fan
H. Water Tank
J. Controller
K. (Vacuum) Driver's Brake Valve
L. Handbrake
M. Brake Cylinder
N. Sand Boxes
O. Motors
P. Fuel Tank
Q. Battery Box
R. Vacuum Brake Reservoirs
S. Screen Wiper
T. Sun Visor
U. Tail Lamp
V. Tool Box
W. Control Cubicle

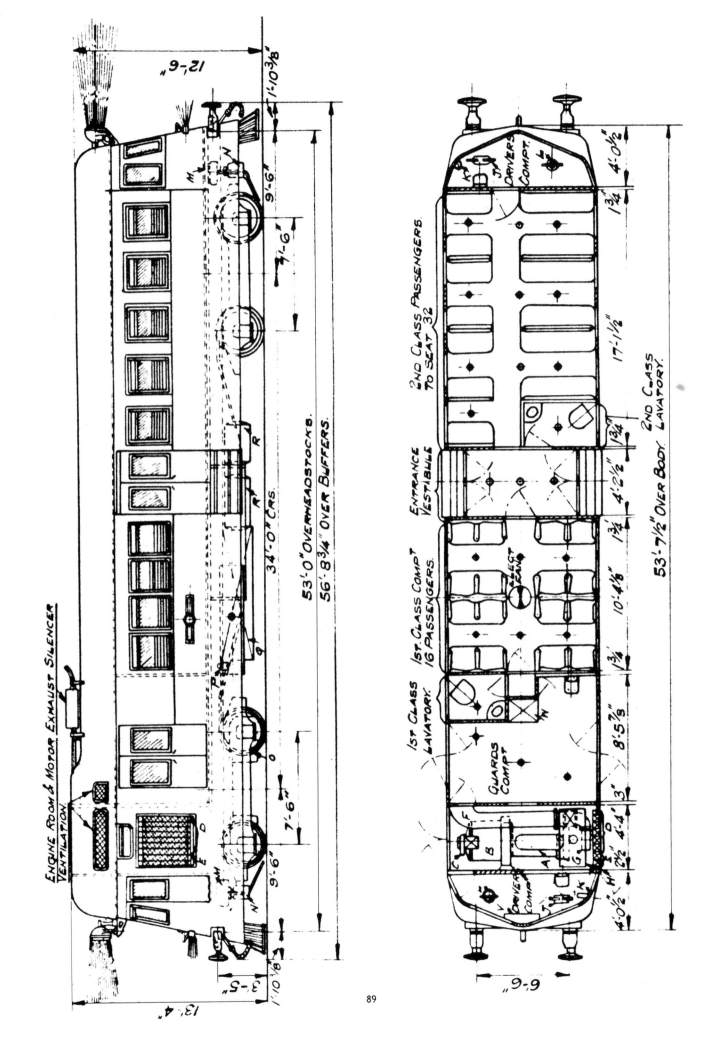

The completed body in full Buenos Aires Western Railway livery in the yard of Park Royal Vehicles Ltd. The body was fitted to the chassis at Scotswood Works.
British Leyland

Details of Service (from official Armstrong Whitworth reports)

Began service	Route	Miles per week	Notes
07.01.35	Haedo-Tabala	550	1.
20.03.35	Haedo-Tabala	1,150	
06.05.35	Haedo-Tabala-Marmol	1,150	2.
23.09.35	Haedo-Tabala-Marmol	1,435	
17.12.35	Haedo-Tabala-Marmol	1,660	
01.37	Canuelas-Empalme Lobos	?	

Notes: 1. Haedo was at the end of the BAWR electrified system.
2. On this route the vehicle often hauled a refrigerated van.

Record of running
A. 7th January - 10th August 1935
B. 10th August 1935 - 31st March 1936

	A.	B.
Miles during period	25,495	24,684
Total miles run	27,635	53,329
Miles per month	3,580	3,200
Fuel oil (mpg)	5.3	7.5
Lubricating oil (mpg)	392	234

The engines were modified on 10th August 1935 to conform to the new pattern of Armstrong-Saurer engines by fitting direct injection, dual turbulence cylinder heads, which altered considerably the average fuel consumption, as can be seen from these figures:

mpg (original) 5.3
mpg (after conversion) 7.0

By the end of 1936 the railbus had covered 65,027 miles.

When compared to the 450 bhp railcar of DT30 the smaller 140 bhp car was not easy to employ – due to its small size and low seating capacity. It did, however, work well on the various branch lines around Buenos Aires. The railcar carried maker's No. D37 of 1934, and BAWR number RM 230. It was taken out of service in May 1971 and was scrapped in February 1972 at the Liniera workshops; its mileage was 628,101 km or 390,050 miles.

DT31 photographed in the Argentine. *Jorge L. San Martin collection*

The 'Universal' locomotive on empty coaching stock trials at Alnmouth.
Brian Webb collection

MAIN LINE LOCOMOTIVES

Armstrong Whitworth's first main line locomotive was that supplied to the BAGSR in late 1933 under order DT4. However, five other locomotives within this category have still to be considered. The first of these was also the second demonstration locomotive suitable for main line railway service, a powerful 'universal' mixed traffic unit designed for British conditions.

With the initiative inherent at Scotswood, Armstrong Whitworth had decided that there was ample scope and opportunity on the British main line railways for a locomotive capable of hauling both passenger and freight trains of medium weight, and, providing a low axle loading was achieved, it would have an almost universal ability to work on most routes, hence its class name.

The locomotive was a rugged, basically simple machine designed to undertake work carried out by a majority of British medium size steam locomotives, with a capability of working 250/270 passenger trains at up to 70 mph and freight trains of up to 800 tons at the usual speeds for loose-coupled unbraked trains.

Armstrong Whitworth envisaged that any railway adopting a fleet of such standard units would be able to use them singly or in multiples of two, or even three, under the control of one crew: a big saving over double-heading with steam, which required separate crews. In addition, it was planned to use them at either end of passenger trains in permanent sets – permitting rapid turnaround at terminals, and enabling improved suburban shuttle services to be worked by controlling both locomotives

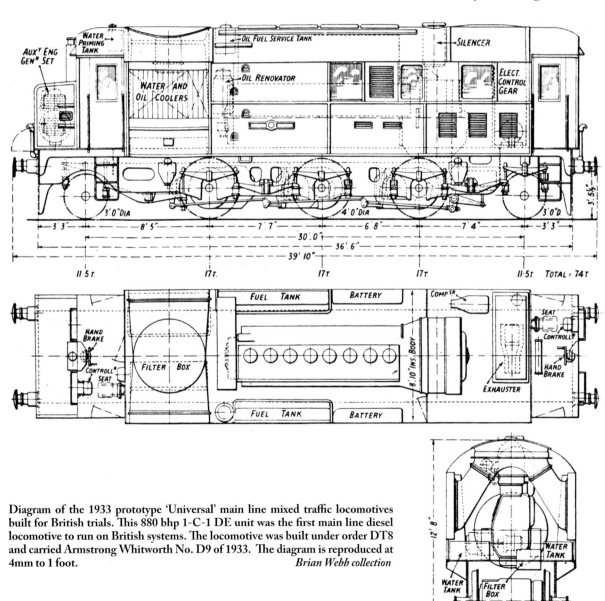

Diagram of the 1933 prototype 'Universal' main line mixed traffic locomotives built for British trials. This 880 bhp 1-C-1 DE unit was the first main line diesel locomotive to run on British systems. The locomotive was built under order DT8 and carried Armstrong Whitworth No. D9 of 1933. The diagram is reproduced at 4mm to 1 foot.
Brian Webb collection

from one cab through control cabling installed in the coaching stock. Smaller trains would have one locomotive at one end to pull or push the train – depending on the direction of travel – and a driving cab provided at the end of the train for use when propelling.

Added to these possibilities was the highly standardised stock of spares required, an arrangement not hitherto attainable with stream traction, due to the multiplicity of types required to operate services which the flexible 'Universal' locomotive could work. It could readily be seen that, provided the conditions were right, Armstrong Whitworth thought they had a 'winner' on their hands.

Built under order No. DT8 in 1933, it carried maker's No. D9, and was a 1-Co-1 diesel electric with a maximum axle loading of seventeen tons and a starting tractive effort of 29,700 lbs. It was fitted for multiple-unit control.

The mechanical design was based on a plate-frame underframe with a pony truck at each end. The frame was deep and very substantial, being decked over with steel plate to give a platform for the power equipment. The superstructure was overall and built of steel sections covered with steel plate. The rigid axles, all powered by their own traction motors, had wheels of four foot diameter and were within the plate frame section, running in Isothermos type axleboxes outside the frames. The guiding pony trucks were of two types, with equalised spring control.

The locomotive had cabs at both ends, with full controls in each. At one end the cab was preceded by a short blunt 'nose' – which was a bonnet housing an auxiliary engine/generator set comprising an Armstrong-Saurer 6BXD six-cylinder engine of 80 bhp, and a generator, mounted transversely. Between the cab and the engine room was the cooling and air filtering section. This had a roof mounted fan which drew in air through floor mounted filters and bodyside radiator panels to cool the engine circulating water and lubricating oil.

The main engine, together with an oil renovator, side fuel tanks, and battery boxes, was housed in the engine room, followed by a steel partition. This separated the main generator, electrical control gear, compressor, and vacuum exhauster from the oily air of the engine room. The second cab followed this.

The prime mover in this locomotive was an Armstrong-Sulzer 8LD28 eight-cylinder vertical engine giving 800 bhp at 700 rpm, with a full load fuel consumption of 0.40 lbs per bhp per hour. The electrical control equipment was fully automatic, having a hydraulic servo-motor operated regulator which enabled the full engine output to be used in the 6-65 mph speed range without series-parallel switches. This servo field control system

A view inside Scotswood Works showing the installation of an Armstrong-Sulzer 8LD28 in the prototype 'Universal' locomotive.
Brian Webb collection

Who says the Americans introduced the nose-type main line diesel locomotive configuration? This view of D9 shows the 'nose' which housed an auxiliary engine/generator set. The locomotive is standing in the yard at Scotswood Works. *Brian Webb collection*

was arranged so that the rheostat controlling the strength of the generator field was operated by an oil-pressure motor, supplied by pressurized oil from the engine lubricating system through a valve controlled by the engine governor. Control at full power was available at all times to the driver. Safety devices prevented overloading of the engine and transmission. A Laurence, Scott & Electromotors main generator, directly coupled to the engine, was installed.

Traction motors, by Crompton Parkinson, were three in number, being self-ventilated axle-hung machines with roller bearings on the armatures and white metal lined, pad-lubricated suspension bearings on the axle. The locomotive was designed to be convertible to one having frame-hung traction motors carried rigidly on the underframe and with flexible drive to the axles.

Engine starting was by motoring the main generator using the current generated by the auxiliary engine/generator set. This auxiliary system obviated the need for larger batteries, while at the same time it drove all the auxiliaries, enabling the whole of the main engine output to be devoted to traction. For this reason the locomotive was often described as being of 880 bhp.

Compressed air sanding was supplied from the small compressor and fed sand to the outer driving wheel axles. Automatic vacuum braking on the locomotive came from two 24-inch cylinders located between the frame plates, applying brake blocks to all driving wheels. Screw down hand braking was also installed.

Driving arrangements were for left hand drive. The driver's main controls, main controller, with power and reverse handles and deadman control; vacuum brake handle; sanding and hand brake; various dials and gauges; plus engine starting switch; speedometer; heating and lighting switches; were all readily to hand from the driver's seat.

A reproduction of an Armstrong Whitworth magazine advertisement of 1933. This includes a faked illustration of two 'Universal' locomotives on a train. In fact, only one was ever built for British use. *Brian Webb collection*

The prototype 'Universal' 880 bhp locomotive at Heaton Sidings, Newcastle-upon-Tyne whilst on freight train trials with the L&NER.
Brian Webb collection

Another view of D9 at Alnmouth on empty coaching stock trials whilst based at Heaton shed. *Brian Webb collection*

The locomotive had a power to weight ratio of 207 lbs per bhp – a good figure for so early a locomotive.

After extensive tests and trials within the confines of Scotswood Works it was tested on the L&NER in mid-summer 1933, on the Newcastle-North Wylam line. With seventeen coaches, the train stopped at the stations en route on its outward run, but ran back non-stop on the return trip. The trial was undertaken under the eye of Armstrong Whitworth engineers, while Nigel Gresley was one of the railway officials present. The locomotive's preliminary tests and trials in the Tyneside area started on 6th July 1933, from Heaton shed, following minor adjustments. Its duties involved runs to Alnmouth and Hexham with empty coaching stock trains.

With intermittent attention at Scotswood the locomotive continued these trials. During September and October 1933 the locomotive was taking ten-coach trains, weighing 275 tons, between Newcastle and Alnmouth with success, and maintaining mile a minute schedules with ease for long distances. Arrangements were then made to run the locomotive on regular goods trains of 45-60 wagons on the L&NER. These started on 19th February 1934 and involved Newcastle-Berwick and Newcastle-York runs, followed by round trips between Berwick, Newcastle, and York. Passenger trials were undertaken on the Newcastle-Carlisle line with duties on regular service trains.

Some of the problems experienced while on main line trials included a burst exhaust manifold while at Heaton shed. The locomotive was run light to Scotswood for attention, and almost poisoned, in the process, the driver and Armstrong Whitworth

A panoramic view of the L&NER empty coaching stock test train, taken at Alnmouth. It is stopped just north of Alnmouth Station alongside the 35 milepost for the official photographer. *Brian Webb collection*

officials who had to ride in the locomotive filled with exhaust fumes. On another occasion the locomotive had to have attention to faulty electrical gear and, whilst being tested in Scotswood Works yard, it was de-railed. After re-railing and examination it was sent back to Heaton for a run to Berwick with a fast goods train, failing at Tweedmouth with a hot intermediate axlebox bearing. Upon its removal from the train it was decided to take it back to Scotswood – the journey back taking three days and needing three new axleboxes fitting en route. The problem was subsequently found to be a bent axle journal sustained in the Scotswood yard derailment.

Braking was found insufficient for handling loose-coupled freights, so additional reservoirs were fitted to actuate new brake blocks on the pony truck wheels. These were fitted between the radius bars of the trucks. Later, on coal train trials on the North Wylam line, one reservoir became detached – while the

D9 speeds past Lamesley on the L&NER main line in 1934. *W. Bryce Greenfield*

locomotive's lack of adhesive weight caused some difficulties when it was unable to halt a 800 ton train, which pushed the locomotive with its brakes on through a set of crossing gates.

The locomotive worked a special train for delegates of the Institute of Transport Congress between Leeds and Darlington on 7th June 1934, when it was reported to be in dark blue livery.

The schedule was as follows:

Leeds (city)	dep	13.25
Crossgates	pass	13.33
Wetherby	pass	13.45
Harrogate	pass	13.56
Ripon	pass	14.08
Thirsk	arr	14.24
Thirsk	dep	15.05
Northallerton	pass	15.15
Croft Junction	arr	15.29
Croft Junction	dep	15.32
Darlington (Geneva loop)	arr	15.34

Visit to P. W. reclamation yard.

The return run:

Darlington (Geneva loop)	dep	17.03
Black Banks	pass	17.06
Northallerton	pass	17.20
Sinderby	pass	17.29
Ripon	pass	17.37
Starbeck	pass	17.53
Arthington	pass	18.06
Holbeck	pass	18.19
Leeds (city)	arr	18.22
Leeds (city)	dep	18.33
Neville Hill	arr	18.43

The train was composed of eight green and cream liveried open tourist stock.

All in all, the locomotive appears to have worked well on its L&NER trials, and a mileage of 26,140 was attained up to the time when the locomotive was taken out of service in June 1934, following an engine crankcase explosion. It returned to Scotswood for repairs, but it was stored minus its power equipment, in the yard until 1937 when it was dismantled.

Armstrong Whitworth recorded that it used 25,000 gallons of fuel: averaging a consumption of 31.60 lbs on passenger service and 16.8 lbs on goods services.

The locomotive was before its time on the rail system under the control of steam minded engineers who only saw diesel traction as something to be equalled, in respect of speed and power, by their beloved steam locomotives, taking no account of the advantages being offered by diesel traction. Perhaps if a pair had been built a more conclusive demonstration would have resulted. As it was, we were to wait over a dozen years before a British railway took a serious look at main line diesel locomotion.

Although the hulk lingered on alongside the paint shop, its power equipment was repaired and used in one of the pair of similar locomotives built for Indian railway conditions in 1934.

Following considerable interest expressed by the officers of the North Western Railway of India in 1932/3 on the subject of main line diesel traction, and in particular the work at Scotswood, the railway said they intended to try some locomotives and probably order them from Armstrong Whitworth. In order to facilitate the work and provide the expected stimulus for the order, AW put in hand an improved version of their 'Universal' locomotive then undergoing tests on the L&NER.

So sure were Armstrong Whitworth of obtaining the order that the work proceeded steadily and performance data graphs were supplied to the NWR. No doubt some surprise and dismay was felt when the order did materialise; for, although it was indeed placed with Armstrong Whitworth, it was for two 1,200 bhp locomotives, not 880 bhp as had been envisaged. After the shock subsided, work proceeded slowly on the two locomotives, but no doubt some serious thought was expended at Scotswood as to what would be the fate of two 5ft 6in. gauge locomotives.

The locomotives were built under order DT23, carried works numbers D27/8, and were completed in 1934. Built to Indian Railway's loading gauge dimensions, they were designed to deal with long distance passenger and goods traffic in shade temperatures of 120°F with tropical humidity, without alteration, and to run distances of up to 1,000 miles without taking either fuel or water. They were designed to operate singly, driven from either end, or in multiple unit, with all starting and running operations controlled from one cab.

Although having an affinity to the British 'Universal' prototype locomotive of order DT8, there was some redesign due to experience gained with that unit. The principle differences were the resiting of the auxiliary engine/generator set, which was moved inside the locomotive body; the provision of forced ventilation for the traction motors; and some simplification of ancillary equipment. The main power unit was the Armstrong-Sulzer 8LD28 eight-cylinder vertical unit running at 700 rpm, but capable of derating from its 800 bhp output to suit climatic requirements. Laurence, Scott & Electromotors supplied the main generator – this being a self-ventilated, ten-pole, double shunt wound, dc machine, with a special series winding used only to motor the main generator when starting the main engine. A sliding roof over the engine/generator set provided access to cylinder heads, walkways being arranged on either side of this opening.

The roof was removable from the cant rails in two sections. One covered the filter compartment and facilitated removal of the main generator, control cubicle, blower and motor, exhauster and compressor contained therein. The larger removable roof covered the engine, and also formed the top part of the silencer casing.

Three Crompton Parkinson traction motors were used, being of the axle-hung, nose-suspended type with forced-ventilation, each having a rating of 250 bhp. They had roller bearing armatures. They drove through a reduction gearing of 61:17.

Auxiliary power came from an Armstrong-Saurer 6BLD engine of 75 bhp at 1,600 rpm driving a 51 KW generator. This

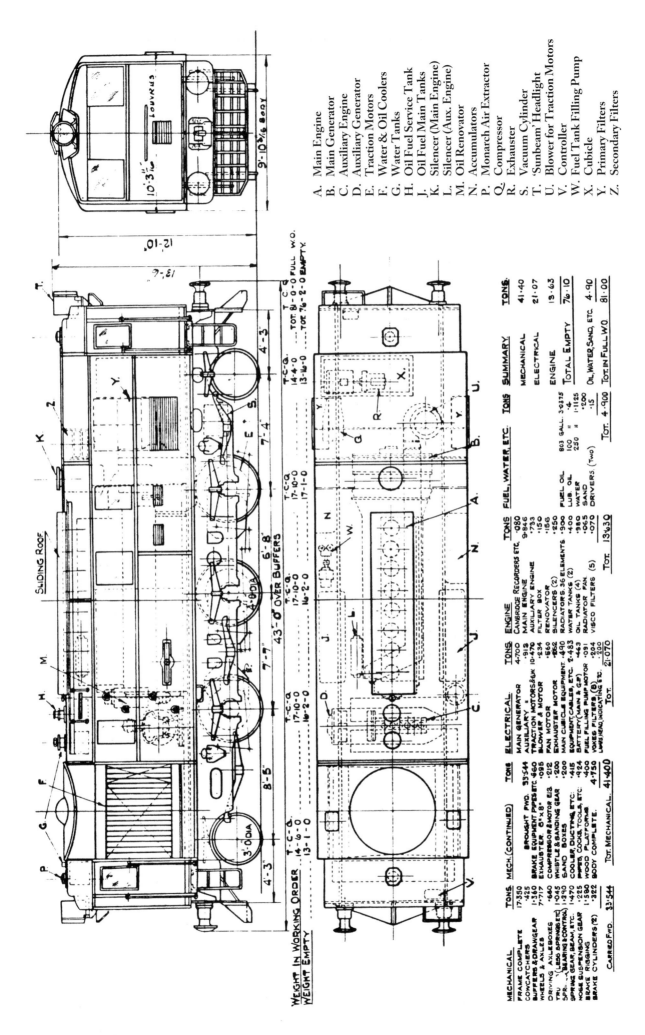

Two 'Universal' locomotives were built hopefully for service in India. However, the sale did not materialise. This is the layout diagram for those locomotives to order DT23, locomotives D27/8 of 1934. 4mm - 1ft.

Brian Webb collection

unit supplied all the auxiliaries and started the main engine; it, in turn, was started from the battery. The auxiliary set was placed transversely across the locomotive in the engine room between the engine and the cooling group partition. The set was arranged to be slid out for attention by removing the bodyside panel.

The cooling group consisted of bodyside oil and water cooling panels with a roof-mounted fan. Other items of equipment were located as follows: 800 gallon (total) fuel tanks in the engine room, one each side, the batteries being arranged similarly; water tanks were roof-mounted, as were the main engine silencers; the main generator protruded through the steel partition into the compartment with bodyside filters, and this also housed the traction motor blower, control cubicle, exhauster, and air compressor; roof mounted Sunbeam headlights and also steel cowcatchers were fitted at both ends.

Westinghouse automatic vacuum brakes were fitted, activating brake blocks on the driving wheels. The brake system was controlled from the driver's brake valve, an emergency valve being interlocked with the master controller. Each cab also had a hand brake.

Control for driving was automatic, and a deadman device with 'delay' was fitted. Sanding was electro-pneumatic, activated by foot switches in each cab. Isothermos axleboxes were fitted.

After completion, arrangements were made to try the locomotives on the Ceylon Government Railway, this being of 5ft 6in. gauge and showing some interest in diesel traction; Armstrong Whitworth hoped that a sale might result.

Both locomotives were shipped in late 1934 under order No. DT59 for a six-month trial period, by permission of the Ceylon Railways, on Colombo-India mail train services. Arriving on the S. S. *Belray* at Colombo, they were landed on 3rd January 1935. The service consisted of hauling the Indian Mail trains of up to eighteen bogie carriages, loading to around 500 tons,

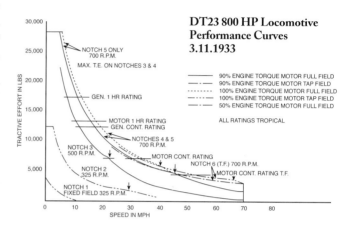

DT23 locomotive (left) and the DT19 train set for Sao Paulo under construction at Scotswood in 1933. *Brian Webb collection*

Two views of the completed DT23 locomotives (AW D27/8). They are seen outside the paint shop at Scotswood Works in the upper view whilst below they are seen from the opposite side in a retouched 'official' view.   *Brian Webb collection*

Mixed gauge multiple unit operation. One of the DT23 locomotives operating in the yard at Scotswood Works with DT1 railcar *Lady Hamilton*. *Brian Webb collection*

One of the 5ft 6in. gauge locomotives in Scotswood Yard prior to being sent to Ceylon for trials. The large headlight has been fitted into the recess on the roof and a cowcatcher attached to the headstock. *Brian Webb collection*

Unloading one of the DT23 locomotives at Colombo, Ceylon (now Sri Lanka) in 1934. *Brian Webb collection*

between Colombo and Talaimanna, with weekly rosters of 2,009 miles in 102 hours and 2,432 miles in 118 hours. Armstrong Whitworth employed their own staff to maintain and operate the locomotives, numbered 800/1 by the CGR, while the CGR paid a fixed charge per train mile, amounting to 75 per cent of the cost of steam traction for the same services.

Early trains were marred by numerous minor faults, especially with the auxiliary power unit and with leaking fuel tanks. Electrical problems included armature banding wires breaking.

Locomotive D27 began services on 17th February 1935, when the banding wire broke on a traction motor. The locomotive was taken into the CGR workshops, and upon being lifted, the crane chain broke – dropping the locomotive 3ft 6in. to the floor. Detailed inspection revealed little damage, apart from a bent axle and some items of framing. After repairs D27 resumed work. The locomotive worked until 27th July when it failed with a broken crankshaft. Examinations revealed that the failure was entirely due to the February mishap, when the fall had put the engine mounting out of alignment. It was unfortunate that this had previously escaped notice.

D28 entered service on 11th February, and worked quite well until it failed on 29th May with a cracked cylinder block.

With D28 out of service, D27 continued until the failure in July. Although the CGR themselves were reported to be interested in purchasing the locomotives, the government

Right: Locomotive D27 on demonstration in Ceylon as Ceylon Government Railways No. 800 in 1934/5. *Brian Webb collection*

turned down the offer, made by Armstrong Whitworth, to sell the locomotives at £15,000 each plus £2,000 worth of spares. The pair were shipped back to the UK and taken into Scotswood Works for attention.

The Ceylon trials proved that the locomotives had in fact operated at half the cost of steam traction, and had covered 34,327 miles in their four months of operation. Each locomotive had been found quite capable of handling singly eighteen-coach mail trains with ease.

An Armstrong Whitworth summary of their running stated:

Locomotive No.	Service days	Official miles	Paid miles	Fuel (gals)	Official mpg	Lub. Oil (gals)
D27	63	18,291	17,622	16,423	1.11	224
D28	55	16,036	15,351	13,424	1.19	227

Cost of operation:
Fuel, lubricants, stores	4.5d per mile
Drivers	1.3d per mile
Maintenance, repairs, overhauls	5.4d per mile
Shed and miscellaneous charges	0.8d per mile
Total	12.0d (5p) per mile

The locomotives were reconditioned at Scotswood under order DT74 with the hope of an eventual sale; this came in 1936 and a further series of modifications put in hand to meet the specification laid down in order DT75. Both were sold to the Buenos Aires Great Southern Railway and shipped from Elswick wharf on the S.S. *Leighton* on 18th December 1937. Shipping specifications show that locomotive D27 had main engine No. 150 and auxiliary engine No. BD296; D28 had main engine No. 108 (ex-locomotive D9 of order DT8) and auxiliary engine BD297. The locomotives were evidently shipped complete with staff exchange apparatus for single line operation, but footsteps and headlamps were stowed in the generator compartment. Cowcatchers were in separate packing cases.

The pair were not welcomed by the BAGSR operating staff, and it was felt that the locomotives had been dumped on them by their London office. They were given numbers CM204/5 and, after tests and trials in early 1938, the locomotives were operated in multiple unit on the night trains between Buenos Aires and Bahia Blanca, alternating with the 1,700 bhp locomotive CM210. The locomotives operated with equal success and with a comparable fuel consumption to CM210.

A piston failure, due to poor design said the BAGSR, resulted in the de-rating of both locomotive engines to 600 bhp. They resumed their duties on the Bahia Blanca trains and worked successfully at the similar running costs to CM210 in spite of their reduced power.

During 1939 CM205 suffered a connecting rod failure which distorted the engine crankcase and fractured the cylinder block. The locomotive was laid up and the damaged components sent to Sulzers at Winterthur for repairs, due to the non-availability of Scotswood under Vickers-Armstrongs for further railway work. The start of the war in 1939 prevented the return of the components. This failure was attributed to a connecting rod bolt

Salvation at last! The DT23 locomotives were subsequently sold in 1937 to the Buenos Aires Great Southern Railway becoming their CM204/5 in which guise they are seen here. For work in the Argentine they have been fitted with much more substantial cowcatchers.
Brian Webb collection

A close-up of CM204. *George L. San Martin collection*

coming loose, due in turn to a broken split pin allowing the bolt to work loose. It was pointed out that apparently Armstrong Whitworth did not follow the usual Sulzer practice of using safety grub screws for locking the castle nuts, and employing a security wire passed through the heads of the grub screws – a process which would have prevented the mishap.

CM204 continued in traffic on less arduous work, being found employment with one of the two Harland & Wolff 1-Do-1 diesel electrics, CM207, on milk train service between Buenos Aires and Canuelas, three times daily. Each unit alternated and covered a daily mileage of 384 kms (238 m). CM204 ceased activity in September 1943, when it caught fire.

In the opinion of the BAGSR it was a liability of plate framed locomotives to harbour dirt and oil and catch fire – for one of the Harland & Wolff units had suffered a similar fate. CM204/5 lacked an unbroken floor plate, due to design problems posed by the plate frames, which also had cross stretchers harbouring oil and dirt in close proximity with electrical cables and was liable to ignite should the cables fail. The fire in CM204 was attributed by the BAGSR to sparks from the brake blocks.

The damage was extensive, and both locomotives were laid up for the war period. As it turned out neither was ever repaired, although according to Argentine Railways records scrapping did not officially take place until December 1963 at the Escalada workshops, their cumulative mileage being 1,918,100 km, or 1,191,140 miles.

Service reports of the locomotives on the BAGSR indicated much trouble with the auxiliary engine, which was through an unnecessary complication, three out of four failures being attributable to this one item of equipment.

Armstrong Whitworth had designed these for use in dry and dusty conditions, and to run with all doors and windows closed to achieve the clean internal atmosphere required. All air was admitted through felt filters in the bodyside, passing via the generator into the engine room. In theory this introduced a slight pressurisation in the locomotive interior to exclude dust and dirt. But in practice the filters soon choked, restricting air flow and combining with the heat given off by the exhaust silencer to make the conditions inside the locomotive unbearable in almost any weather conditions, but considerably aggravated in the summer. These problems were overcome by fitting wire gauze air filters, moving the silencer outside the locomotive on the roof and providing additional ventilation doors in the engine room roof.

The BAGSR were more convinced than ever of the desirability for bogie locomotives and their loss of interest in plate-framed units is hardly surprising.

Armstrong Whitworth's magnum opus in diesel electric locomotion was to be the ordering in April 1934, by North Western Railway of India, of two 1,200 bhp main line locomotives. They were intended for use on the Sind mail train service between Lahore and Karachi. Great care was taken with the design work on these locomotives, which were intended to be able to handle express passenger and heavy goods trains in shade temperatures from 32°F to 120°F and in conditions of tropical humidity at altitudes ranging from sea level to 1,000 feet.

The Indian Railways Board allowed RS. 7,000,000, or £52,500 for the locomotives, but surviving reports put the cost at £24,809 per locomotive. Construction was done under the supervision of Messrs Rendel, Palmer and Tritton, the railway's consulting engineers.

Armstrong Whitworth's largest single-unit main line locomotives were built in 1935 under order DT51 for the North Western Railway of India. Armstrong Whitworth numbers D44/5 were 1,200 bhp 1A-Co-2 units. Here what was to become NWR No. 332 is seen inside Scotswood Works. *Brian Webb collection*

The Armstrong Whitworth adherence to plate frames was again continued in these units. They had officially the 2-Do-1 axle layout, but 2-Co-A1 would be more strictly accurate – due to the fact that the trailing driving axle was incorporated into a bogie, so reducing the rigid wheelbase and providing a bogie of equal guiding efficiency at both ends to permit similar quality running in both directions.

Bogie design followed steam locomotive practice on the Indian railways: incorporating laminated control springs on one bogie and helical on the other, thus allowing full freedom for all oscillations and asymmetrical movements. All axleboxes had Timken tapered roller bearings with oil lubrication.

The braking system was of the vacuum type with two twenty-four inch diameter cylinders operating on the three rigid axled wheels, and two eighteen inch cylinders on the motored bogie wheels. A rotary vacuum exhauster was fitted behind the leading cab, being motor driven. A Westinghouse compressor, in the same location, operated the air-sanding gear.

The locomotive body was of twin cab layout, flat fronted with end doors to permit inter-locomotive access when operating in multiple. The cabs were lined internally with teak and had double roofs, ventilated as in normal Indian practice. Between the cabs the body was divided, behind the leading cab, with a steel partition separating the main generator, brake equipment, and main electrical control cubicle from the engine room.

The engine room housed the main engine/generator set, battery boxes, and the auxiliary engine/generator set, arranged symmetrically along the body centreline. Immediately behind the trailing cab were the water and oil cooling radiators and roof mounted fan. The engine room was force ventilated by air discharged from the main generator, this preventing ingress of dust. The generator compartment had Vokes panel-type flannel filters, protected externally by louvres to allow only cool filtered air access to it. Cooling air for the main generator, traction motors, and auxiliary engine group was taken from the generator compartment, the same source supplying Visco filtered air to the engine intake manifold.

The main engine was an Armstrong-Sulzer type 8LD34 eight-cylinder in-line unit with Bosch direct fuel injection pumps and nozzles. The engine had a continuous output of 1,200 bhp at 630 rpm. The engine weighed 14 tons empty, giving a ratio of 26 lbs per bhp; in service weight, with oil and water, the engine/generator group weighed 22.3 tons.

Under test conditions at Scotswood the engines ran continuously for 150 hours with an average fuel consumption figure of 0.37 lbs per bhp hour and a maximum rating of 1,260 bhp was obtained. In their installed state the engines were derated to 984 bhp.

A feature of the engines was their welded steel crankcases, which were stiffened laterally by double-triangulation of the lower side members. Cylinder blocks, of cast iron, were in two groups of four, bolted together and to the crankcase. Separate

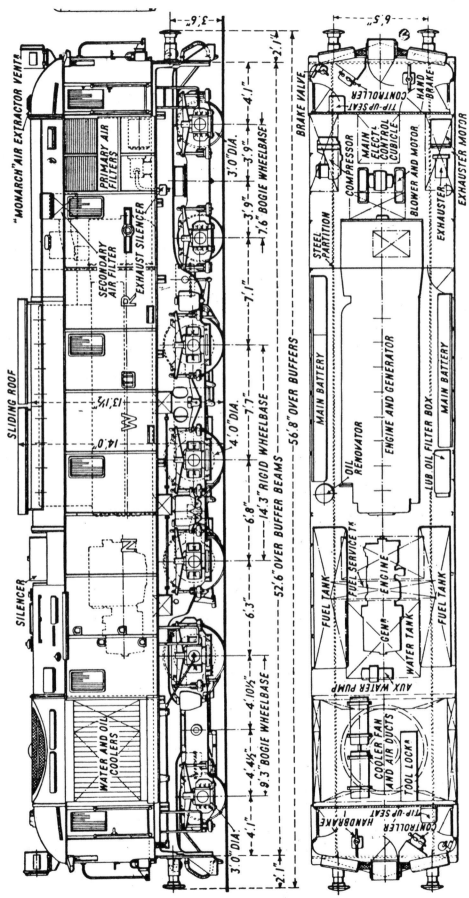
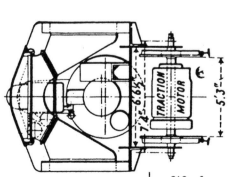

Layout diagram of DT51. 4mm – 1ft.

Brian Webb collection

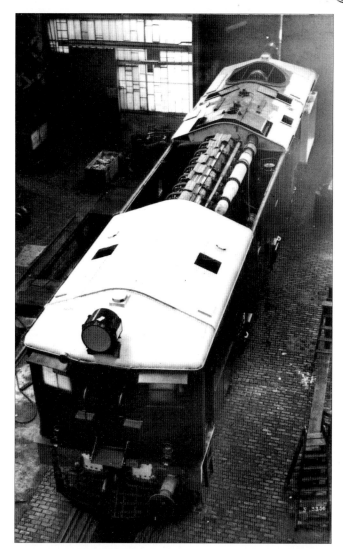

A view from above DT51 locomotive with part of the roof removed in Scotswood Works. *Brian Webb collection*

cylinder liners and cooling water jackets for each cylinder incorporated water cooling passages to cool the cylinder head.

Pistons, of heat treated aluminium alloy, had hollowed out crowns to provide a symmetrical combustion space suited to the multi-hole fuel injection nozzle. Fully-floating gudgeon pins carried the nickel-chrome steel connecting rods which ran on big-end bearings of gunmetal shells lined with white metal. Open-hearth, oil-treated steel, in one piece, was used for the crankshaft. It ran in bearings lined with white metal on a steel shell.

Easy access to the big-end and main bearings was via large aluminium doors covering the joint between crankcase and cylinder block. The camshaft, carried on bearings mounted on the cylinder block, was driven by gearing at the coupling end of the crankshaft. Vertical push rods actuated the inlet and exhaust valves on each cylinder head. The camshaft also drove the centrifugal three-speed engine governor – the change between speeds being controlled by air-operated pistons actuated through electro-pneumatic valves controlled by the driver.

Fuel injection was arranged so that timing varied for each change of speed. Each cylinder had its own fuel pump, fed with fuel by gravity via an Auto-Klean filter, the tank being overhead. This tank was kept filled from the main tanks by a gear-driven transfer pump.

The gearing at the coupling end of the engine also drove a centrifugal coolant water pump, and pumps at the opposite end for forced lubrication and oil circulation. The engine stopped automatically if oil pressure fell.

The auxiliary equipment was almost all powered by the auxiliary engine/generator set comprising an Armstrong-Saurer 6BXD six-cylinder engine and generator giving 110 bhp at 1300 rpm, started from the battery.

The main generator was by Laurence, Scott and Electromotors, being a dc double shunt wound machine, arranged for motoring to start the main engine – power for this coming from the auxiliary set.

Four Crompton Parkinson force-ventilated, axle-hung, nose-suspended traction motors were fitted to each locomotive. The fuel tanks were mounted on each side of the auxiliary engine/generator set, and the water tank was roof-mounted above the name set.

Photographs of the locomotives under construction show them numbered 32 and 33, but they were delivered as 332 and 333.

The locomotives were built under order DT51 and carried works numbers D44/5. Shipped in fully erected condition from Elswick wharf, they were lifted on to the deck of the Christen-Smith *Belship* for the journey to Karachi. They arrived in Karachi on 3rd/4th September 1935.

Intentions to operate these locomotives over the Sind desert were really to gain operating experience with diesel units under conditions similar to those expected on the proposed direct route between Bombay and Karachi. On their scheduled sphere of operations between Lahore and Karachi they were to haul trains of up to 600 tons weight at 60-65 mph in multiple unit, carrying enough fuel for the return journey of 1,564 miles. Further trials envisaged single-unit operation on slow passenger and goods trains.

Troubles were immediately experienced at Karachi with flashovers at the generators and traction motors. While locomotive D45 (NWR No. 333) was being hauled dead by 332, the reverser drum of the traction motor closed due to vibrations, and the motors began to generate. Severe damage to the motors resulted, two needing complete rewinding and the remainder extensive repair work. Lack of facilities at Karachi for heavy repair work necessitated the locomotives being sent to Lahore. On 7th October 332, hauling 333 and a 40 ton carriage, set off – to arrive there two days later. The 752 mile journey used 400 gallons of fuel oil.

At Lahore, 333 was laid aside, and trials recommenced with one locomotive, which continued to give trouble with flashovers. Experiments with air-blast over the commutator were tried successfully. The trials, a series of short runs totalling some 1,000 miles with loads of between 110 and 350 tons, ran into trouble once track speeds of 50 mph were exceeded, when flashovers occurred.

Investigations showed that the main generator was unstable at 850 volts to meet the railway's required speeds and loadings.

DT51 No. 332 seen at Lahore, India in 1935 whilst on trials. *P. S. A. Berridge*

Vibration troubles caused difficulties to the relays, but modified contractors were fitted which, to some extent, overcame the trouble.

Subsequent enquiries showed that bench tests at the maker's works were carried out at fixed voltages, and the generators were evidently not run for long periods at maximum service voltage. With this information trials ceased on 12th June 1936.

The following table gave meagre indication of their performance:

Locomotive No.	Main Engine hours	Auxiliary Engine hours	Locomotive hours	Mileage
332	182	206	241	5,102
333	51	84	70	1,387

The only solution to this unhappy state of affairs was to replace the generators with ones of improved capacity, modify the traction motors, or replace them with new ones and recondition the engines, although these had proven entirely satisfactory. The whole power equipment was shipped back to the UK in late 1936, an official report stating that 1,400 miles of trials had been carried out, but that the trials on the 1,500 mile mail train service had been postponed until early 1937.

A long report on the locomotives prepared by the Armstrong Whitworth Indian representative, Mr Rudd, gave the following observations in May 1936:

1. The locomotive did not need an overall body design because the staff were afraid to use the engine room lighting, due to the risk of running down the battery.
2. The heat inside the body when standing was overpowering due, of course, to the lack of air movement (as when the locomotive was moving).
3. The roof section removal was laborious, and could cause less than conscientious maintenance. The need to remove hundreds of bolts and use a crane was an inconvenience.
4. The requirement to remove the roof for at least three monthly attentions to the auxiliary set would provide damage to the roof flanges etc.
5. The overall body retarded cooling down to permit quick turn around or essential running maintenance work. In summer in India it was not possible to work inside the engine room for some hours after the locomotive had gone on shed.
6. Inefficiency of compartment doors, which did not exclude dust nor hot air, and made futile attempts to exclude dust through efficient filtration.
7. Streamlining was not necessary from a technical viewpoint at 60-65 mph, for which these locomotives were intended.
8. The plate-framing was not as good for access to traction motors, and a bogie design would be better, obviating the need to lift the heavy locomotive to gain the necessary access. It was far easier to jack up a locomotive body and run out the bogies while the provision of spare engines enabled the locomotive to be kept in service.

9. On the driver's cab, Mr Rudd said it was too small and should contain all the instruments and fuses. All instruments should be larger and within the driver's range of vision. The lookout windows were too large and made the cab too hot. Safety glass should be used and protected. The cab doors did not fit, and the locks were poor. The doors rattled and much sand entered during running. Gaps on doors into the generator compartment allowed fine sand to gain constant access to this area. The heating up of metal doors was a constant problem after long periods of running.
10. Many other items, such as the fuel gauges, fuel filters, and fuel tanks, gave much trouble.

Work to modify the electrical equipment had started when the end of Armstrong Whitworth came – work ceasing on 20th January 1937. Vickers Armstrongs wanted the works for armament work and, although allowing outstanding contracts of Armstrong Whitworth to be completed, they managed to get the work on these two locomotives stopped.

The Indian Railways agreed, with some reluctance, to the whole contract being terminated, and the mechanical portions were scrapped in India. The engines were taken over by a Sulzer Bros subsidiary and sold in due course to the BBC for standby duties at their Rampisham Down station.

Laurence Scott took back the generators: one was converted to a motor to drive an alternator on the test bed. Both were still in service as late as 1975 at the maker's Norwich works.

The failure of this bold project was very unfortunate for the evolution of British diesel rail traction, but it was felt that the experience was at least telling for the designers who had failed to appreciate the severe conditions for diesel electric traction in India – with its extremes of temperatures, humidity, dust and sand storms, flooding, badly equipped maintenance facilities, and unskilled and illiterate staff.

British colonialisation at its peak! DT51 locomotive No. 332 at Lahore in 1935. *P. S. A. Berridge*

Table 3
Main details and dimensions of mobile powerhouses and main line locomotives built by Armstrong Whitworth

Order No., AW No.	Axle layout	Engine make, type, and bhp	Generator make	Traction motor make	Weight in working order	Length	Overall width	Overall height	Driving wheel diam.	Carrying wheel diam.	Rigid wheel-base	Bogie centres	Bogie wheel-base	Total wheel-base	Maximum Tractive Effort lbs	Top Speed mph
DT3 D4-6	Bo-2+2-Bo	Sulzer 8LV34 2 x 850 bhp	BB	EE	132^{TOC}	67ft 9in. * 65ft 0in.†	10ft 2in.	13ft 9in.	3ft 1½in.	3ft 1½in.	–	20ft 0in.	8ft 4in. driving 6ft 6in. carrying	65ft 0in.	60,800	60
DT4 D7	1A-Bo+Bo-A1	Sulzer 8LV34 2 x 850 bhp	BB	EE	145^{TOC}	75ft 3½in.* 71ft 6in.†	10ft 2in.	15ft 0in.	3ft 6in.	3ft 1½in.	–	21ft 0in.	8ft 5in. and 9ft 0in.	65ft 4in.	63,500 (40,000 at rail)	62½
DT8 D9	1-Co-1	Armstrong-Sulzer 8LD28 800 bhp	LSE	CP	71^{TC}	39ft 10in.* 36ft 6in.†	8ft 10in.	13ft 0in.	4ft 0in.	3ft 0in.	14ft 3in.	–	–	30ft 0in.	29,700	70
DT23 D27/8	1-Co-1	Armstrong-Sulzer 8LD28 800 bhp	LSE	CP	81^{TOC}	49ft 0in.* 38ft 6in.†	10ft 3¹¹⁄₁₆in.	13ft 6in.	4ft 0in.	3ft 0in.	14ft 3in.	–	–	30ft 0in.	29,700	70
DT51 D44/5	1A-Co-2	Armstrong-Sulzer 8LD34 1,200 bhp	LSE	CP	117^{TOC}	56ft 8in.* 52ft 6in.†	9ft 10in.	14ft 0in.	4ft 0in.	3ft 0in.	14ft 3in.	36ft 2½in.	1A bogie 9ft 3in. 2 bogie 7ft 6in.	44ft 4in.	39,400	70

* over buffers
† over bufferbeams

The second sale from order DT22 was D25 to the North Sunderland Railway. Here it was modified and properly braked and is seen here on a passenger train at Seahouses. It was named *The Lady Armstrong*.

H. C. Casserley

Order DT22 was for six 85/95 bhp Armstrong-Saurer engined 0-4-0 DE industrial shunters (AW D21-26) which were built in 1933 as a stock order. Here one example is seen on a demonstration shunting task, possibly at Dorman Long & Co's Cleveland Works on Teeside.
Brian Webb collection

THE 0-4-0 SHUNTERS

Two basic standard gauge designs of 0-4-0DE were on offer by Armstrong Whitworth in 1933/4. Both of these were similar in appearance, but differed in engine power and service weight. The smaller was the 15 ton unit of 85/95 bhp, designed for light continuous service; the larger, a 20 tonner with a 122 bhp engine. Both had final drive by jackshaft from behind the driving cabs.

Another variant on offer was intended to replace steam in the 36 ton range. It was itself a 30 ton unit, but of quite different design from the others in having final drive by a worm drive gearbox mounted on one axle. It was intended for heavier duties in the steel, engineering, and coal mining industries.

Of these three types, six of the 15 ton and one of the 20 ton locomotives were built.

In March 1934 Armstrong Whitworth had available a simple table of average working costs:

Working costs per eight hour shift	Steam	Diesel	Steam	Diesel	Steam	Diesel
Locomotive Weight	18 T	15 T	30 T	25 T	36 T	30 T
Cylinder Size (steam)	12in. x 18in.		14" x 22"		16in. x 24in.	
Starting t.e. (lbs)	8,000	8,400	13,300	14,000	15,000	16,800
Fuel (s/d)	6s 1d	1s 10½d	18s 7d	6s 8d	23s 2d	12s 2d
Water	5d	–	1s 6d	–	1s 11d	–
Repairs and Maintenance (s/d)	6s 0d	5s 4d	6s 8d	6s 0d	7s 4d	6s 8d
Lubricants (s/d)	5d	6d	7½d	1s 5½d	9½d	2s 7d
Wages (s/d)	15s 7d	12s 0d	14s 8d	12s 0d	20s 7d	2s 7d
Total working cost (s/d)	28s 6d	19s 8½d	42s 1d	26s 1½d	53s 9½d	33s 5d

Preparation and washing out time of a steam locomotive was added to the wages. There was no equivalent for the diesel locomotive.

Cost of coal per ton on locomotive	18s 0d
Cost of fuel oil per gallon on locomotive	5½d (incl. Tax)
Cost of water, per 1,000 gallons	1s 0d

The costings were those expected for the various units of both types, steam or diesel, working on duties suited to their capacities.

The first batch of shunters was built as a project under order DT22 and was made up of six 15 ton units for demonstration to as wide a range of industries and prospective customers as possible. As we know, the order was for stock, and it was a very different product than the one built under order DT11.

The six locomotives were completed in 1933, carrying maker's numbers D21-26. They were conventional by today's standards, but at their time advanced, as the first attempt by a UK locomotive builder to produce a quality, rugged, yet comparatively simple industrial diesel electric on two axles.

The underframe was of deep steel plate, well stayed, and with a floor plate extending the length of the engine area and cab. The bonnet was low enough to provide good visibility from the off-centre cab, behind which was the sloping topped casing housing, the traction motor, gearbox/final drive unit, and jackshaft. An Armstrong Saurer 6BLD engine with six cylinders was fitted, giving 85 bhp at 1700 rpm.

The engine, together with its directly coupled main generator, was set longitudinally in the locomotive, supplying current to the rear, transversely mounted traction motor. Both these were by Laurence, Scott & Electromotors. Final drive was by jackshaft and side rods.

It had been originally intended to run the engines at 2,000 rpm, and the decision to reduce this to 1,700 was taken after the generators were ordered in May 1933. This, AW recorded, was the cause of the low peak speeds—7.8 mph for these machines.

The locomotives were simple to drive, with controls at both sides of the cab. The engine control handle had four positions: stop, glow, start, idle. The 'glow' position was used for a few seconds, prior to starting the engine, to heat the glow plugs in the cylinder head. Both hand and air braking were fitted, together with air-operated sanding for both directions of travel. The transmission was of the patent ABE type, the generator doing the battery charging. An auxiliary compressor motor of 1 hp was fitted for engine starting purposes.

Although extensive demonstrations were undertaken by these locomotives, sales were slow—only three of them readily found purchasers. The remainder lingered on until 1937, these three spending a long period stored in a corner of the paint shop, still in works grey paint.

The first locomotive, D21, was demonstrated at the North Eastern Electric Supply Company's Dunston generating station. They, it will be remembered, tried the 1932 15 ton shunter in 1933 for a period. D21 was sold to the N.E.E.S. Co. in February 1934 under order No. DT45. A report, dated 27th October 1936, gave the following details on the Dunston shunter:

The first DT22 locomotive to be sold was D21 to the North Eastern Electric Supply Company at Dunston Power Station. Here it is seen on the 18th July 1968 by which time it was fitted with a Gardner 6LW engine. The locomotive is now preserved by the National Railway Museum and is on loan to Beamish Museum.
Brian Webb

15 tons, 85 bhp, Diesel Shunting Locomotive

Period (inclusive)	Feb 1934 Mar 1935	Apr 1935 Apr 1936	Total
Months	14	13	27
Routine maintenance:			
Materials	£4.7.0d	£15.1.4d	£19.8.4d
Labour	£7.15.6d	£7.1.9d	£14.17.3d
Overhauls†:			
Materials and labour	£50.3.3d	£57.1.3d	£107.4.6d
Total	£62.5.9d	£79.4.4d	£141.10.1d
Cost per year	£53.12.0d	£73.4.0d	£62.18.0d
Approx hrs worked	2,200	3,300	5,500
Approx cost per service hour	6.80d	5.76d	6.17d

† Comprised engine examination at each half year, and locomotive overhaul (combined with the engine overhaul) every year.

At the latter, yearly, overhaul the N.E.E.S. Co. asked for the supervision of an Armstrong Whitworth engineer, the actual work being done by the N.E.E.S. Co. men. If the cost of the supervision was included in the foregoing costings, we get:

Total	£83.9.9d	£93.10.4d	£177.0.1d
Cost per year	£71.14.0d	£86.6.0d	£78.14.0d
Cost per service hr	9.14d	6.80d	8.17d

The duty of the locomotive involved handling average loads of 220-250 tons of coal in 20 ton wagons, to a total of 3,000 tons each week. It was also involved in the tipping of the coal, and on ash removal work – in which it hauled five bogie tippler trucks of 25 ton capacity each on 1 in 33 gradients and 60 ft radius curves.

Between February 1934 and April 1936 the locomotive had worked from 07.30 to 17.30, Monday to Saturday, and five hours on Sunday for 27 months: totalling 5,500 hours, at a fuel and repair cost of 6.17d per hour.

After 1,100 engine hours, on 13th September 1934, the engine was examined and found to require six piston rings, gaskets, and some rejointing, costing 17s 4d. 1,100 hours later, on 11th November 1935, it was found necessary to fit thirteen piston rings, renew the fuel pump driving pinion, a crankshaft nut, refit gaskets and joints, at a total cost of £1.16.6d. Again, no electrical spares were required. On 21st April 1936, 3,000 engine hours later, the items for replacement were six cylinder liners, thirty piston rings, a silentbloc bush, joints and hose connections. The cost was £13 9s 11d.

This locomotive remained in use among the works steam units until 1973, by which time it had a Gardner diesel engine. In 1975 it was acquired for preservation by the Hexham Rolling Stock Group and restored to its elaborate lined black livery. In 1978 it was on exhibition at the National Railway Museum, York, a fitting tribute to the diesel electrics of Armstrong Whitworth.

The second locomotive sold was D25, under order DT42, to the North Sunderland Railway which, like Dunston, had some success by using the 15 ton DT11 unit during 1933. The NSR directors evidently suggested to Armstrong Whitworth, on 16th November 1933, that a diesel locomotive should be given to them for advertisement purposes, and that it would benefit Armstrong Whitworth to have a diesel unit in regular service for demonstration within easy reach of Newcastle.

The NSR directors decided to wait and see if Armstrong Whitworth would approach them regarding a new locomotive, as the one they had on loan '…*was much worn after use in collieries, etc.*' On 6th December 1933 Armstrong Whitworth said they could supply a new locomotive for £1.914 16s 0d: for a £1,000 deposit and six-monthly payments of £317 12s 0d, £311 12s 0d and £285 12s 0d. This was accepted the following day by the NSR.

Upon examination of the NSR requirements, the locomotive required modifications which put the cost up to £2.053 4s 0d and altered the payments to £300, £300, and £453 4s 0d respectively. Before delivery the locomotive was fitted with a larger battery, larger and heavier generator to give it a better performance on line-service at speeds of 15-20 mph, main line buffing and drawgear, front and rear headlights, and Westinghouse air brake.

It was purchased for £2,092, painted plain black, and named *The Lady Armstrong* after the wife of Lord William George Armstrong, the founder of Armstrong Whitworth. Some doubt about the cost of the locomotive arises from the NSR records of 13th April 1934: '…*agreement drawn up for the locomotive, and cost now £2,098 7s 9d, cash on delivery £1,000, payments at six, twelve, and eighteen months of £321 1s 3d, £315 1s 3d, £462 5s 3d.*

To meet this 'revitalisation' of motive power, the NSR Directors did some work on their rolling stock by fitting electric lighting to their saloon carriage to replace the oil lamps, and repainting it. They stated '…*the little train is now smart and inviting instead of, as formerly, a spectacle of abandoned hope.*'

The locomotive was put to work on the 4½ mile railway which connected Chathill, on the L&NER main line, with the fishing port of Seahouses, Northumberland. It handled all the line's traffic, and enabled the railway's only other locomotive, an 1888 Manning Wardle 0-6-0ST named *Bamburgh* to be kept spare to the diesel. As such the NSR was probably one of the first public railways in the world to be completely dieselised.

Extracts from the annual NSR directors' reports found in official Armstrong Whitworth material make convincing reading of the locomotive's success.

North Sunderland Railway Diesel Locomotive

1. Capital Expenditure:

	1931	1932	1933	1934	1935
Steam locomotive	–	–	–	–	–
Diesel locomotive (incl. Spares)	–	–	–	£2,092	£15

2. Maintenance of Rolling Stock:

	1931	1932	1933	1934	1935
Steam locomotive	£90	£31	£23[1]	£224	£8
Diesel locomotive	–	–	£2[2]	£12	£57

Notes: 1. Ten months running.
2. DT11 diesel locomotive on loan, two months running.

The Lady Armstrong standing at Chathill. *Brian Webb collection*

3. Locomotive Running Expenses:

Steam locomotive	1931	1932	1933[1]	1934	1935
Wages	£292	£218	£147	---	---
Fuel	217	208	159	---	---
Water	10	8	10	---	---
Lubricants	21	18	21	---	---
Stores	20	13	12	---	---
Totals	£560	£465	£349	---	---

Diesel locomotive	1931	1932	1933[2]	1934	1935
Wages	---	---	£32	£125	£139
Fuel	---	---	18	94	61
Water	---	---	---	1	2
Lubricants	---	---	4	45[3]	13
Stores/Misc.	---	---	---	---	8
Totals	---	---	£54	£265	£223

Notes: 1. Ten months running.
    2. Two months running with DT11 locomotive. All 1933 costs apply to this locomotive.
    3. Includes purchase of stock of spares.

4. Engine mileage:

	1931	1932	1933	1934	1935
Train miles	12,910	12,912	12,814	13,258	13,790
Shunting miles	3,906	3,938	3,912	3,999	4,059
Total engine miles	16,816	16,850	16,726[1]	17,257[2]	17,849[2]

Notes: 1. Includes 2,822 run by diesel locomotive DT11 while on loan.
    2. All run by diesel locomotive *The Lady Armstrong*.

5. Passenger and Goods Traffic:

	1931	1932	1933	1934	1935
Passengers	8,554	7,909	10,462	15,325	17,744
Goods (tonnage)	4,792	3,666	4,032	3,646	3,744

6. Operating Costs (excluding maintenance)
Engines per mile:

	1931	1932	1933	1934	1935
Steam	7.9d	6.6d	6.0d[1]	---	---
Diesel	---	---	4.6d[2]	3.7d	3.0d

Operating costs (including maintenance)
Engines per mile:

	1931	1932	1933	1934	1935
Steam	9.3d	7.1d	6.4d[1]	---	---
Diesel	---	---	4.8d[2]	3.9d	3.8d

Notes: 1. Steam locomotive ten months running.
    2. Diesel locomotive DT11 on loan, two months running.

From these figures Armstrong Whitworth stated that the steam locomotive cost £616 per year to operate, averaging 8.80d per mile. The diesel locomotive, at £283, cost 3.88d per mile. A saving of 3½d per mile by the diesel locomotive, or £255 per year over steam, was the outcome.

The locomotive paid off its initial cost over steam traction in eighteen months work, showing a saving of 5d per train mile, or £330 per year. It covered 6,000 miles in its first five months duty, and by 1936 its monthly mileage was 1,460, with a yearly mileage of 17,928, with an availability of 100 per cent. Its average working day was 8 hours, 5 days per week, and in 201.2 months it had covered 8,175 miles at a total cost of 8.41d per mile.

By the end of the war the diesel was rather the worse for wear and journied to the Darlington works of the L&NER for attention. Its last visit to Darlington was its end, for it was dumped in the yard, beyond repair, until sold for scrap on 11th October 1949, to W. H. Arnott Young & Co. Ltd for the sum of £42 10s 0d.

The remaining four DT22 shunters were sent out on demonstration to the following locations:

D22   Dorman Long & Co. Ltd, Britannia Works, Middlesbrough.
Warner and Co. Ltd, Cargo Fleet.
D23   War Dept. Tramway, Shoeburyness.
Gas Light & Coke Co. Ltd, Beckton.
Admiralty Chatham Dockyard.
D24   Bass, Ratcliff & Gretton Ltd, Burton-upon-Trent; ICI Ltd Metals Division, Kynoch Works, Witton Birmingham; the Austin Motor Co. Ltd, Birmingham; Dunlop Rubber Co. Ltd Birmingham; Nevills Dock Co. Ltd, Llanelly; Bede Metal & Chemical Co. Ltd Hebburn.
D26   Not recorded as being sent out on demonstration.

They were finally sold as follows:

D22   A Reyrolle & Co. Ltd, Hebburn, painted battleship grey with white lettering and numbers under order DT77 in 1937. Sold in December 1970 to W. F. & J. R. Shepherd & Co. scrap metal dealers for use in their St. Peter's yard, Newcastle-upon-Tyne. Locomotive fitted with Gardner 6LW engine in 1963. After a period out of use the locomotive was acquired for preservation on the Tanfield Railway in 1978.
D23   Admiralty Chatham – named *Walmer Castle*: purchased under order DT65 in 1934 and scrapped in March 1966.
D24   Thames Board Mills Ltd, Warrington, under order DT76 on 17th November 1936 painted in green livery. Locomotive cost £1,510 plus £36 worth of spares. New engine fitted in 1944. Sold for scrap for £250 in 1957.
D26   Sold under order DT78 in 1937. Painted black with M. E. L. on bonnet sides in aluminium paint, to Magneseum Elektron Ltd, who had a works with very restricted siding accommodation in a portion of the old Clifton Power Station of the LMS (ex-L&YR Manchester-Bury electric line). Locomotive believed disposed of by mid-1962.

The Armstrong Whitworth table of the demonstration periods of three of these locomotives was as follows:

Locomotive D29 was in due course purchased by the Admiralty for use at Chatham Royal Navy Dockyard. Named *Walmer Castle* it is seen here at Chatham on 24th September 1962.
Brian Webb

In addition to the Dunston locomotive, the ex-Reyrolle locomotive D22 survived to be fitted with a Gardner engine and lasted until 1978, latterly at the Tyneside scrapyard of W. F. & J. R. Shepherd where it was seen on 29th July 1974. This locomotive is preserved at the Tanfield Railway.
Brian Webb

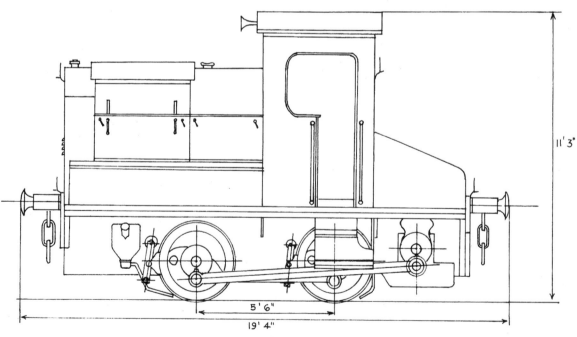

Side elevation of the DT22 shunters. Reproduced at a scale of 7mm to 1ft.
Brian Webb

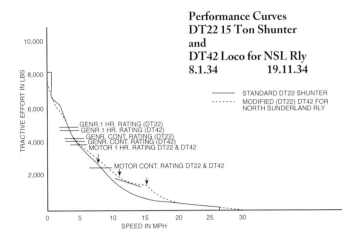

Performance Curves
DT22 15 Ton Shunter
and
DT42 Loco for NSL Rly
8.1.34   19.11.34

Locomotive No.	D22	D23	D24
Service days	39	139	136
Service hours	275	1,010	1,213
Locomotive hours	258	794	886
Fuel (gallons)	270	848	1,220
Lubricating oil (gallons)	1½	15	18
Maintenance (man hours)	53	263	104

The only example of the larger 0-4-0 shunter built by Armstrong Whitworth was that built under order DT44 in 1934 for the Ceylon Government Railways. Carrying works No. D43, it was a 20 ton 5ft 6in. gauge machine costing £3,000. It was fitted with an Armstrong-Saurer 6BXD engine of 122 bhp at 1,400 rpm, but de-rated to 116 bhp.

Laurence, Scott & Electromotors supplied the traction equipment. The engine/generator set had three-point suspension and was capable of removal as a single unit for overhaul. The generator supplied power to one rigidly fixed traction motor, set transversely in the frame at the rear of the cab. The drive was through single reduction gear to the jackshaft drive unit mounted under the motor, final drive was by coupling rods. The transmission was of the ABE type. Duplicated controls were fitted in the cab, and hand and vacuum brakes and both direction sanding were fitted.

The locomotive was No. 500 in CGR stock, and entered service as yard shunter at the Ratmalana works on 15th October 1934.

During its first twelve months service (up to September 1935) the locomotive was only out of service for three days. This was in April when after completing 1,595 miles, it had its first engine overhaul. By September it had done 3,957 miles, using 2,082 gallons of fuel. On 28th May 1936 the CGR reported to Armstrong Whitworth that the locomotive was performing well, it having undergone its second and third six-monthly engine overhauls after further mileages of 2,752 and 2,731. These took twelve days and four days each, respectively, no other days being lost at all.

It worked a five day, forty hour week, and by the end of June 1936 it had covered 8,175 miles in 20½ months. Apart from overhauls it had been in service as scheduled. Total expenses – fuel, lubricants, spares, driver's and fitter's wages, etc. – was put at 8.41d per mile.

The locomotive was capable of hauling 500 ton loads round 5 chain radius curves at 5 mph, routine servicing being done on Saturday mornings. On its normal work it covered 25 miles per day with 4½ hours engine running time.

DT44 was an order for a larger 0-4-0 DE, this time of 122 bhp and of 5ft 6in. gauge for Ceylon Government Railways. It was AW D43 of 1934, carrying CGR No. 500. Here it is seen in Scotswood Works yard prior to delivery. *Brian Webb collection*

A. Engine & Generator
B. Traction Motor
C. Cooling Water Tank
D. Radiator & Fan
E. Oil Fuel Tank
F. Silencer
G. Control Cabinet
H. Battery Box
J. Belt Driven Exhauster
K. Brake Cylinder
L. Toolbox

Brian Webb collection

Layout diagram of DT44, reproduced at 7mm - 1ft.

Ceylon Government Railways' No. 500 is seen again in Scotswood Works yard. *Brian Webb collection*

A November 1973 shot of D43 shunting at the Ceylon Government Railways' workshops at Ratmalana. Classified 'G1' by Sri Lankan Railways it is believed that this locomotive too is still in existence, maintained by apprentices at Ratmalana Workshops. *Les Nixon*

Some of the infrequent problems encountered included rapid cylinder wear – overcome by fitting treated liners; imperfect white-metal adhesion on the big end bearings; piston head wear around the top ring, necessitating renewal. Electrical problems included some resoldering of computer connections on the traction motor armature.

The first serious problem occurred in 1953 when an engine connecting-rod fractured and smashed through the side of the crankcase, damaging the water spaces. The crankcase was patched by riveting, and Saurers in Switzerland was approached for a new crankcase, or alternately a new engine. The latter move was not made for, during 1959, it was rebuilt with a new Rolls Royce type C6 SFL 127C engine and BTH traction and control equipment.

Narrow gauge shunting locomotives did not appear in large numbers from Scotswood Works, but during 1934/5 three such machines were built in the gauges 2ft 6in., 3ft 0in., and 3ft 3⅜ in. All were quite different in concept; no attempt at a standard design for their mechanical portions was made. In spite of this, all had similar characteristics, in that all were 0-4-0 in layout, had Armstrong-Saurer engines, and final drive was through a worm axle drive unit.

The first example was built under order No. DT36. It was ordered in the autumn of 1933 by Messrs Hensckell, Du Buisson & Co. for use at their sugar factory at Basseterre, St. Kitts in the West Indies, as part of a scheme to replace steam traction. Of conventional design, this 2ft 6in. gauge unit was powered by an Armstrong-Saurer type 6BLD six-cylinder engine rated at 85 bhp at 1,700 rpm, but de-rated at 78 bhp. The engine and its generator had a three point suspension designed for easy removal for maintenance.

The electrical equipment was by Laurence, Scott & Electromotors, and comprised a main generator which supplied power to one rigidly fixed, rear, frame-mounted, traction motor which drove a worm reduction gearbox mounted on the leading axle by means of a cardan shaft. Both axles were coupled by rods.

Duplicated controls were provided in the cab, and both hand and air braking were provided. Although ABE transmission was installed, cutting out the need for an auxiliary battery charging generator, a one horse power compressor motor was fitted. Pneumatic couplers were fitted.

Carrying work's No. D40 of 1934, the locomotive was designed for haulage and shunting service in the 3 to 12 mph range, with a maximum of 20 mph, and to operate in tropical conditions with average shade temperatures of 86°F. It was delivered in May 1934, and out into service by the local mechanic. Set to work hauling trains of sugar cane between the fields and the factory, it also worked to the pier with sugar and molasses. On the 31st May, after two weeks service, it had some electrical troubles due to contactor arcing and burning but these were easily rectified.

The owners reported to Armstrong Whitworth that the locomotive was '...*extremely well thought out, well finished, and every part is accessible. The instruction book and drawings are also models of care and thought...*'. They concluded by stating that they '...*think it remarkably cheap at the price.*'

This 2ft 6in. gauge shunter (order DT36, AW No. D40/34) was built for use on a sugar plantation railway on St. Kitts in the West Indies. Here it is seen on a works flat wagon at Scotswood. *Brian Webb collection*

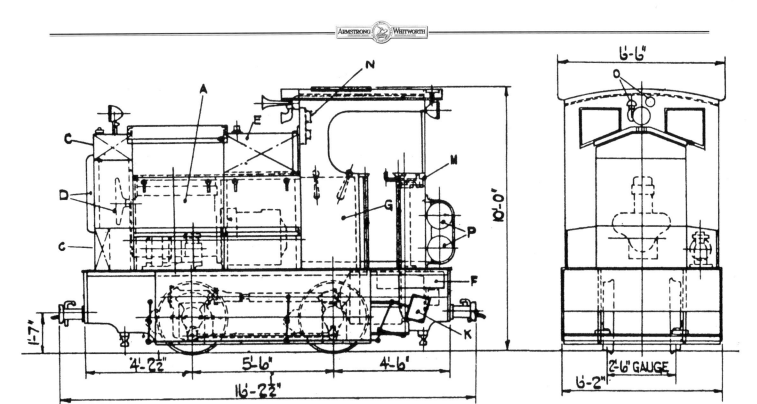

A. Engine & Generator
B. Traction Motor
C. Cooling Water Tank
D. Coolers & Fan
E. Oil Fuel Tank
F. Silencer
G. Control Cabinet
H. Battery Box
J. Compressor & Motor
K. Brake Cylinder
L. Toolbox
M. Compressor Governor
N. Instrument Panel
O. Horns
P. Compressed Air Reservoir
Q. Gearbox

Layout diagram of DT36 when built.
7mm - 1ft *Brian Webb collection*

In October 1934 the locomotive was reported on pier service, where the average gradient was 1 per cent, operating at up to 12 mph with loads of 100 tons. Further details informed Armstrong Whitworth that the machine was also working loads over 2 per cent gradients with 150 ft radius curves for up to 20 hours per day during the season, at an average fuel consumption of 5.8 mpg. During February 1936 it was working between the cane fields and the factory with 75 ton trains, returning with the empty wagons weighing 15-20 tons, at an average fuel consumption of 3.74 mpg.

Its makers noted in early 1937 that the fact that little had been heard of the locomotive showed it had apparently worked very satisfactorily. The locomotive was still hard at work in March 1974, after being fitted, about 1950, with a Cummins type HB1 engine and completing between 300,000 and 500,000 service hours. The only complaint – after forty years – was that its wheelbase was too long for some of the small radius curves on the railway, hence its use mainly as a factory and harbour shunter.

A 1974 photograph of D40, the St. Kitts 0-4-0 DE, still in use. By this date it had been re-engined with a Cummins diesel unit. The locomotive was still in service in 1991. *Brian Webb collection*

Order DT60 was for a metre-gauge 0-4-0 DE of 92 bhp (AW D52) delivered in 1935 for use at Penang Harbour in the Straits Settlements (now Malaysia).
Brian Webb collection

Armstrong Whitworth's second narrow gauge shunter, a metre gauge (3ft 3³⁄₈in.) unit, was completed under order DT60. It was delivered during July 1935 for service on the wharves at Prai Harbour, Straits Settlements, to the order of the Penang Harbour Board. Carrying works number D52 of 1935, this conventional unit was powered by an Armstrong-Sauer type 6BLD six-cylinder engine of 100 bhp at 1,700 rpm, de-rated to 92 bhp.

The electrical equipment was by Laurence, Scott & Electromotors, and consisted of a directly coupled main generator which, with the engine, was mounted by three point suspension and was easily removable for overhaul.

The traction motor was mounted rigidly between the frames under the cab and drove through a cardan shaft to a double reduction worm gearbox on the leading axle, both axles being coupled by side rods. The cab was fitted with duplicate controls, and both hand and air brakes were installed. Although the ABE transmission system was fitted it only obviated the provision of an auxiliary compressor motor, as an auxiliary CAV generator was installed for engine starting purposes. Pneumatic sanding for both directions was fitted.

The locomotive began service on 10th August 1935, handling loads of 40 tons over distances of around ¼ mile. An interesting table, dated June 1936, comparing this locomotive with steam, has come to light:

Penang Harbour Board. Comparison of Running Costs between Diesel Electric Locomotive and Steam Locomotive

Diesel Locomotive	Steam Locomotive
0-4-0 ABE transmission	0-4-0 ST in steam 10 hrs/day
Weight: 15 tons 13 cwt	Weight: 18 tons
	Cylinders (2): 10in.x14in. stroke
Wheels: 3ft 3in.	Wheels: 2ft 8in.
	Pressure: 150 lbs psi
Tractive effort: 8,500 lbs	Tractive effort: 5,600 lbs
Fuel, Lubricants and stores (d/hr): 5.5	Coal: 600 lbs/day (d/hr): 6.4
	Water: 1,000 galls/day (d/hr) 0.3
	Lubricants (d/day): 2.1
Maintenance and repairs (d/hr): 4.4	Maintenance and repairs (d/hr): 7.0
Total: 9.9d/hr	Total: 15.8d/hr
Wages: not available	Wages: driver 26s 0d per week
	fireman
	shunter 14s 0d per week
	engine cleaner
	Total: 8.9d/hr

For the diesel locomotive, the wages of the driver and shunter only are debited. If we assume £1 per week and 7s 0d per week as being the wages of fireman and cleaner we get:

Layout diagram of order DT60. Reproduced at 7mm - 1ft scale.
Brian Webb collection

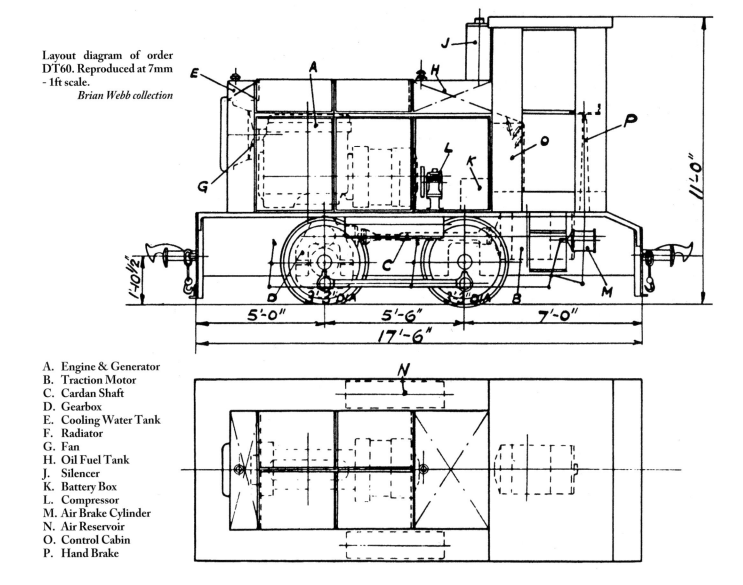

A. Engine & Generator
B. Traction Motor
C. Cardan Shaft
D. Gearbox
E. Cooling Water Tank
F. Radiator
G. Fan
H. Oil Fuel Tank
J. Silencer
K. Battery Box
L. Compressor
M. Air Brake Cylinder
N. Air Reservoir
O. Control Cabin
P. Hand Brake

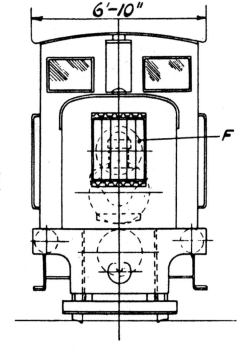

Steam locomotive wages: 8.9d/hr
Diesel locomotive wages: 5.3d/hr
Saving: 3.6d/hr

This brings the total operating costs to:
Steam, running costs including wages: 24.7d/hr
Diesel, running costs including wages: 15.2d/hr
Saving: 9.5d/hr

On the basis of 10 hours per day, 330 days per year, the saving amounts to £131 per year. The diesel locomotive has a greater tractive force, and is capable of hauling heavier trains. Where wage rates are higher, the savings will be correspondingly higher.

Detail of Diesel Locomotive Costs:

1936	Hours	Fuels, lubricants and stores	Maintenance and repairs	Total
Jan		£3.1.5d	£2.1.9d	£5.3.2d
Feb		£3.5.0d	£3.16.8d	£7.1.3d
Mar		£2.15.11d	£2.0.2d	£4.16.1d
Apr		£3.12.9d	£2.7.6d	£6.0.3d
Total	558	£12.15.1d	£10.6.1d	£23.1.2d

Locomotive working 10 hours per day.

Maintenance and repairs include minor modifications dictated by local conditions and are seen to be reducing. However, taking into account periodic overhauls, it could be taken as an average figure.

The locomotive continued to work successfully until it became redundant during 1959 when Malayan Railways took over the harbour shunting work. Its life did not end there, for it was sold in October 1959 to Associated Pan Malaysian Cement, and delivered to their works at Rawang, Selangor in the same month. It worked there until its gearbox failed in early 1973 and it was cut up during July, following its replacement by an English Electric 'Stephenson' diesel hydraulic shunter which had formerly been at the Dunbar works of APCM in Scotland.

The only narrow gauge locomotive built by Armstrong Whitworth for use in the UK was that completed under order No. DT61 for the 3ft 0in. gauge industrial railway of the Penmaenmawr & Welsh Granite Co. Ltd of Penmaenmawr, North Wales. Carrying works No. D53 of 1935 and named *Alice*, it was quite conventional, but with a very short wheelbase.

The engine was an Armstrong-Saurer type 4BOD four cylinder 60 bhp engine running at 1,700 rpm, de-rated to 58 bhp. Electrical equipment was by Laurence, Scott & Electromotors. The main generator was, with the engine, given a three point suspension, and supplied power to one longitudinally set, rigidly fixed, frame-mounted, traction motor placed between the frames at the leading end of the locomotive. Drive was through a cardan shaft to an axle-mounted, worm reduction gearbox on the rear axle, both axles being rod coupled.

Duplicated driving controls were fitted, and braking was by hand only. Two direction sanding was fitted. The ABE transmission system was fitted, but a CAV auxiliary generator was installed for battery charging.

It was designed for shunting and haulage work at an altitude of 970ft, on trains of up to 250 tons of granite per hour, over 1,000-1,400 yards of fairly level track cut into the mountainside, on curves of down to 143 foot radius. The locomotive was put into service on 1st July 1935.

The only Armstrong Whitworth report on this machine was as follows:

Running Costs per Hour (DT61)
Fuel	4.2d
Driver	23.8d
Lubricants	1.5d
Maintenance and labour	8.2d
Stores	2.7d
Total	40.4d

The steam locomotive costs on the same duty were put at 56.6d per hour. For hauling 1,000 tons/mile the diesel cost 41.1d per hour and the steam locomotive cost 57.6d per hour. The diesel used one gallon of fuel per hour and 2.95 gallons of lubricating oil in 100 hours. The locomotive averaged 3,290 hours service per year, as opposed to the steam locomotive's average of 1,760 hours.

Little trouble had been experienced with this unit by 1937,

The Penang locomotive was sold in 1959 to Associated Pan Malaysian Cement and used at their Rawang Works, Selangor. It was photographed there in December 1970.
John Benson

The only narrow gauge Armstrong Whitworth 0-4-0 DE for the British Isles was built to order DT61 for the 3ft 0in. gauge system of the Penmaenmawr & Welsh Granite Co. Ltd in North Wales. The locomotive was named *Alice* and was No. D53 of 1935. It is seen here outside the paintshop at Scotswood Works loaded on a venerable dropside wagon. *Brian Webb collection*

apart from with the worm axle drive unit, which required a complete spare set to be maintained to facilitate quick replacement and continuity of service.

The locomotive worked until 1967, when the progressive abandonment of the Penmaenmawr rail system rendered it redundant. By this time it had aquired an AEC diesel engine, necessitating a slight increase in the length of the engine housing or bonnet. Attempts to secure this locomotive for preservation failed, although it was still operable in 1967. It was finally cut up in its lofty and almost inaccessible position during 1969.

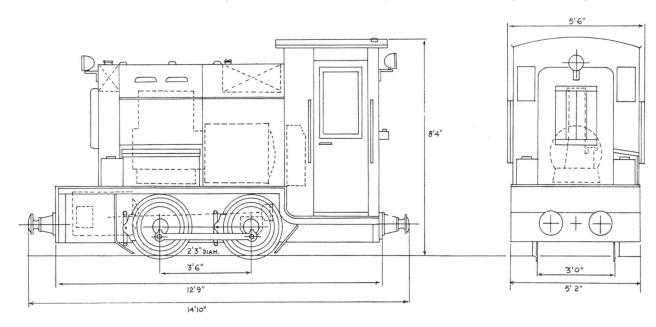

Layout diagram of order DT61. Reproduced at a scale of 7mm - 1ft. *Brian Webb*

Taken in August 1965 this view shows *Alice* to be apparently well looked after. The name has now been painted above the radiator and the headlight capacity doubled. Notice also the bonnet has been extended to house an AEC diesel unit.

Brian Webb collection

The Penmaenmawr locomotive survived until 1969, being out of use but still operable when photographed from both sides in June 1968. There had, however, been an apparent decline in the standard of care from the view on the previous page. *Brian Webb*

Order DT19 was for this luxury diesel electric train set for the Sao Paulo Railway, Brazil, in 1933. It was tested thoroughly at Scotswood before despatch, a special broad gauge track being installed through the erecting and tender shops for the purpose.
University of Glasgow

ARTICULATED TRAIN SETS

1933 saw the first large luxury diesel electric train set exported from Scotswood. This was a part-articulated, three-coach train and power car, described by Armstrong Whitworth as a 'motor train', for the Sao Paulo Railway in Brazil. It was designed for service between Santos and Sao Paulo, a distance of forty-nine miles, involving a climb of approximately 2,600 ft from sea level via the famous Serra incline about seven miles from Santos.

The level tableland of the state of Sao Paulo was reached by the 1 in 12½ rope-worked incline, 11 km (6.83 miles) in length, opened in 1900 to replace an earlier one with a continuous rope haulage system. It was worked by small, special rope-gripping steam tank locomotives, built by Robert Stephenson & Co., which employed a steam-operated gripping device to grip the 1¾in. diameter steel rope. The locomotive coupled on to the train it was to pilot on the incline, and this was ascended or descended as the case might be. The problems to be faced by Armstrong Whitworth in designing the train in question were set out by the demand that it should be able to work equally well at different altitudes, its weight was limited, as was the train length due to the length of the passing loops on the incline. Built to the requirements and inspection of Messrs Fox & Mayo, consulting engineers, the train was completed in late 1933 under order No. DT19.

It was a four unit set. One unit was the powerhouse, which was articulated to the first coach. The second and third coaches were articulated together, and the two sections were coupled with simple drawgear.

Designed for a top speed of 65 mph, it was driven by four traction motors located on the leading bogie of the power vehicle, and on the rear bogie of the train. Driving cabs were provided at both ends to allow a shuttle service operation and obviate turning. The underframes were built up by welding from braced longitudinal girders; the cross-members supporting the coachwork were of light channel sections bolted to the main longitudinals. The bodywork was of light, all-metal construction mounted on the underframes but not integrally with the underframes. The body framing was of 'U' section pressed steel pillars. The flanges were riveted to the waist rails and cant rails to allow easy removal of windows and louvres. The windows of the passenger compartments were of the full drop type.

A view from above of the DT19 power vehicle under construction at Scotswood showing part of the articulating-bogie and the Armstrong-Sulzer 6LD25 450 bhp engine. The power vehicle carried Armstrong Whitworth number D16. *Brian Webb collection*

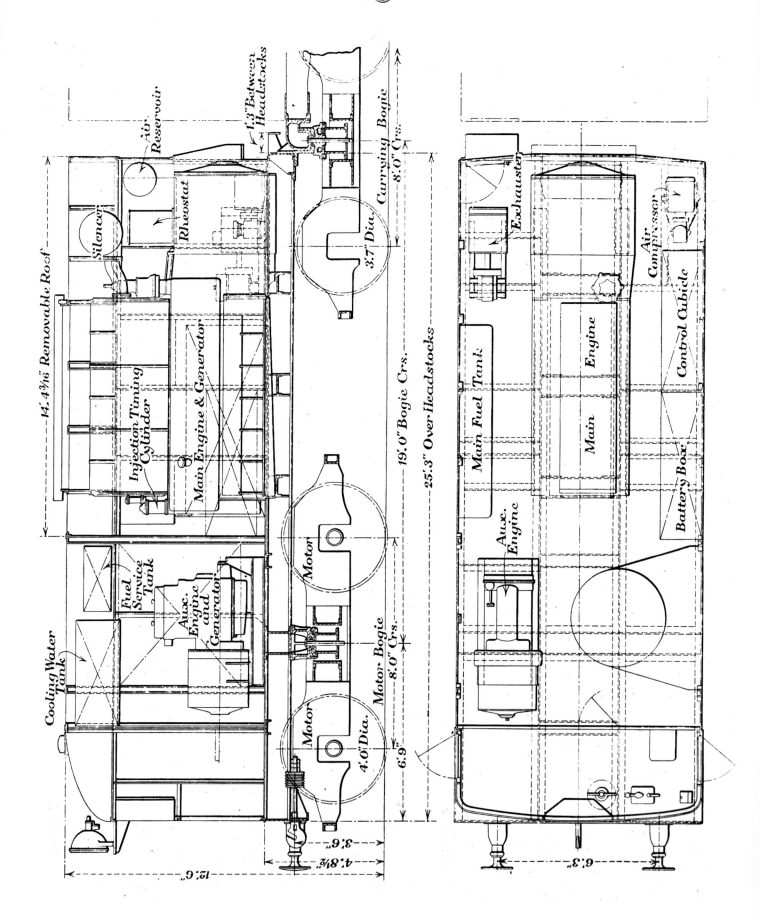

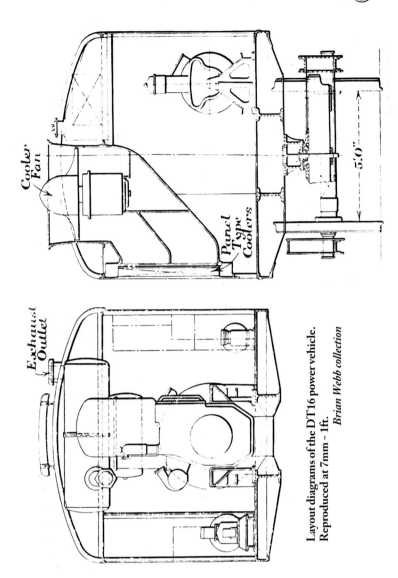

Layout diagrams of the DT16 power vehicle. Reproduced at 7mm - 1ft. *Brian Webb collection*

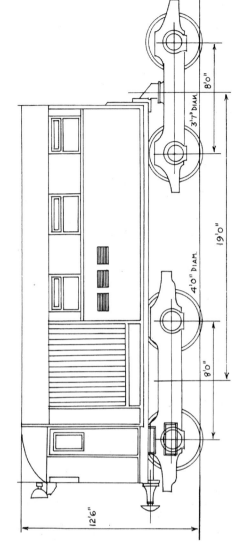

The external appearance of DT16, reproduced at 4mm - 1ft. *Brian Webb*

Seating capacity was provided for the 100 first class and 68 second class passengers, all seats being reversible. Interior panelling was of plywood, covered with leather to the waist line in the first class. The second class compartments were painted cream and brown. First class seating was covered with rattan and fitted with head rests, while the second class seats were of polished ash slats. Three toilets were provided, and there was a buffet fitted with racks and cupboards and with a small ice chest. The buffet was in the coach articulated to the power vehicle, at its leading end.

The coach bodies were entirely built and fitted out by the Gloucester Railway Carriage & Wagon Co. Ltd, but fitted to the underframes at Scotswood. Armstrong Whitworth built the power vehicle at Scotswood. Its mechanical structure was based on two longitudinal 'I' section steel members with channel shaped cross stretchers; the superstructure was similar to that of the coaches, and light in weight.

The power vehicle powered-bogie and rear carriage power-bogie were of identical design, with plate sides, Isothermos axleboxes, and springing by laminated springs, as usual in Armstrong Whitworth practice. They were light in weight, but without loss of strength and rigidity. Articulation bogies were similar, and used the Gresley type articulating joint, designed to transfer the load to the bogie frames by double helical springs by means of the bolster. Axlebox springing was orthodox, using leaf springs. Braking on the power bogies was by clasp brakes on both sides of the wheels, with a similar system for the carrying bogies. All braking was on the vacuum system with the exhauster driven by an electric motor in the power vehicle.

Motive power for the train was provided by an Armstrong-Sulzer type 6LD25 six-cylinder vertical engine of 450 bhp, de-rated to 382 bhp, running at 750 rpm. This was directly coupled to a Laurence, Scott & Electromotors generator supplying power to four Crompton Parkinson axle-hung, nose-suspended, traction motors. The engine/generator set was capable of being lifted out through removable roof sections for overhaul. The power equipment was located centrally, towards the rear of the power vehicle – the generator drawing in air through filters in the rear bulkhead. Alongside the generator were placed the exhauster and air compressor, one each side. The main fuel tank was to the right of the engine and the battery box to the left.

The 33 KW auxiliary power unit, comprising an Armstrong-Saurer four cylinder BOD 50 bhp engine and generator was used to motor the main generator for engine starting and to drive all

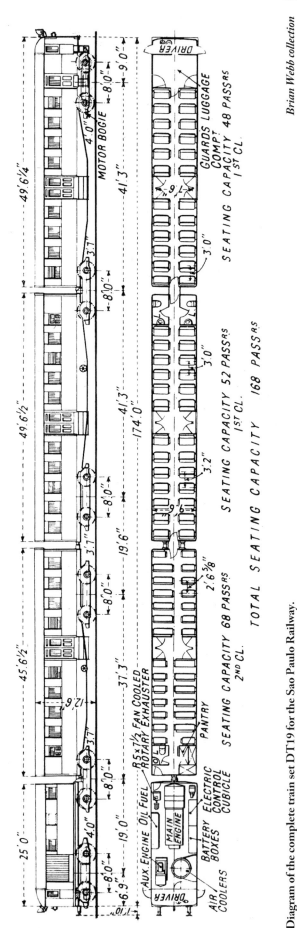

Diagram of the complete train set DT19 for the Sao Paulo Railway. *Brian Webb collection*

auxiliaries. This unit was arranged to the right side of the engine compartment, balanced by the cooling group on the left. The cooling radiator was on the left body side, and air circulation was achieved by a roof-mounted fan. The water tank was in the roof, as was the exhaust silencer. Control gear was electromagnetic, and an automatic load regulator was fitted.

The whole trainset was given running trials at Scotswood. Although this was usual, the size of the trainset presented problems. Special 5ft 3in. gauge rails were put down inside the works, through the erecting and tender shops, complete with curves to test the articulation and bogie check chains. The whole train ran to and fro, presenting an unusual sight, according to eye-witnesses. The train was shipped from Elswick in late 1933, and it is interesting to note that the whole train of four vehicles was given works numbers D16-D19.

Following arrival in Brazil and test running, the Sao Paulo Railway undertook some modifications of the seating accommodation by altering the two outer carriages to seat 84 first class passengers. The centre vehicle was refitted as a deluxe car with 19 seats in a lounge and a smoking saloon. The latter had a buffet bar, and the lounge a small library. A supplementary fare was levied for the use of this car.

The train set, called *Cometa*, was put into regular service following a ceremony at Alto De Serro, attended by government and railway officials, on 25th June 1934. Prior to this, the party had travelled from Sao Paulo Luz station in a special train to Alto De Serra, where the operation of the Serra Incline was inspected and an exhibition of old and new locomotives and rolling stock and the new diesel train set was held.

The party then travelled in the new train, driven by Dr Francisco Machado De Campos, Brazilian Government Secretary of Transport, for some 200 yards, and declared the diesel service officially opened. Following luncheon and speeches, the train set off on its first run to Sao Paulo.

The 30 miles run, with severe curvature and gradients, took 35 minutes, at an average speed of 51 mph and a maximum of 67 mph being attained. Public service began on 1st July, when the train replaced the 08.00 steam service from Sao Paulo, as well as the 13.00. It returned from Santos at 10.00 and 17.00. The 13.00 was a new train, and was accelerated to cover the 49 miles run in 97 minutes which included 41 minutes on the Serra Incline.

The initial service of the two return trips daily was operated six days per week, giving a total of 1,036 miles under power and 164 miles on the cable of the incline. The total mileage was 1,200 per week. Between 9th July and 2nd September 1934 the train had completed 10,000 miles. It was then out of service for four days while a broken traction motor banding wire was attended to and some modification to the bodywork was carried out.

From 9th September until 30th December 1934 the mileage was 26,700. During this period the train was out of service for 38 days for periodic engine overhaul, inspection of bogies, tyre turning, and internal bodywork and passenger accommodation repairs. Also in this period it was off duty for 6 days, to spend five days on trial running and one day on a special working. During the period 17th February to 19th May 1935 it covered 42,700 miles without any trouble; its only lost time was four days when not required.

The train was then given an additional duty to add to its two daily round trips: one return journey from Sao Paulo to Alto De Santos on a Sunday. This increased its mileage to 1,293 per week.

Between 26th May and 24th November 1935 the mileage increased from 43,993 to 64,268. During this time it was out of service for 108 days. 52 days were for examination and modifications, 36 days for repainting, 4 days for engine overhaul (at 59,310 miles), 3 days for trial running, 2 days not required, and 1 day lost through a failure of the Serra Incline.

More demanding services involving three round trips per day started in January 1936. It was working three trips Monday to Friday, and two on Sunday, raising the weekly mileage to 1,988. Of these, 1,715 miles were under power, and 273 miles were on the incline. By October the train's mileage stood at 135,590 miles. This period saw it out of service for a total of 36 days: 7 for repairs, 5 due to failures, 2 days of trials and 22 days not required.

In its first twenty-four months service the train covered 110,000 miles without failure, though it suffered bogie suspension troubles during the first half of this period. By the end of October 1936 its mileage stood at 139,590 which had been in 602 days at an average fuel consumption of 3.24 gallons per powered mile.

The Armstrong Whitworth report on DT19, received from Mr Gregson, their South American area representative, has happily survived, and the following points of interest are selected from it:

1. Flooding of the line – up to 24in. of rain had been recorded in twenty-four hours – made it necessary to sling traction motors higher and, to improve access to them, provide floor hatches.
2. The main generator air should not be discharged into the engine room as the room became too hot.
3. The engine silencer and exhaust pipes could be more efficient to lessen excessive noise and radiated heat, which would benefit the engine room conditions. Gregson suggested moving the silencer outside on to the roof.
4. Ventilation was vulnerable, as were roof and body joints, to ingress of rain. Cab doors should open inwards. Windows in carriages should have had removable panels below in the interior to allow access to operating gear. The cabs need rearrangement and better quality and finished apparatus.
5. Swing bolsters should be used on articulating bogies together with buffers on the headstocks, to improve riding curves.
6. As the Sao Paulo track was very noisy, better sound insulation was required.
7. Dust was no problem on the main line, but on branch lines track was earth ballasted and dust exclusion must be a priority.

The first serious failure took place in the May-June period of 1944, when heavy repairs were deemed necessary following failure in traffic. Examination revealed that the main engine crankshaft had fractured. Some time was needed to rectify this, only to have it fracture again in June 1949. By the end of 1947 585,000 miles had been covered.

In August 1959 the Armstrong-Sulzer engine was replaced by an American Cooper-Bessemer unit of 720 bhp, and the auxiliary Armstrong-Saurer engine set by a Buda engine of 110 bhp. Electrical troubles were very few.

In the autumn of 1975 *Cometa* was still in service, but increasing maintenance costs were putting its future in doubt after over forty years of service.

DT19 *Cometa* derelict at Lapa Works, Sao Paulo in 1978. *Sergio Martire A.B.P.F.*

Order DT30 was for this twin-unit articulated railcoach for the Buenos Aires Western Railway, in 1934. It was powered by an Armstrong-Sulzer 6LD25 engine giving 350 bhp. Here it is seen in Scotswood Works.
Brian Webb collection

In 1934 Armstrong Whitworth supplied, under order DT30, a twin-unit articulated railcar to the Buenos Aires Western Railway. The decision to order this and a lightweight railbus was due to the success of the BAGSR with diesel electric traction, and to the desire to regain lost traffic by offering greater comfort and higher speeds, while at the same time gaining economy and higher mileages.

The twin-unit railcar was somewhat similar to the Sao Paulo train set: it comprised a short power vehicle articulated to a passenger carriage. The main difference was that, although designed as a self-contained unit, it was capable of hauling up to two trailers. These could be attached at either end of the railcar, as corridor access was provided throughout and there were cabs at both ends. Mechanically the railcar was very similar to the Sao Paulo train, but was of rather better appearance. Technically it was much improved on its predecessor.

Described by Armstrong Whitworth as an 'articulated motor coach', it was powered by a six-cylinder Armstrong-Sulzer type 6LD engine of 450 bhp at 750 rpm. De-rating adjustable to 350 bhp, according to altitude, was possible. The engine was directly coupled to Laurence, Scott & Electromotors main generator. An overhung auxiliary generator supplied power for battery charging, lighting, heating, braking, cooling, etc. The auxiliary engine/generator set was eliminated in this vehicle. The main generator had a series field winding for use when starting the engine. The engine/generator set could be lifted out through the removable roof.

The engine roof contained: the battery used for engine starting and supplying control and lighting circuits; fuel pump exhauster, etc.; the exhauster – motor driven – for the brakes; motor driven air compressor for engine control; the control cubicle; automatic rheostat; cooler fan for water and oil radiator cooling; the radiators were mounted in the bodyside; roof-mounted water tank for cooling; and main fuel tank, sited alongside the engine. The driving cabs had the usual controls and dead man pedal.

The railcar had two axle-hung, nose-suspended, self ventilated traction motors by Crompton Parkinson. These were both on the leading bogie of the power vehicle. Electrical equipment was designed to operate at altitudes up to 1,570ft and at temperatures of between 28 and 140°F. Maximum power could be developed up to a speed of 64 mph, and the top speed was 72 mph. The articulating bogie was on Gresley principles, but in common with usual Armstrong Whitworth bogie work complied to their standard design with plate side frames and Isothermos axleboxes.

Gloucester Railway Carriage & Wagon Co. Ltd built the complete carriage body, which was attached to the welded, lightweight underframe, built by Armstrong Whitworth at Scotswood Works. Passenger accommodation was First Class only: very comfortable fixed seats with portable tables between, as well as toilet and luggage accommodation, were provided. The body was built of metal, but lined internally with wood. The windows had sunblinds. Sound and heat insulation, double roof, electric lighting, electrically driven cooling fans, and heaters for winter were also included.

The railcar began trials on 14th September 1934, and ran a special Eucharistic Congress service from Buenos Aires (Once) to Lujan, and then ran the following services:

Date	Service: Once to	Intermediate stops	Miles/day	Days/week
05.11.1934	Bragado	7	260	6
10.12.1934	Nuevo De Julio	8-10	326	7
01.02.1935	Carlos Caesares	12	400	7
15.12.1936	Pehuajo	?	466	7

Dynamometer car trials to Carlos Caesares and back were carried out on 9th August 1935. A general overhaul was carried out, after 126,918 miles, beginning on 5th November 1935.

According to Armstrong Whitworth, up to the end of 1936 no engine failure had occurred. But motor bogie hot axleboxes were frequent, so that in 1936 the Isothermos axleboxes were replaced by waste packed ones. This was necessary due to the dust guards of the Isothermos boxes not being proof against the fine pampa dust. It was felt that not enough account had been taken of the train's operation over unballasted tracks.

The train had been in service 595 days, out of service 212 days, and done a mileage of 228,300 miles. The fuel consumption of approximately 5 mpg was improved by 10 per cent during 1936 by increasing engine temperature and re-timing the journey.

A preliminary engine inspection in December 1934 enabled the railcar to run until 2nd April 1935 after completing 53,000 miles for periodic engine examination. The examination showed it necessary to replace 15 piston rings and 12 carbon brushes for the generator. One engine big end shell showed signs of cracking and was replaced. The railcar resumed work on 12th April and worked until the next inspection, at 80,000 miles, during July.

In six years the railcar ran 126,000 miles and cost £336.50 in labour costs, and £234.25 in materials to maintain. It was the victim of being a 'one off' job, for the railcar had to spend long periods off duty when under repair, due to the small number of spares carried by the BAWR for the diesel engine, generator, traction motors, etc. A fleet of this type of car would have allowed the requisite spares to be kept.

A report on the failures over six years service gave the following facts:

1. Diesel engine.
   Until a few months before the report the engine had been very good, not failing once. The only troubles previously had been water leakage into the engine sump and only five days were lost due to this.
2. Electric transmission.
   This proved excellent apart from some early minor faults.
3. Traction motors.
   Some short circuits in the armature windings occurred in one traction motor. As no spare motor was carried, rewinding was necessary. However, failure again occurred, due to one of the new coil insulators failing and short circuiting. This saw the car out of service for 57 days. After six years the motor gears were found excellent.
4. The Isothermos axleboxes.
   These were replaced by waste-packed boxes and, apart from needing constant attention due to ingress of dust, they

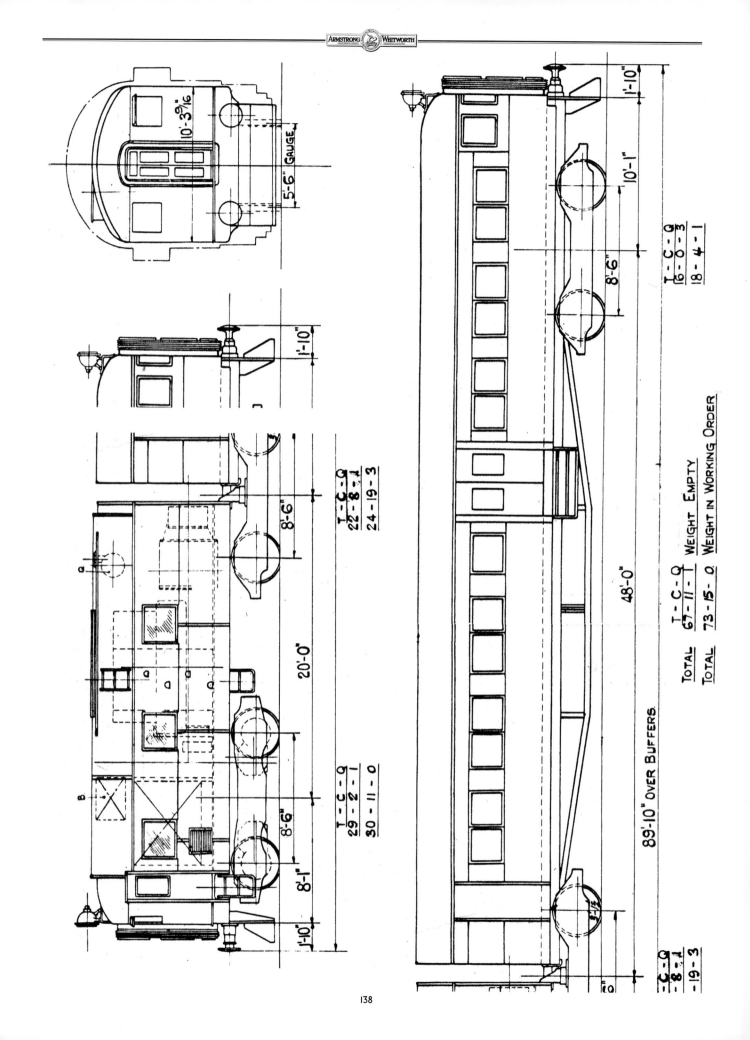

A. Controller
B. Cooling Water Tank
C. Vacuum Exhauster
D. Lubricating Oil Filters
E. Oil Fuelling Pump
F. Oil Fuel Tank
G. Air Compressor
H. Control Cubicle
J. Batteries
K. Engine & Generator
L. Battery Container
M. Radiator
N. Fan Casing
O. Tool Box
P. Hand Brake
Q. Silencer

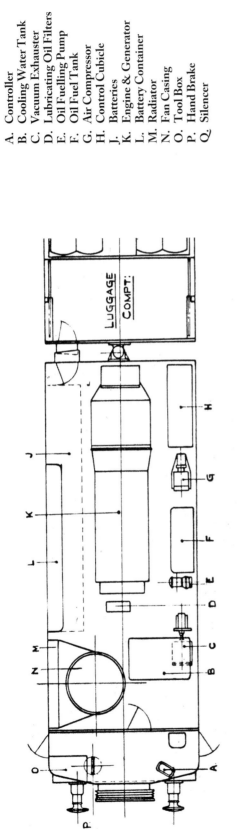
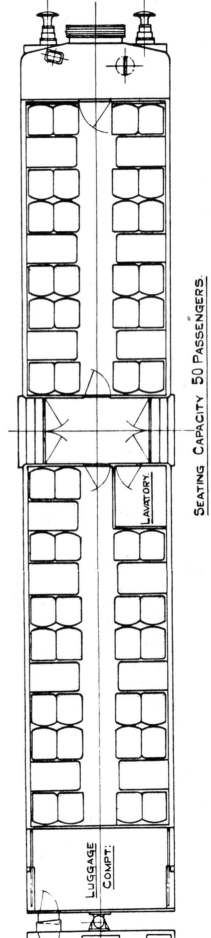

Layout diagram of DT30.

Brian Webb collection

A 1934 snapshot taken by an Armstrong Whitworth engineer of DT30 on test at Scotswood. *Donald C. Plyer*

worked better. The answer, according to the BAWR, lay in using roller-bearing boxes.

5. Mechanical portion.
Cracking of bogie frames needed attention. In spite of reinforcing the power-bogie bolster, it finally had to be rewarded. A spring bolster was used. The trouble was attributed to poor track conditions.

6. Passenger accommodation.
The railway had set up a small buffet in the luggage compartment, and opined that one should have been fitted at the start. The loss of the luggage space aggravated the luggage stowage position, which was already limited to rather inadequate racking. The provision of air-conditioning equipment was deemed a must to prevent the practice of opening carriage windows, which allowed the intake of dust when running.

7. General.
The railcar's seating capacity of 50 was insufficient and an additional coach was contemplated. This finally materialised as a larger body with a seating capacity of 80-90 placed in the position of the leading coach, which was removed to the rear to preserve its driving cab position. Both vehicles were articulated by a further bogie. The buffet was moved into the new carriage. The railcar was thus formed into one three-unit all articulated set. The new carriage body and underframe was designed by Armstrong Whitworth under diagrams LD977 & 978 dated September 1935.

One point, which attracted some critics, was the apparent over powering – with a high power to weight ratio of 6 bhp per ton. However, the fact that it always had ample power reserve meant it was rarely worked continuously at full power, thus giving long life and low maintenance to offset higher initial cost. The car was operated mostly by one man, except when, after repairs, engineers or inspectors travelled as observers.

As with other 'one off' railcars, replacement by steam trains was inevitable when out of traffic density exceeded accommodation. At the end of 1947 the train set had completed over 1,125,000 miles running. Of the maker's numbers carried by the railcoach the power vehicle was No. D35 and its coach portion D36 of 1934.

Argentine sources indicate that the train was retired during the 1968-1970 period, being scrapped at the old BAWR shops at Liniera during 1971. The mileage recorded at the end of its career officially 925,410 km or 574,679 miles, this being quite at variance with the figure quoted above.

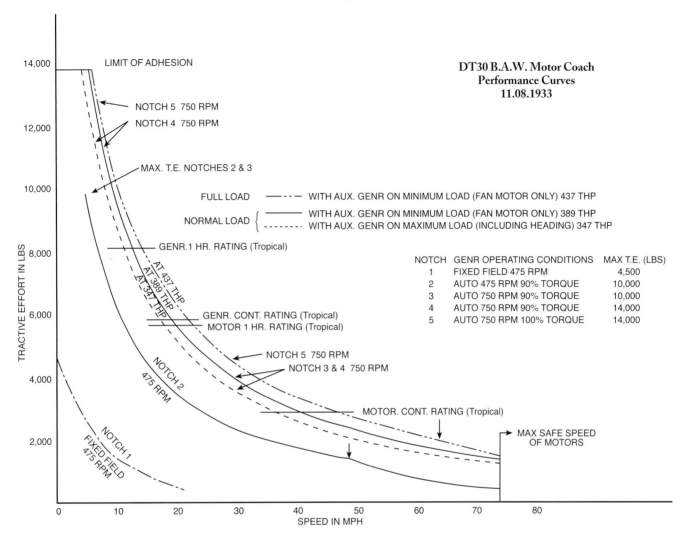

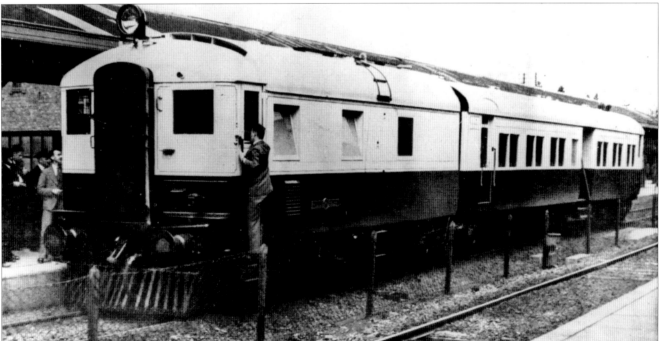

The DT30 railcoach (D35 and D36 of 1934) on the Buenos Aires Western Railway. *Jorge L. San Martin collection*

The first 0-6-0 DE owned by a British main line railway was this 250 bhp Armstrong–Sulzer powered unit for the LMSR in 1934. Built under order number DT20, it carried Armstrong Whitworth number D20 and LMS 7408 (later renumbered to 7058). Here it is seen at Scotswood Works with preparations for its 'official' photograph going on behind – note the workman with the white sheet!
Brian Webb collection

LARGE 0-6-0 SHUNTERS

The first order to originate from one of the British main line railways was received from the LMS in 1933. At this time the LMS was embarking on an experimental programme of diesel traction for shunting duties, a step which earmarked the onset of the dieselisation of British railways, although few at that time would accept the fact.

The LMS decision to acquire eight two- and three-axle diesel mechanical locomotives in the 150-180 bhp range, and one 250 bhp diesel electric to supplement their 0-6-0 diesel hydraulic of Derby-Paxman-Haslam and Newton type was a bold one. The variety of equipment used was interesting, but it has, nonetheless, been covered elsewhere and is not our concern here.

It was the diesel electric unit which had the most profound effect on the LMS future shunting policy, and it was Armstrong Whitworth who supplied the locomotive in question. At this time Armstrong Whitworth were the only British manufacturers with diesel electric locomotives at work, and as such were the originators of the main line diesel electric shunter so prevalent in the UK today.

Built under order DT20 and carrying works number D20, the locomotive was numbered 7408, but soon became 7058 in LMS locomotive stock. Generally the same as the 1932 Armstrong Whitworth unit D8 (order DT7), it had larger fuel capacity, vacuum brake equipment, and shunting steps as its most important differing features.

This 0-6-0 unit used the Armstrong-Sulzer 6LV22 engine to drive its Laurence, Scott 640 V, 800 A dc generator, which in turn supplied power to the frame-mounted, force-ventilated, traction motor of the same manufacture. The traction motor was located above the final drive unit with jackshaft – within the locomotive wheelbase. Completely automatic control limited current at starting, while at the same time it kept the engine output at full load on the last notches of the controller, and prevented overloading of the engine and generator.

Weighing 40 tons and having a maximum axleloading of 13.5 tons, the locomotive exerted 24,000 lbs tractive effort at start, and had an adhesion factor of 3.74. Engine starting was by motoring the main generator from the battery. An auxiliary generator was driven by chain-drive from the end of the main generator shaft and this also drove cooling fan and water pump. The cooling for the traction motor was obtained through ducting from the motor-driven blower mounted on top of the main motor. The driving motor was connected to the road wheels through a 121:21 single spur reduction gear to a jackshaft, connecting and coupling rods. Braking was by compressed air to all wheels, the air being supplied from a compressor mounted in the underframe. Fuel oil tanks were on the footplate alongside the bonnet, but the service oil tank was in the cab roof, filled by the driver by a semi rotary pump.

The locomotive was delivered to the LMS in February 1934, and between 14th February and 2nd March 1934 it was used for driver training prior to starting regular marshalling yard duties on 6th March. The first duties were at the Brent yard near Willesden, London; these extended until 20th May. It then moved on to Crewe between 23rd May and 10th June, and Beeston (Nottingham) for four days (week ending 17th June).

Service at Toton yard occupied six days (week ending 24th June 1934), followed by four days at Bescot, near Walsall (week ending 1st July). Duties at Brent restarted on 20th July 1934. At Brent the locomotive worked twenty-four hour duties, six days per week, being on duty from 02.22 on Monday until 06.00 Sunday. During this time it was driven by three shifts of drivers each twenty-four hours.

Armstrong Whitworth recorded that its average daily mileage was only 40, indicating its low speed of operation, which was, over a twenty-four hour period, an average of only 1.66 mph: Speeds rarely exceeded 10 mph. Fuel consumption at Brent was put at 60 gallons in twenty-four hours, but sufficient was carried for a week's work. Loads hauled at Brent varied considerably, but tests showed the locomotive able to take 1,000 tons with complete ease. At the time of the closure of Armstrong Whitworth to locomotive work, in February 1937, it was recorded that this locomotive was working 6,000 hours per year, and had completed 9,200 miles during its first twelve months in service.

The following figures on the locomotive's performance during its first twenty-four weeks service, 14th February-26th August 1934, were recorded by Armstrong Whitworth on 1st September 1934:

Days in service	125
Service hours	2,772
Locomotive hours	2,551$\frac{1}{2}$
Fuel (gallons)	6,467
Lubricating oil (gallons)	88$\frac{1}{2}$
Maintenance (man hours)	314$\frac{1}{2}$
Average hours/day in service	22.2
Average locomotive hours/day in service	20.4
Fuel, gallons/service hour	2.33
Fuel, gallons/locomotive hour	2.53
Load factor, based on engine continuous rating and on locomotive hours	20.6 per cent

The success of this locomotive over the mixed bag of low speed, low-power diesel mechanicals was marked, and it was this locomotive which was to pave the way for a complete sweep, so far as British main line railways were concerned, for the diesel electric shunter. It was not until the 1950s that the mechanical and hydraulic drive locomotive made a brief comeback, albeit in some quantity.

Practical problems were that the cab was far too small, and that the layout and size of the control desk required attention in future locomotives of the type. The cab was poorly ventilated, and soon became hot and stuffy: the close proximity of the engine exhaust system and silencer passing up the front of the cab assisted this process. Engine room ventilation was considered quite deficient

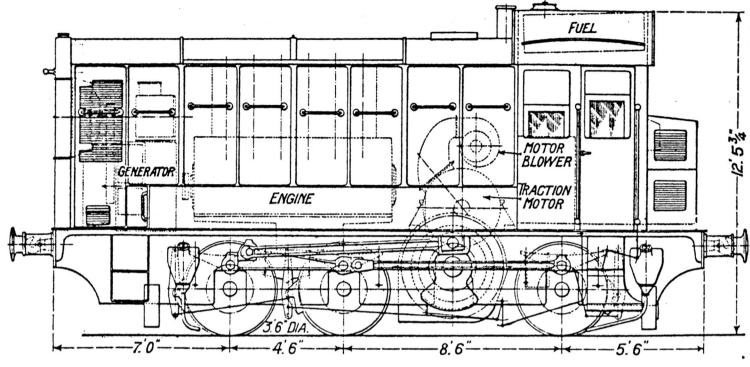

Side and end elevations of order DT20. Reproduced at 7mm - 1ft.
Brian Webb collection

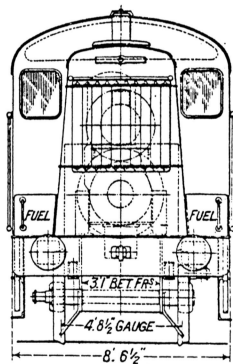

and the locomotive often ran with the sliding bonnet top covers open, an unsatisfactory practice due to the amount of dirt and rainwater allowed access thereby.

Following its activity at Brent and Crewe, the locomotive was based at Willesden. During the war it was lent to the War Department, returning in 1943. Its final years were spent at Willesden and Toton.

Although allocated number 13000 in the BR diesel locomotive numbering series, the locomotive did not carry it, having been withdrawn as 7058 in late 1949.

The largest locomotive order executed by the diesel traction department was one for ten 350 bhp 0-6-0 DE shunters for the LMS. Following the success of the 250 bhp locomotive, the LMS ordered two batches of ten diesel electric shunters – from Armstrong Whitworth and English Electric. The latter were built by R. & W. Hawthorn, Leslie & Co. Ltd as subcontractors – coincidentally at Newcastle also. These two Tyneside builders supplied their locomotives in 1935/6. Although the Armstrong Whitworth units were completed at Scotswood, the English Electric examples had to journey from the Hawthorn, Leslie works to Preston for installation of power equipment.

Armstrong Whitworth supplied their locomotives under order DT63, carrying works numbers D54-D63, and LMS numbers 7059-7068. The design of these locomotives followed closely that of orders DT7 and DT20, the 250 bhp units. The superstructure housed the engine/generator, radiator, and single traction motor. It was of sheet steel fabricated by welding and riveting, as was the cab. Large sliding covers were provided in the bonnet over the engine. A 545 gallon main fuel tank was mounted between the power unit and the cab on top of the frames; the 90 gallons service tank was above it.

The underframe of $1^{1/4}$in. thick plate had the usual vertical and horizontal stretchers, but additional strengthening was necessary to hold the jackshaft bearing hornblock casting on each frameplate. This resulted in a transverse bracing connecting the frame plates by way of the motor bearer. This arrangement rigidly braced the frames and jackshaft unit against the racking and alternating thrusts of the driving rods.

Unequal spacing of the wheels to provide accommodation for the reduction gear and frame-mounted jackshaft drive unit was again necessary. The result of this was that the relatively small wheels of 4ft 3in. diameter had to be spread over a wheelbase of 14ft 6in. To allow for flexibility on sharp curves, a side play of ³/₄in. each side was allowed on the centre wheels.

The battery box was on the left hand running plate, necessitating shorter bonnet side access doors over it – otherwise full length doors were fitted. The end cab was provided with lookout windows alongside the bonnet but, for some reason, had only small size rear windows. Driving controls were on a central control desk, with dual control for either side operation. Braking was by straight air and hand screw systems, with one block on each wheel fully compensated. Fine control for shunting was obtained by the self-lapping driver's brake valve incorporated into the system.

The engine was the Armstrong-Sulzer type 6LTD22, a six-cylinder vertical unit with 220mm x 280mm cylinders and a top rating of 400 bhp at 1,000 rpm, but set to give 350 bhp at 975 rpm. This engine was of lighter weight and higher speed than the 250 bhp engine used in the two previous 0-6-0 shunters, but, as its top rating was 400 bhp at 1,000 rpm for one hour, in this application its rating was quite conservative. With a weight of around four tons, complete with generator support formed by extending the crankcase, its power to weight ratio was 22½ lbs per bhp.

Engine construction was given some prominence by Armstrong Whitworth with these locomotives, for the combination of cast and welded construction techniques had been chiefly responsible for the reduction in weight. The crankcase was of welded steel plating, together with its five inner transverse stays supporting the main crankshaft bearings. However, the end members carrying the outer bearings were steel castings attached by welding.

The top part of the cylinder block was a casting, while the cylinder heads were separate iron castings encased in cast aluminium alloy and had 'T' section nickel steel connecting rods attached by fully floating gudgeon pins.

The crankshaft and pins were hollow bored and ran on seven white metal lined, steel shell bearings. The big end bearings were white metal on bronze shells. Welded steel was used for the bottom part of the crankcase and provided the engine bedplate and generator support.

Each cylinder head had suction and exhaust valves and a multi-hole, centrally placed fuel valve with direct injection, via strainers and filters, by CAV-Bosch fuel pumps. The camshaft was gear driven, located on the intake side of the engine and operating the air and exhaust valves through push rods and rockers. The opposite side had the camshaft for driving the fuel pump and governor.

These locomotives had their generators at the cab end of the bonnet – or the engine/generators mounted the opposite way to that of LMSR 7058, or the Preston Docks 250 bhp locomotives.

Crompton Parkinson manufactured the electric traction equipment. The main generator, having a continuous rating of 234 KW, supplied current to the single springhouse traction

DT20 survived into British Railways ownership as 7058 and is seen here at Derby Works on 27th February 1949. It was withdrawn later the same year.
Les W. Perkins

The largest locomotive order received by the Armstrong Whitworth diesel traction department was for ten 350/400 bhp 0-6-0 DE for the LMS. Built under order DT63 (AW D54-63) in 1935 they were LMS 7059-68.
Brian Webb collection

The production line for the LMS shunters at Scotswood Works. Note the jackshaft unit over the pit to the right of the nearest locomotive.
Brian Webb collection

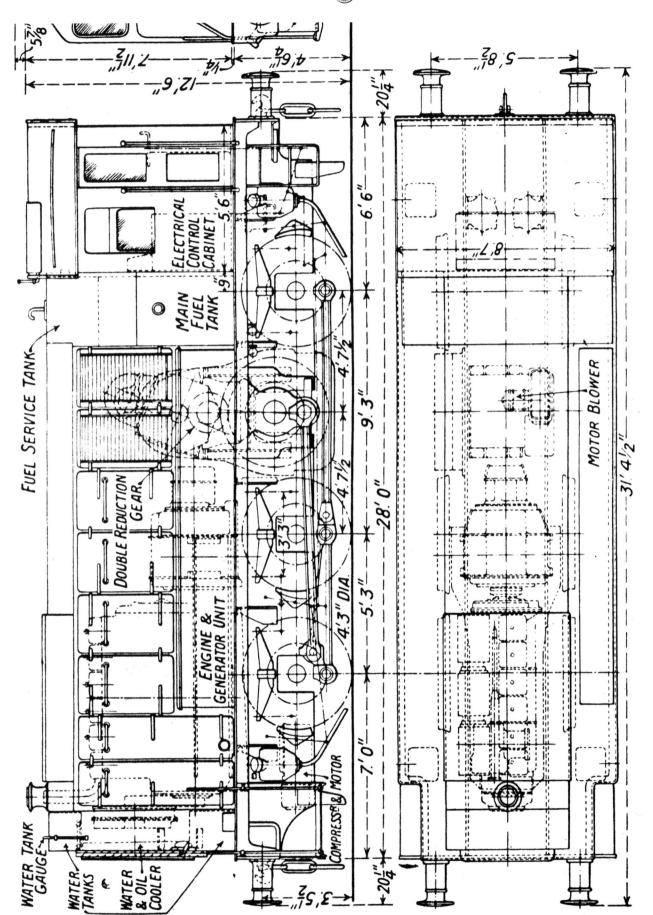

Drawing of DT63 reproduced at 7mm - 1ft. See overleaf for front elevation.

Brian Webb collection

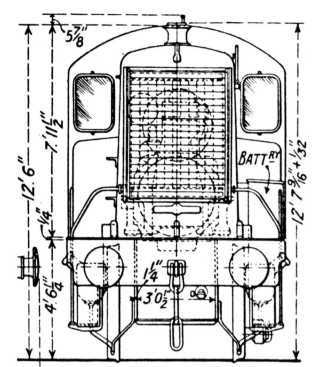

Left: The front elevation for DT63.

Below: LMS 7063 displays the often unphotographed side of the DT63 shunters. Note the absence of battery boxes and the end of the double reduction drive unit located directly over the final drive clearly visible on the bonnet side. *Les W. Perkins*

motor located at the rear of the bonnet housing. This drove to the jackshaft via double reduction gears with a ratio of 11.1:1. The jackshaft drove via fly-cranks and an 'I' section driving rod of 'Vibrac' steel, forked over the triangular coupling rod – to which the driving rod was connected by a spherical joint.

All ten LMS shunters were despatched to Carlisle for acceptance trials in the local shunting yards, then allocated to Crewe South, Carlisle, and Willesden sheds. All ten locomotives were officially taken into stock on 31st December 1936. At this time, 7059-63 were at Crewe; 7064-8 at Carlisle, Kingmoor. Subsequent movements saw them at these same depots until 1940/1 when the War Department started to acquire them, together with others of different makes.

Armstrong Whitworth recorded the following information for the locomotives on 11th March 1937:

Works No.	Date into service	Days in service (total)	Days in service (actual)	Service hours	Locomotive hours	Engine hours	Mileage
D54	12/05/36	300	128	2,644	2,510	1,982	2,769
D55	29/07/36	222	171	3,527	3,252	2,676	3,189
D56	13/06/36	268	180	4,122	3,638	2,818	4,203
D57	03/08/36	252	162	3,562	3,370	2,776	3,898
D58	04/09/36	217	149	3,034	2,859	2,314	3,567
D59	04/09/36	185	120	2,809	2,692	2,568	3,100
D60	16/09/36	173	112	2,459	2,359	2,298	3,019
D61	28/09/36	161	100	2,118	2,030	1,963	2,370
D62	10/10/36	149	95	1,959	1,876	1,832	2,407
D63	28/11/36	100	70	1,539	1,468	1,436	1,784

By 7th March 1937 five locomotives were at Crewe (D54-D58), and five at Carlisle.

On 2nd November 1936 dynamometer car trials were conducted by the LMS, proving that the locomotives more than fulfilled their maker's figures quoted in the tender for the locomotives.

The locomotives were involved in transfers to and from the War Department (WD) during the period leading up to the 'D' day, as follows:

7059 To WD 9/40. To LMS 5/41. To WD 8/41. WD No. 70213. Worked in France and Belgium. Became SNCB 23001, then 230001. Withdrawn 3/58.

7060 To WD 1/41. WD MEF No. 19, later 70019. Sent to Egypt; worked at Suez. Withdrawn 1945, dismantled for spares.

7061 To WD 11/40. Became WD 70214. Worked in France, Belgium, and Holland. Lent to NS as NS 521 in 1945/6. Became SNCB 23002, then 231001. Withdrawn 2/65.

7062 To WD 11/40. To LMS 12/41. To WD 12/41. WD No. 70215. Worked at Long Marston, Bicester, Chatham. Sent to Germany BAOR 1958. Sold for scrap 1959 as WD 882. It was still in existence in Germany in 1976 when up for sale at 20000 DM.

7063 To WD 9/40. To LMS 11/42. To WD 11/44. Wd No. 70216. Worked at Cairnryan and Bicester. Became WD 883. Sold to E. L. Pitt Ltd, Brackley 1963. Lent to CEGB Hams Hall in 1966. Since scrapped.

7064 To WD 9/40. To LMS 1/44. To WD /44. WD No. 70217. Worked in France, Belgium, and Holland. Lent to NS as NS 521 in 1945/6. Became SNCB 23003, then 231002. Withdrawn 5/61.

7065 To WD 2/41. WD No. MEF 20, later 70020 and 880. Sent to Egypt; worked at Suez. Became ESR No. 4022 in 1954. Fate not known.

7066 To WD 2/41. WD No. MEF 21, later 70021. Sent to Egypt; worked at Suez. Dismantled for spares, but not scrapped until c1951.

7067 To WD 8/41. WD No. 70218. Worked in France and Belgium. Became SNCB 23004, then 231103. Withdrawn 1/66.

7068 To WD 2/41. WD No. MEF 22, later 70022. Sent to Egypt; worked at Suez. Became WD 881. Became ESR No. 4021. Fate not known.

It will be appreciated that the locations of the above locomotives during military use is not easily traced. It is known that some locomotives worked at Martin Mill Military Railway in Kent and also at Elham, Longmoor, Catterick and Long Marston. Of locomotives sent overseas, those sent to the Middle East Forces (MEF) at the Suez Canal Zone were left behind when British troops left Suez.

The locomotives were withdrawn from LMS stock as follows:
12/42 7060/5/6/8
11/44 7059/61-4/7
12/49 7058

LMS 7061 as Belgian State Railways (SNCB) number 23002 seen at Brussels Nord in October 1952. *R. C. Riley*

One of two of the order DT63 locomotives to do a long spell with the War Department in the United Kingdom was ex LMS number 7063 as WD 883. It is seen here in the yard of E. L. Pitt at Brackley in April 1965 who used it on contracts for some years. *Sydney A. Leleux*

Concurrently with the LMS shunters a similar locomotive was put in hand for the Bombay, Baroda & Central India Railway who numbered it DE800 in their stock. Built under order number DT68 (works number D64) it was lighter in weight due to a limiting axle load of 16 tons and was to Indian loading gauge and rail gauge of 5ft 6in. The double-reduction gear was different, at 9.3:1, compared with 11.1:1 on the LMS units.

Both vacuum and hand brakes were fitted. The former was supplied by a rotary exhauster, electrically driven. Indian national friction drawgear was fitted and such items as axles, springs, brake blocks and fittings plus lubrication components were standard, as far as possible, to Indian steam locomotive standards.

Special anti-dust filtered ventilation was fitted to suit Indian conditions, air being drawn in through filters in the roof of the bonnet and slightly pressurised to prevent ingress of dust. The engine air intake incorporated a further filter. Air for the radiators was drawn in at the sides of the engine casing.

Side play on the centre axle of the LMS units was not necessary on the Indian locomotive, as it was not called upon to negotiate curves less than 300 feet radius. The wheel diameter was 3ft 7in., or 8 inches less than the LMS locomotives, but the wheelbase remained at 14ft 6in.

Despatch of this locomotive was by road trailer and steam road locomotive – evidently to Glasgow for shipment according to former employees. The locomotive arrived in Bombay on the 2nd October 1936. Training in its use was begun on the 19th and continuous service commenced on the 22nd at Bandra hump yard, Bombay.

By 19th January 1937 it had been in service 75 days, having proved very successful and capable of moving 2,000 ton train loads on level track. It replaced the 'G' class 2-8-0 tender locomotives of 120 tons weight.

In spite of being a 'one off' job, operating reports gave it a qualified success, maintenance was entrusted to fitters trained by Armstrong Whitworth engineers upon the locomotive's arrival, while the drivers were recruited from ordinary shunting locomotive staff. The locomotive normally returned to the Bandra locomotive shed once weekly for refuelling and examination; a simple system of recording of periodic examinations ensured all items were treated on the weekly basis.

During its first three years service the locomotive had two heavy and six intermediate repairs. In general, the engine was given a heavy repair after 36 weeks working and an intermediate after 12 weeks. The heavy repair included a complete dismantling and overhaul of the engine and a systematic check and maintenance of the electrical equipment, which, in fact, gave very little trouble. The intermediate repair comprised removal of the engine cylinder covers, valve grinding, decarbonisation of pistons, examination of bearings and alignment of crankshaft.

In the three year period the locomotive was in service 14,144 hours, with standing time of 2,572 hours - giving it an availability of 65 per cent. Repair times were aggravated by delay in obtaining spare parts from the United Kingdom, a problem which could have been overcome if a fleet of such locomotives had been in use.

Above: Similar to the LMS 0-6-0 DE was this solitary shunter built under order DT68 (AW D64) for the Bombay, Baroda & Central India Railway in 1936. *Sulzer Bros UK Ltd*

Right: View of traction motor and gearing to final drive mounted in the frame of DT68 at Scotswood whilst under construction. *Brian Webb collection*

By 1940 it was again reported to be satisfactory and had given little trouble. The diesel engine had suffered troubles due to thin bronze shells and white metal linings on main and big end bearings but, this apart, only normal replacements had been necessary.

Bewteen 2nd March 1939 and 1st June 1939 the following figures were recorded for this locomotive:

Total time in period	2,208 hours
Time in service	1,709½ hours
Time standing by	232¼ hours
Time under maintenance	266¼ hours
Fuel consumption	5,070 gallons
Lubricating oil	129 gallons
Average shunting time daily	19.5 hours
Fuel use per shunting hour	2.965 gallons
Locomotive availability	88 per cent
Operating costs (gross)	16.75 Annas per mile
Operating costs	6.34 Annas per mile
Interest and depreciation	10.01 Annas per mile
Heavy overhaul	0.40 Annas per mile

The cost of the locomotive after landing and re-erection was RS 130,000.

The locomotive was still known to be at work in the 1950s.

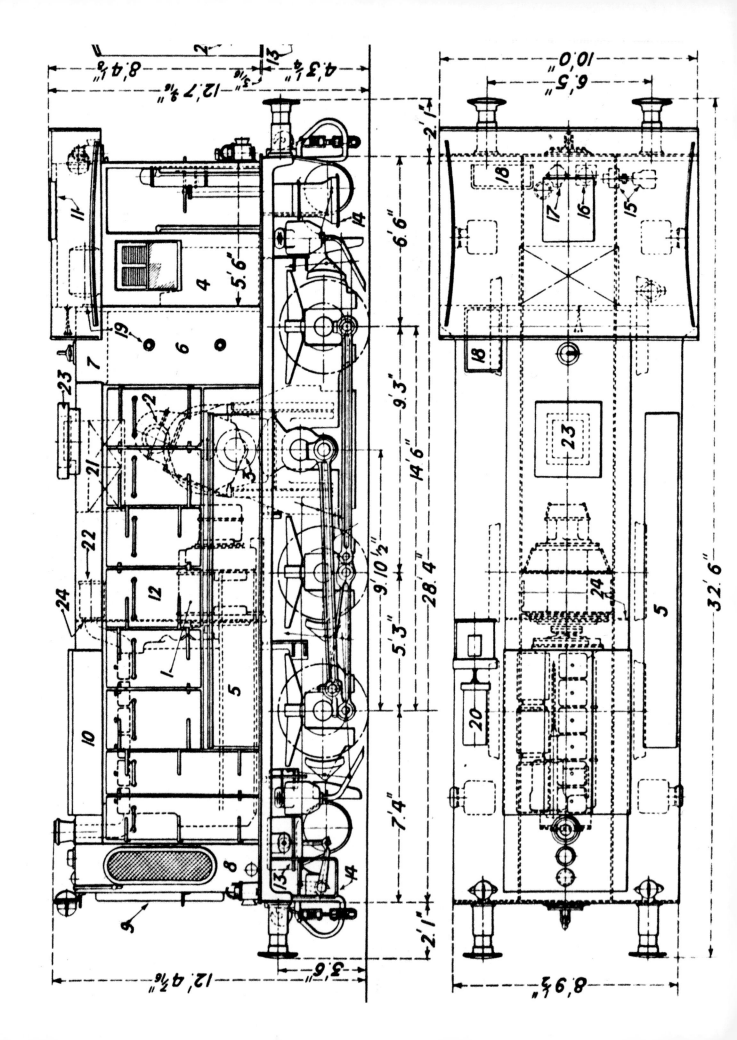

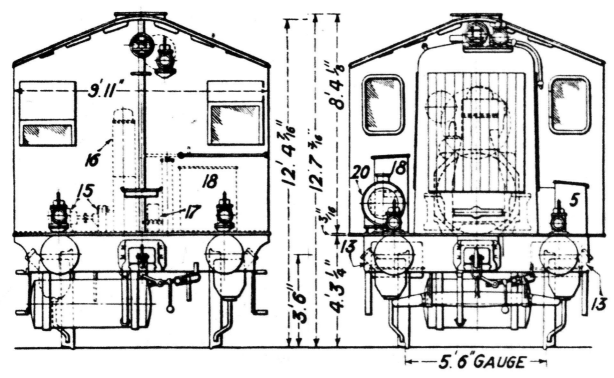

Layout diagram of DT68, reproduced at 7mm - 1ft.
Brian Webb collection

1. Engine, Generator and Auxiliary Generator
2. Traction Motor & Motor Blower
3. Double Reduction Gear
4. Electrical Control Cabinet
5. Battery
6. Main Fuel Tank
7. Fuel Service Tank
8. Water Tanks
9. Water & Oil Cooler
10. Sliding Roof
11. Cab Ventilator
12. Hinged Doors
13. Brake Cylinders
14. Foot Steps
15. Compressor & Motor
16. Oil Renovator
17. Vacuum Automatic Governor
18. Tool Boxes
19. Fuel Tank Gauges
20. Exhauster & Motor
21. Primary Air Filters
22. Secondary Air Filters
23. Filter Cowl
24. Partition between Engine & Generator

Right: A head-on view of DE 800. *Brian Webb collection*

Table 4: Main details and dimensions of diesel shunting locomotives built by Armstrong Whitworth

Order No., AW No.	Axle Layout	Engine Make, Type, and bhp	Generator make	Traction Motor Make	Weight in Working Order	Length	Overall Width	Overall Height	Wheel Diam.	Rigid Wheel Base	Rail Gauge	Maximum Tractive Effort lbs	Fuel Capacity galls	Min. Curve Negotiable feet	Max Speed mph
DT7 D8	0-6-0	Armstrong-Sulzer 6LD22 250 bhp	LSE	LSE	39T 5C	29ft 0in.* 25ft 6in.†	8ft 6in.	12ft 3in.	3ft 6in.	13ft 0in.	4ft 8½in.	24,000	40	160	20
DT11 D10	0-4-0	Armstrong-Saurer 6BLD, 95 bhp	LSE	LSE	15T 0C	20ft 0in.• 13ft 2½in.†	8ft 6in. (9ft over roof)	10ft 0 13/16in.	2ft 9in.	6ft 3in.	4ft 8½in.	8,150	40	–	27
DT20 D20	0-6-0	Armstrong-Sulzer 6LD22 250 bhp	LSE	LSE	40T 5C	29ft 0in.* 25ft 6in.†	8ft 6½in.	12ft 5¾in.	3ft 6in.	13ft 0in.	4ft 8½in.	24,000	570	160	30
DT22 D21-26	0-4-0	Armstrong-Saurer 6BLD 85/95 bhp	LSE	LSE	15T 0C	19ft 4in.* 19ft 10in.† (Loco D25 16ft 2in.†)	8ft 0in.	11ft 3in. (D25 10ft 10in.)	3ft 0in.	5ft 6in.	4ft 8½in.	8,400	120	60	25 (D25 30)
DT36 D40	0-4-0	Armstrong-Saurer 6BLD 85 bhp	LSE	LSE	12T 0C	16ft 2½in.* 14ft 2½in.† over couplers	6ft 6in.	10ft 0in.	2ft 9in.	5ft 6in.	2ft 6in.	7,500	–	60	25
DT44 D43	0-4-0	Armstrong-Saurer 6BXD 122 bhp	LSE	LSE	20T 0C	21ft 0in.* 17ft 1in.†	8ft 8in. (10ft 2in. over cab roof)	11ft 0in.	3ft 0in.	5ft 6in.	5ft 6in.	12,000	–	60	20
DT60 D52	0-4-0	Armstrong-Saurer 6BLD 100 bhp	LSE	LSE	15T 13C	19ft 6in.* 17ft 6in.† over couplers	6ft 10in.	11ft 0in.	3ft 0in.	5ft 6in.	metre	8,500	94	55	25
DT61 D53	0-4-0	Armstrong-Saurer 4BOD, 60 bhp	LSE	LSE	9T 0C	14ft 10in.* 12ft 9in.†	5ft 6in.	8ft 4in.	2ft 9in.	3ft 6in.	3ft 0in.	4,500	40	50	24
DT63 D54-63	0-6-0	Armstrong-Sulzer 6LTD22 400 bhp	CP	CP	52T 0C	31ft 4½in.* 28ft 0in.†	8ft 7in.	12ft 7 9/16in.	4ft 3in.	14ft 6in.	4ft 8½in.	30,000	630	200	23½
DT68 D64	0-6-0	Armstrong-Sulzer 6LTD22 400 bhp	CP	CP	48T 0C	32ft 6in.* 28ft 4in.†	10ft 0in.	12ft 7 9/16in.	3ft 7in.	14ft 6in.	5ft 6in.	26,400	429	200	22

* over buffers   † over bufferbeams

Two extremes of the diesel electric shunter. Above is D10 of 1932 built to order DT11 a 15-ton 0-4-0 95 bhp model whilst below is LMS number 7059 (AW D54 of 1935) built under order number DT63. These 0-6-0s were rated at 350/400 bhp. *Brian Webb collection*

The Western Australian Government Railways 3ft 6in. gauge railcar 446 *Governor Stirling*. This highly successful batch of six cars were built under order DT71 (AW D65-70) in 1937.
Western Australian Government Railways

THE FINAL CONTRACTS

The only Australian order completed by Armstrong Whitworth was that completed in April 1937. This order, number DT71, was for six twin bogie railcars for the Western Australian Government Railways. Carrying works numbers D65-D70, the cars were the result of an order placed in early 1936. They were shipped as five complete chassis ready for body mounting and one complete railcar. The five outstanding bodies were to be completed in Australia, using sets of body framing, window, seats, etc., supplied by Armstrong Whitworth.

The vehicles were built to the requirements of J. W. R. Broadfoot, WAGR Chief Mechanical Engineer. Park Royal Coachworks Ltd built the one body and supplied the five sets of components.

The mechanical portion consisted of an underframe following closely standard Armstrong Whitworth practice. It was built up from two longitudinal side members, with lattice girder and stretchers to give rigidity and to carry such items as water tank, brake cylinders, the traction motor, etc. The whole was fully welded.

Bogie design followed previous Armstrong Whitworth designs: using box-girder side frames which permitted the placing of laminated bearer-springs between the sides of the box-girder. The bogie frames were similar, but the springing was arranged to cater for the weight of the engine, etc., at one end of the railcar. Isothermos axleboxes were fitted.

Of 3ft 6in. gauge, the railcars had 40 seats, luggage space and two lavatories. There were driving compartments at both ends. The bodywork framing was largely electrically welded, except in areas where repairs and replacements were likely and these were riveted. The body floor bearers consisted of two channel sections back to back and electrically welded. These were secured to the body pillars with gusset plates, while the roof was supported on mild-steel angles laid in pairs on steel distance pieces. An air-space was provided in the roof between the inner and outer linings. Body panelling was of steel, lined on the inside with asbestos sheet; interior panels were of plywood.

The front driving compartment had its partitions insulated from the engine room by Insulwood. Access to the engine room was by fume-proof doors in the partition, in addition to bodyside doors.

Flooring was covered in Insulwood and linoleum. The latter was laid over radiused panels at the sides and carried up to the seat rails to ease cleaning and give a full length kicking-panel. Interior finishes were of Rexine with polished mahogany trim and rails.

Passenger compartment windows, by Beclawat, were of half-drop type and were fitted with spring-loaded roller blinds of Rexine. Parcel racks were fitted, and semi-flush lighting fittings were fitted underneath them. Seating, arranged back to back, was also upholstered in Rexine.

Due to the fact that the railcars were operated on routes without proper station facilities, they were fitted with vacuum

451 *Governor Bedford* working with a specially built trailer car. *Western Australian Government Railways*

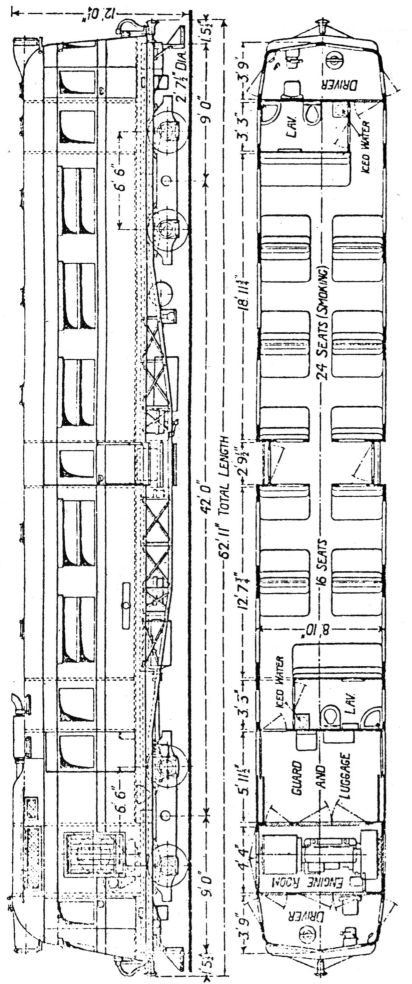
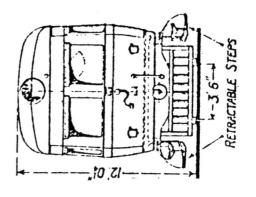

Layout of IDT71 railcar. 4mm – 1ft. Brian Webb collection

operated, interlocking, Ross system, folding steps on both sides. These were interlocked with the vacuum brake system and could only be lowered and raised when the vehicle was stationary.

Standard WAGR centre couplers were fitted, as the railcars were set to work with some old saloon type coaches as trailers, operating with these until 1940. From this time six new all-steel trailers (class ADT) were available, seating 16 non-smoking and 20 smoking passengers, in addition to containing a large compartment for luggage and parcels; two toilets were provided. The trailers weighed 13 tons (tare).

The railcars were powered by Armstrong-Saurer 6BXD 140 bhp six-cylinder engines running at 1,500 rpm. These drove a Laurence, Scott generator. The complete power pack was mounted in a subframe and placed transversely across the underframe behind one driving compartment, separated from the passenger saloon by the luggage/guard's compartment. The whole power unit was easily removed for maintenance or replacement, a spare set being kept for this purpose.

The single Laurence, Scott self-ventilated traction motor was hung from the chassis, driving to the inner axle of the bogie under the engine end of the vehicle via a cardan shaft and a worm-axle drive unit. Above the engine room, the roof had a pronounced hump to house exhaust silencers and exhaust system.

Service reports on the railcars stated that they operated at 40-45 mph. Based initially at Perth (four cars), Bunbury and Geraldton (one car each), they served a variety of areas – agricultural, coastal, and mining – with runs ranging up to 225 miles and 340 miles for the Perth-Albany services. In their first four to five months regular service they aggregated 140,302 miles, with operating expenses of 9.49 pence per mile and earnings of 23.8 pence per mile. During this time they carried 35,763 passengers. Gross earnings were £13,931, with working expenses of £5,552, interest charges of £1,088, depreciation of £1,752. The surplus, after meeting all accounts, was put at £5,539.

The railcars were classified ADE (A=passenger, DE=diesel electric), and known as the 'Governor' class, being numbered and named after Western Australian governors:

446 *Governor Stirling*
447 *Governor Lawley*
448 *Governor Hutt*
449 *Governor Weld*
450 *Governor Hampton*
451 *Governor Bedford*

In 1948 the cars were operating in the Perth area on the following routes:

Perth-Merredin-Narembeen-Narrogin.
Perth-Albany-Denmark.
Perth-Katanning-Ongerup-Pigerup.
Perth-York-Brucerock-Narrogin.
Perth-Miling.
Mullewa-Geraldton.

A common arrangement in Armstrong Whitworth railcars was the ease of engine removal/exchange afforded by using compact Armstrong-Saurer engine/generator sets. Here the installation of the engine is demonstrated at Scotswood Works on railcar D65 of order DT71.
Brian Webb collection

So effective were these cars that in 1949 the WAGR put in hand six new railcars to augment the 'Governor' class on the longer runs. The 'Governors' were then transferred for use in more remote inland areas – including routes from Kalgoorie to Laverton (211 miles) and Esperance (258 miles)--replacing steam traction. In 1950/1 it was reported that the cars were gaining a fuel usage of 6 1/2 mpg, while the electrical gear was doing 80,000 miles between repairs.

The railcars were withdrawn in April 1962, after a very busy life on country services and travel on most lines, with mileages over one million miles. They were never re-engined, and some cars were still stored at Midland workshops in early 1974.

Order No. DT67 was an unusual and unique one, in that it comprised the supply of engines, fluid couplings, gearboxes, transmissions, radiators, and auxiliaries mounted on a sub-frame for installation in the power bogies of a batch of diesel-mechanical railcars for the Central Argentine Railway. In this 1936 subcontract, for Armstrong Whitworth were supplying the equipment for use in vehicles designed and built by the Birmingham Railway Carriage & Wagon Co. Ltd, the Scotswood-built components were to be fitted in patented box-frame welded bogies of BRC&W build and design.

The railcars were all-steel, streamlined units in two variants. Four were single-unit twin bogie cars, and two were twin-unit triple-bogie articulated ones. The former had one power bogie and the latter two, each. All were powered by identical Armstrong-Sulzer engines, but two types of transmission were employed. Two of the single-units, and both the articulated cars had SLM-Winterthur gearboxes, while the remaining two single cars had Wilson epicyclic gearboxes with Vulcan-Sinclair fluid couplings.

The sub-frame assembly was to be fitted, engine leading, in the bogies. From the front it consisted of: diesel engine, fluid coupling, gearbox, dynamo, compressor, final-drive with cardan shafts extending fore and aft, cooling radiator unit alongside the 85 gallon fuel tank (both these items overhanging at the rear of the subframe and bogie). The engine was arranged so that it projected through the floor of the railcar body to give access for maintenance.

The engine was of the Armstrong-Sulzer type 6LF19, a six-cylinder vertical four stroke unit with a maximum rating of 275 bhp at 1,150 rpm, or 260 bhp at 1,075 rpm. The design of the bogie enabled all the power and auxiliary equipment to be mounted in a sub-frame running throughout the main bogie and to be insulated from the bogie frame itself by resilient rubber mountings. The whole sub-frame was fitted with slinging points to allow its removal for maintenance purposes.

The transmissions of both SLM and Wilson gearboxes had five speeds in both directions, with a top speed of 68 mph. The SLM-Winterthur boxes were made by Armstrong Whitworth at Scotswood. Final drive was by fore and aft cardan shafts to worm gear boxes on both axles of the power bogie, these being by Bostock and Bramley. The SLM gearbox was bolted directly to the sub-frame, but the input shaft from the engine had two universal joints to allow for the vibration of the engine on its rubber mountings. The Wilson gearbox had a three point suspension with rubber mountings attached to the sub-frame – its input shaft, too, having two universal joints. The Vulcan-Sinclair hydraulic coupling unit had an outboard bearing bracketed to the engine. Aft of the gearbox both types of transmissions used identical equipment.

Both gearboxes were electro-pneumatically controlled, but the electro-pneumatic valves were located differently. The SLM one had them on a separate manifold: admitting air to a control cock on the rear of the gearbox and directing oil pressure to respective gear clutches. On the Wilson box, the valves were on the gearbox itself: admitting air directly to the cylinders operating the epicyclic band brakes. The control system was standard, and suited both varieties of transmission to allow full interchange of power units.

In all, eight sets were supplied, plus one spare unit. The work was carried out to the inspection, and under the supervision of Messrs Livesey and Henderson, consulting engineers to Mr W. P. Dakin, Chief Mechanical Engineer of the Central Argentine Railway.

The success of the 1934 articulated diesel electric train *Cometa*, supplied by Armstrong Whitworth to the Sao Paulo Railway, prompted the placing of a further order during 1936. Two non-articulated train sets were ordered, powered by 600 bhp engines, in the summer of 1936. They were close-coupled luxury train sets of semi-streamlined design, comprising one short twin-bogie power vehicle and three passenger vehicles, and seating 134 passengers – as opposed to 100 in the 1934 train. With the pressure-charged engine they had some 33 per cent more power.

Under the supervision of the Sao Paulo Railway consulting engineers, Fox and Mayo, the overall design was carried out by Armstrong Whitworth, who supplied the complete power vehicles, and by Birmingham Carriage & Wagon Co. Ltd, who were given the job of building the carriages. One train was painted blue and named *Estrella* (Star) and the other red and named *Planeta* (Planet); both had cream roofs.

Intended for operation, along with the 1934 train, on the luxury first class passenger traffic between the port of Santos and the city of Sao Paulo they also had to negotiate the celebrated Serra incline by rope haulage. As with the 1934 train, severe restrictions were placed on the design of the train sets and their overall lengths were restricted to not more than 194 feet, with an appoximate weight of 108 tons without passengers and luggage. The top speed was to be 60 mph.

The distance between Santos and Sao Paulo was 49 miles, the summit of the route was 2,600 ft above sea level, and the trains had to run over six chain curves. Each train was formed with a power car at one end, housing the power equipment which supplied power to the two traction motors on this vehicle's bogies and the one on the opposite end coach. Three coaches completed the sets; the outer one was shaped like the power car and provided with a second driving cab.

The power vehicle itself weighed 47 1/2 tons and had an all steel underframe, built in the usual Armstrong Whitworth practice. The superstructure was built upon a light, flanged steel, channel section framework. Front end panelling was of steel but aluminium was used for the roof and side panels to keep weight under control. The bogies themselves were standard Armstrong

An artistically enhanced image of the train set designed for the Sao Paulo Railway. This gives a contemporary impression of the design for these luxury train sets, albeit the power vehicle is possibly not the most pleasing of shapes. *Brian Webb collection*

Whitworth units and accounted for 10¼ tons of the vehicle's weight.

Housed within the power vehicle was also a small buffet and guard's compartment. The roof was removable to allow access to the power equipment. The prime mover was an Armstrong-Sulzer 6LDA25 six-cylinder vertical engine with pressure charging, giving 600 bhp at 750 rpm. A Büchi exhaust-gas turbo charger attached to a seating above the main generator provided the pressure charging.

The engine control system allowed the engine to run at speeds of 450 and 620 rpm with bhp ratings of 203 and 462 respectively. CAV-Bosch fuel injection equipment was fitted.

For the electrical equipment, a return to the English Electric Co. Ltd was made. The equipment included a main generator of six pole type, directly coupled to the diesel engine. It had a continuous rating of 750 A, 525 V at 750 rpm, and a one hour rating at 750 rpm of 850 A, 430 V.

The three traction motors were mounted on the underframes and drove via cardan shafts, each to one axle via a worm reduction gearbox on the axle. The power vehicle had two motors driving the inner axles of the bogies and a third motor driving the inner axle of the bogie at the opposite end of the train. Driving compartments were provided at both ends.

The carriages were built on welded underframes and ran on bogies with individual laminated springs and rubber auxiliaries above Timken roller bearing axleboxes. The bogie bolsters were supported on helical springs. The bodywork was of aluminium on a steel frame, similar to the powerhouse.

In order to maintain a smooth, unbroken external appearance between power car and train a full-width outer vestibule

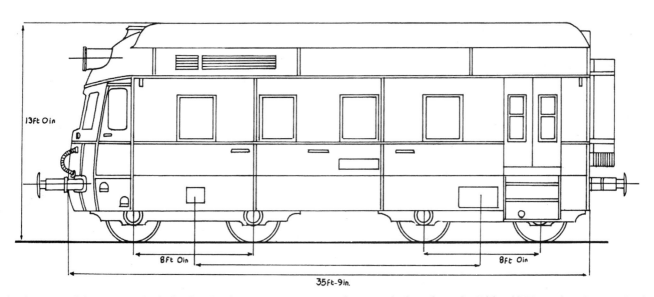

Side elevation of the power vehicle for Sao Paulo train sets *Estrella* and *Planeta* built under order DT73 (AW numbers D71 & D72). Reproduced at 4mm to 1ft. *Brian Webb*

The three Sao Paulo train sets are here grouped together with, from right to left, *Planeta*, *Estrella* (both to order DT73) and *Cometa* (order DT19). The fourth vehicle is a railcar used as an ambulance.

RFFSA, Brazil

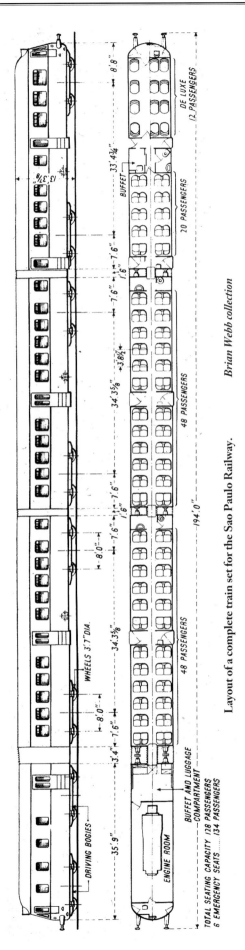

Layout of a complete train set for the Sao Paulo Railway.
Brian Webb collection

sheathing was fitted, to cover the normal coupling arrangement and corridor connection.

Though built under order DT73, some mystery surrounds the construction of these trains. The coaches were all built at Birmingham by the Birmingham Railway Carriage & Wagon Co. Ltd, and this same company may indeed have built the power vehicles also. However, these carried Armstrong Whitworth works numbers D71/2. The lack of surviving records, coupled with the statements of people who worked at Scotswood at the time of the closure to locomotive work seems to indicate that they were probably not built at Scotswood, although the power equipment was tested there.

Another point in this theory is the fact that the train sets were considerably delayed in delivery, so that in spite of assurances in October 1937 of delivery by early 1938, it was not until early autumn 1938 that shipment actually took place from Liverpool.

Estrella entered service on 16th February 1940, and is reported to have worked well until, in April 1960, troubles with engine and drive shafts together with water leakage from the engine became common. These persisted until the 1970s. In 1972 the seating of the train was replaced, and in late 1975 the train was still at work. The remains of the unit could still be seen in Paranapiacaba Yard in 2001.

Planeta entered traffic in December 1939, and ran well until, in August 1946, two piston failures occurred – another followed in May 1948. Crankshaft problems gave troubles during 1960 and 1964. The latter even caused the train to be out of action for some years. By late 1975 the train had been out of service since November 1972. Consideration was being given to possible permanent withdrawal of it and its sister train, due to the increasing expense of maintenance. Indeed, photographic evidence from 1978 shows that the power car was badly damaged at the front end, possibly due to collision but whether this was sustained in service or whilst stored is unknown.

The 'nameplate' of DT73 train set DE No. 2 *Estrella*.
Sergio Martire - A.B.P.F.

Driving trailer of former Sao Paulo Railway train set *Estrella* as Estrada De Ferro Santos A Jundiai DE No. 2 dumped at Lapa Works Sao Paulo in 1978. *Sergio Martire - A.B.P.F.*

The power car of set DE No. 3 *Planeta* could also be found in a badly damaged condition at the same location. *Sergio Martire - A.B.P.F.*

Table 5: Main details and dimensions of single unit railcars built by Armstrong Whitworth.

Order No., AW No.	Axle Layout	Engine Make, Type, bhp	Generator Make	Traction Motor Make	Weight in Working Order	Length	Overall Width	Overall Height	Wheel Diam	Bogie Wheelbase/ Centres	Min Curve Negotiable feet	Max Tractive Effort lbs	Fuel Capacity galls	Seating Capacity	Max. Speed mph
DT1 D1-3	Bo-2	Armstrong-Sulzer 6LD22 250 bhp	LSE	GEC	49T13C3Q	63ft 3in.* 59ft 6in.†	8ft 11¾in.	12ft 8in.	3ft 3in.	8ft 0in. 42ft 0in.	198	6,800	80	60	65
DT12 D11-14	2-A	Armstrong-Saurer 6BLD 100 bhp	LSE	LSE	12T18C	26ft 3⅜in. over couplers 23ft 0in.†	7ft 5⅜in.	10ft 2in.	2ft 0in.	4ft 3in. —	?	3,840	?	6	30
DT16 D15	1A-2	Armstrong-Saurer 6BLD 95 bhp	LSE	LSE	17T13C2Q	53ft 0in.*	8ft 11½in.	11ft 11¼in.	2ft 9in.	7ft 0in. 30ft 0in.	200	2,850	?	57	60
DT31 D37	Bo-2	Armstrong-Saurer 6BXD 122 bhp	LSE	CP	36T18C2Q	56ft 8¾in.* 53ft 0in.†	10ft 7in.	13ft 4in.	3ft 1½in.	7ft 6in. 34ft 0in.	308	6,880	70	48	57
DT34 D39	2-B	Armstrong-Saurer 6BXD 122 bhp	LSE	LSE	13T0C	27ft 9in.* 30ft 1in. over cowcatchers	7ft 6in.	10ft 0³⁄₁₆in.	2ft 0in.	4ft 6in. 15ft 0in.	90	2,900	?	16	25
DT41 D41	1A-2	Armstrong-Saurer 6BXD 140 bhp	LSE	LSE	20T14C	48ft 8⁵⁄₁₆in. over couplers 45ft 0in.†	7ft 6in.	10ft 0in.	2ft 0in.	4ft 6in. 31ft 6in.	330	3,020	60	58	40
DT43 D46-51	1A-2	Armstrong-Saurer 6BXD 140 bhp	LSE	LSE	32T0C	73ft 4in.* 69ft 0in.† 72ft 8in. over body	9ft 9in.	11ft 5⁷⁄₃₂in.	3ft. 0in.	8ft. 0in. 45ft 0in.	573	3,285	60	110	40-45
DT71 D65-70	1A-2	Armstrong-Saurer 6BXD 140 bhp	LSE	LSE	?	52ft 11in. over couplers 60ft 0in.†	9ft 0in.	12ft 0¼in.	2ft 7½in.	6ft 6in. 42ft 0in.	?	?	?	40	40-45

* over buffers
† over bufferbeams

Table 6: **Main details and dimensions of the four articulated, semi-articulated, and close coupled train sets built by Armstrong Whitworth**

Order No., AW No.	Axle layout	Engine make, type, bhp	Generator make	Traction motor make	Individual bogie loading	Length over body	Overall width	Overall height	Wheel diam.	Bogie wheelbase/ centres	Seating capacity	Maximum tractive effort lbs	Fuel cap. galls	Notes
DT19 D16	Bo-2 Power vehicle	Armstrong-Sulzer 6LD25, 450	LSE	CP	Bo: $25^T3^C2^Q$ 2: $22^T4^C2^Q$	25ft 0in.	9ft 6in.	12ft 6in.	4ft 0in. on Bo bogie 3ft 7in. on trailing bogie	8ft 0in. 19ft 0in.	Nil	12,100 includes motor bogie on D19	?	1.
D17	- - 2 No. 1 Carriage articulation to D16	Nil	Nil	Nil	2: $14^T15^C0^Q$	45ft 6½in.	9ft 6in.	12ft 6in.	3ft 7in.	8ft 0in. 37ft 3in	68 2nd class	Nil	?	
D18	2-2 No. 2 carriage	Nil	Nil	Nil	2: $14^T4^C2^Q$ 2: $16^T6^C0^Q$	49ft 6½in.	9ft 6in.	12ft 6in.	3ft 7in.	8ft 0in. 41ft 3in.	52 1st class	Nil	?	
D19	- Bo No. 3 carriage articulated to D18	Nil	Nil	CP	Bo: $17^T11^C0^Q$	49ft 6¼in.	9ft 6in.	12ft 6in.	4ft 0in. on Bo bogie 3ft 7in. on non-power bogie	8ft 0in. 41ft 3in.	48 1st class	combined with D16	?	
DT73 D71/2	1A-A1 Power vehicles Armstrong-Sulzer 6LD25, 600	Armstrong-Sulzer 6LD25, 600	EE	EE	?	35ft 9in.	9ft 7½in.	13ft 11in.	3ft 7in.	8ft 0in. ?	Nil	?	?	2.
Two vehicles	2-2 No. 1 carriage	Nil	Nil	Nil	?	49ft 1½in.	9ft 7½in.	13ft 3⅞in.	3ft 7in.	8ft 0in. 34'3⅝in.	48	Nil	?	
Two vehicles	2-2 No 2 carriage	Nil	Nil	Nil	?	49ft 1½in.	9ft 7½in.	13ft 3⅞in.	3ft 7in.	8ft 0in. 34ft 3⅝in.	48	Nil	?	
Two vehicles	2-A1 No 3 carriage	Nil	Nil	EE	?	49ft 4¾in.	9ft 7½in.	13ft 3⅞in.	3ft 7in.	8ft 0in. 34ft 4¾in.	20 + 12 luxury class	combined with power vehicle	?	
DT30 D35	Bo-2 power vehicle	Armstrong-Sulzer 6LD25, 450	LSE	CP	Bo: $30^T11^C0^Q$ 2: $24^T19^C3^Q$	27ft 9⅞in.	10ft 3⁹⁄₁₆in.	12ft 11in.	3ft 1½in.	8ft 6in. 20ft 0in.	Nil	14,000	220	3.
D36	- - 2 carriage articulation to D35	Nil	Nil	CP	2: $18^T4^C1^Q$	57ft 6⅛in.	10ft 3⁹⁄₁₆in.	12ft 7in.	3ft 1½in.	8ft 6in. 48ft 0in.	50 1st class	combined with D35	Nil	

Table 7: Order and works numbers of diesel electric rail vehicles built by Armstrong Whitworth 1931-1938

Order No.	AW No.	Year	Brief Description of Order	General Comments
DT1	D1 D2 D3	1931 1932 1932	250 bhp twin bogie railcars Bodywork by Cravens Ltd Built for demonstration in UK on LNE, LMSR and SR	D1 named *Tyneside Venturer*, sold to LNE under order DT17. D2 named *Lady Hamilton*, sold to LNE under order DT53. D3 named *Northumbrian*, sold to LNE under order DT53. D3 operated as Armstrong-Shell Express for a short period.
DT3	D4 D5 D6	1933	1,700 bhp twin-unit mobile powerhouses for Buenos Aires Great Southern Rly (BAGSR)	D4 BAGSR No. UE3. D5 BAGSR No. UE4. D6 BAGSR No. UE5.
DT4	D7	1933	1,700 bhp twin-unit main line mixed traffic locomotive for BAGSR	BAGSR No. CM210.
DT7	D8	1932	250 bhp shunting locomotive for demonstration in UK	Demonstrated on L&NER; SR under order DT26; Hartley Main Colliery Railway under order DT47; Lever Bros Ltd, Port Sunlight, under order DL4. Demonstrated and sold to Ribble Navigation Ltd, Preston, under order DT64, named *Duchess*.
DT8	D9	1933	880 bhp main line mixed traffic 'Universal' locomotive for UK	Demonstrated on L&NER under order DT46. Locomotive stored at Scotswood Works and finally scrapped in 1937.
DT11	D10	1932	95 bhp light shunting locomotive for demonstration in UK	Demonstrated at Frodingham Iron & Steel Co., Scunthorpe under order DT21; J. Lyons & Co. Greenford under order DT25; North Eastern Electric Supply Co., Dunston under order DT37; L&NER York under DT38; Rowntree & Co., York under order DT39; North Sunderland Railway under order DT40. Locomotive used as Armstrong Whitworth works shunter until scrapped in 1957.
DT12 D12	D11 1932 D13 D14		100 bhp light locomotive-tractor railcar chassis for Gaekworks Baroda State Rly, India. Bodies and trailer cars built in India. One chassis tested on Leek & Manifold Rly	D11 Baroda State Rlys No. 101 named *Economy*. D12 Baroda State Rlys No. 102. D13 Baroda State Rlys No. 103. D14 Baroda State Rlys No. 104.
DT16	D15	1933	95 bhp twin bogie light railbus for demonstration in UK	Demonstrated on LNE and sold to LNE under order DT51. Bodywork by Park Royal.
DT19	D16 D17 D18 D19	1933	450 bhp semi articulated train set for Sao Paulo Railway, Brazil	Named *Cometa*.
DT20	D20	1934	250 bhp shunting locomotive for LMS	Similar to DT7/D8. LMS No. 7408, later 7058.
DT22	D21	1933	95 bhp light shunting locomotives built for stock and demonstration in UK	D21 demonstrated at North Eastern Electric Supply Co., Dunston, and sold to them under order DT45.
	D22	*		D22 demonstrated at Dornan Long & Co., Middlesbrough under order DT50; Warner & Co., Cargo Fleet, under DT54; demonstrated and sold to a Reyrolle & Co., Hebburn, becoming their No. 2 under DT77 3/37.
	D23	1933		D23 demonstrated at W. D. Royal Engineers, Shoeburyness under DT48; Gas Light & Coke Co., Beckton, under DT57. Demonstrated at Admiralty Chatham Dockyard under DL2 and sold to them under order DT65.
	D24	*		D24 demonstrated at Bass Ratcliff & Gretton Burton-on-Trent under DT49; ICI Ltd metals division, Witton, Birmingham under DT55; Austin Motor Co. Ltd, Birmingham under DL1; Dunlop Rubber Co. Ltd, Birmingham under DL3; Nevills Dock Co., Llanelly under DL5; Bede Metal & Chemical Co., Hebburn under DL6. Demonstrated and sold to Thames Board Mills Ltd, Warrington under order DT76. 02/1937.
	D25 D26	1933 *		D25 sold to North Sunderland Rly under DT42. Named *The Lady Armstrong*. D26 stored at AW Works until sold to Magnesium Elektron Co. Ltd, Manchester under order DT78. 04/1937.
			*D22/4/6 built 1933, dates later removed from plates.	
DT23	D27 D28	1934	880 bhp main line mixed traffic 'Universal' locomotives for demonstration in India	D27 & D28 demonstrated on Ceylon Govt Rlys as CGR 800/1 under order DT59. Returned to UK for reconditioning under DT74. Locomotives sold under DT75 to BAGSR becoming their numbers CM204/5.
	D29 to D34		Cancelled orders, numbers not used.	
DT30	D35 D36	1934	450 bhp twin-unit articulated train with bodywork by Gloucester Railway Carriage & Wagon Co. for Buenos Aires Western Rly (BAWR)	Sold to BAWR under order DT69.

Order No.	AW No.	Year	Brief Description of Order	General Comments
DT31	D37	1934	122 bhp twin bogie railcar with Park Royal bodywork for BAWR	BAWR No. RM230. Sold to BAWR under order DT70.
	D38		Cancelled order, number not used.	
DT34	D39	1934	122 bhp twin bogie railcar with body by Gloucester RC&WCo. for Kalka – Simla section of North Western Railway of India. (NWR)	NWR railmotor No. 14.
DT36	D40	1934	85 bhp shunting locomotive for St. Kitts Basse Terre Sugar Factory, West Indies	Numbered 12.
DT41	D41	1934	122 bhp twin bogie railcar chassis for Central Provinces section of Great Indian Peninsula Rly India. Body built by GIPR in India.	
	D42		Cancelled order, number not used.	
DT43	D46 D47 D48 D49 D50 D51	1934	140 bhp twin bogie railcar chassis for Madras and Southern Mahratta Rly India. Bodywork built in India.	
DT44	D43	1933	122 bhp shunting locomotive for Ceylon Govt Railway (CGR)	CGR No. 500.
DT51	D44 D45	1935	1,200 bhp main line mixed traffic locomotives for North Western Railway of India (NWR)	D44 NWR No. 332. D45 NWR No. 333. Both locomotives power equipment returned to UK for modifications but not carried out. Mechanical parts scrapped in India.
DT60	D52	1935	100 bhp shunting locomotive for Penang Harbour Board, Straits Settlements.	
DT61	D53	1935	60 bhp shunting locomotive for Penmaenmawr & Welsh Granite Co.	Named *Alice*.
DT63	D54 D55 D56 D57 D58 D59 D60 D61 D62 D63	1935	400 bhp shunting locomotives for LMS	D54-D63 LMS numbers 7059-68.
DT68	D64	1936	400 bhp shunting locomotive for Bombay, Baroda & Central India Rly (BBCIR)	BBCIR No. DE800.
DT71	D65 D66 D67 D68 D69 D70	1936	140 bhp twin bogie railcars for Western Australian Govt Rlys. Six chassis, one complete Park Royal built body and five body kits supplied	Numbered and named: 446 *Governor Stirling* 447 *Governor Lawley* 448 *Governor Hutt* 449 *Governor Weld* 450 *Governor Hampton* 451 *Governor Bedford*
DT73	D71 D72	1937/8 1937/8	600 bhp twin bogie power cars for use with three car train sets built by Birmingham Railway Carriage & Wagon Co. Ltd. For Sao Paulo Rly, Brazil	Named *Estrella* and *Planeta*.

ARMSTRONG WHITWORTH DIESELS IN COLOUR

COMPILED BY DAVID KELSO

The late Brian Webb completed his manuscript in 1979 when the world of railway book publishing was far different from what has become the norm today. There was very little colour photography in railway publications at that time and it is clear that the book was planned as a black and white production. Brian's original text was supplemented by a host of black and white material both photographs and diagrams. These have been reproduced where Brian noted they should be placed within the text.

We did not know whether any original colour photographs of Armstrong Whitworth locomotives exist. It was thought to be unlikely as very few railway photographers were using colour film when the locomotives and railcars were in service. Also in 1979 the British railway preservation movement was a very small part of what it is today and there was even less preservation activity overseas. Brian makes reference more than once in the text that a particular locomotive or railcar is destined for preservation.

This then begs the question in 2010: Which, if any, Armstrong Whitworth locomotives and railcars survive today and where are they located? Are there working examples or perhaps just static exhibits at a preservation site or in a local, national railway or transport museum?

In an attempt to bring the story up to date the RCTS has used its extensive contacts worldwide to try and establish the true position. The results of this research are presented in the following pages to compliment Brian's original work. It goes without saying that if any reader can add to or update the information presented here both the RCTS and Lightmoor Press would be delighted to hear from you so that any future edition of the book can be brought up to date. Information can be sent by e-mail or letter to either or both of the addresses shown in the front of the book.

Acknowledgements

The RCTS and Lightmoor Press are very appreciative of the help received from many people in our search for equipment still in existence and for colour photographs. The Internet also played a part. In addition to the photographers we particularly wish to thank Alan Thompson and Peter Weightman of the Tanfield Railway, Paul Jarman, Keeper of Transport at Beamish Museum, Colin Churcher, Roger Darsley, Bob Ellison, Dr. David Hyatt and Eric Palmer for up to date information regarding India, Sri Lanka and St. Kitts. Also anybody else who we have overlooked.

THE TANFIELD RAILWAY, MARLEY HILL, GATESHEAD, COUNTY DURHAM, UK.
ARMSTRONG WHITWORTH NO. D22
STANDARD GAUGE 95HP 0-4-0 DIESEL-ELECTRIC SHUNTER OF 1933

On a cold November morning D22 stands at Andrews House station platform. *Peter Weightman*

D22 was used as a demonstration locomotive at both Dorman Long & Co. Ltd, Middlesborough and at Warner & Co. Ltd, Cargo Fleet until sold in 1937 to A. Reyrolle & Co. Ltd. Its duties included work at both of the rail connected plants in Hebburn and it worked between the two works along the L&NER South Tyneside line. At some time, perhaps the late 1940s, the original Armstrong Saurer engine gave trouble and was replaced with a Gardner 6LW. In December 1970 it was sold to W. F. & J. R. Shepherd Ltd and transported to their Byker, Newcastle, scrapyard and used to shunt that yard. It went into disuse and then had its wiring and some of its switchgear and brushes stolen. Mr Stanley Weightman sought to purchase it, having recollections of the North Sunderland Railway example, D25, from when he lived for a while at Bamburgh. D22 was partly buried in scrap but was purchased and recovered in July 1978 when it was delivered to the Tanfield Railway. Stan Weightman restored it with assistance of workers at Marley Hill. Much of the sheet metal superstructure had to be replaced due to having been crushed in the scrapyard, the engine unit was removed and overhauled, generator overhauled, brush gear replaced, wiring, switchgear and resistances replaced, radiator replaced etc. Details of the exact livery were hard to establish so the loco was painted black with the number 2 - its Reyrolle number. Vacuum brake equipment was fitted to permit haulage of passenger trains. During repair, efforts were made to obtain original information concerning the design. The makers of the traction motor and generator, Laurence Scott Electromotors, were very helpful and provided replacement brush gear and confirmed some wiring details of the original batch D21 to D26. A specification sheet (from AW?) for Order No. DT22 was obtained from a third party. This sheet shows all the batch to have been practically identical. The only exception being the North Sunderland Railway locomotive had a larger battery, train lighting equipment and Westinghouse air brake equipment extended for the train brakes. That they were all designed for 30 mph speed is confirmed by the original notice still written in D22's cab: 'MAXIMUM SPEED 30 MPH'. The locomotive has been used extensively at the Tanfield Railway over the last twenty five years or so and continues to undertake shunting on several days every week. It may now be reasonably said to be the oldest diesel electric locomotive in regular use anywhere in the world.

D22, Tanfield Railway No. 2 shunts the goods yard at Marley Hill during the Legends of Industry Gala, 11th/12th September 2009.
David Ford

No. 2 shunts the passenger stock at Marley Hill carriage sheds on 23rd May 2010 as it does every Sunday morning during the railway operating season.
Alan Thompson

BEAMISH MUSEUM, BEAMISH, COUNTY DURHAM UK
ARMSTRONG WHITWORTH NO. D21
STANDARD GAUGE 95HP 0-4-0 DIESEL-ELECTRIC SHUNTER OF 1933

Looking resplendent D21 stands outside the shed at Beamish Museum. *Paul Jarman, Beamish Museum*

D21 was the first of the batch of five 0-4-0 shunters to be sold in 1934 and was bought by the North Eastern Electricity Supply Company, Dunston Green Power Station. Its history is well documented in the chapter entitled 'The 0-4-0 Shunters'. After restoration it was exhibited at the National Railway Museum at York in 1978. Since then a further restoration was carried at York in 2004 and the locomotive was present at the opening of 'Locomotion' at Shildon in September of that year. The move to Beamish Museum took place in 2008 and D21 still resides there at the time of writing.

The rear of D21 showing the gearbox cover. *Terry Pinnegar*

INDIAN RAILWAYS, RAIL TRANSPORT MUSEUM, CHANKYAPURI, NEW DELHI–110021, INDIA.
ARMSTRONG WHITWORTH NO. D39
2FT 6IN. GAUGE 122HP DIESEL-ELECTRIC RAILCAR OF 1934

D39, Kalka-Simla Railway railcar No. 14 stands outside the Indian Railways Museum in New Dehli. *Bob Ellison*

The story of the North Western Railway's Kalka - Simla railway No. 14 is fully described in the chapter entitled 'Railcars for India' and Brian Webb indicates in his final paragraph that it was due to find a place in the Indian Railways collection for preservation. The Indian Railways Rail Transport Museum was six years in the making and opened its doors on the 1st February 1977. According to a museum catalogue, published in 1992 and obtained by two RCTS members during a visit at that time, the museum building houses only the smaller artifacts and models. The heavier rolling stock exhibits being displayed outside. Unfortunately No. 14 fell into the latter category and the catalogue contains a picture and brief details of No. 14 showing it as an outside exhibit. Subsequently an RCTS member visited the museum seventeen years later in March 2009 and was able to obtain this photograph of No. 14 still outside looking in need of some tender loving care but never the less it appears intact 75 years after delivery.

CEYLON GOVERNMENT RAILWAYS (SRI LANKA RAILWAYS), SRI LANKA
ARMSTRONG WHITWORTH NO. D43
5FT 6IN. GAUGE 122HP 0-4-0 DIESEL-ELECTRIC SHUNTER OF 1934

No. 500 shunting in the works yard at Ratmalana in 1999. *John Polley*

D43 was classified G1 by the Ceylon Government Railways and accorded No. 500. It was delivered to the main workshops of the CGR at Ratmalana where it entered service and acted as the yard shunter and appears to have remained there for all its working life. Latterly it was taken in hand by apprentices at the workshops and its restoration and upkeep has been part of the Sri Lankan Railways apprentice training programme.

In this photograph, taken in 2002, No. 500 is shown after restoration standing in the yard at Ratmalana workshops. *David Hyatt*

ST KITTS SUGAR MANUFACTURING CORPORATION, BASSETERRE, ST KITTS.
ARMSTRONG WHITWORTH NO. D40
2FT 6IN. GAUGE 85HP 0-4-0 DIESEL-ELECTRIC SHUNTER OF 1934

This picture, taken in 1984, shows No. 12 coupled to one of the passenger coaches used on the system. *Roger Darsley*

The centuries old sugar industry of St Kitts built a centralised sugar processing mill at Basseterre in 1912 together with an extensive 2ft 6in. railway system to haul the sugar cane from the many estates to the mill. Steam began to be replaced in the 1930s and D40 arrived as part of the steam replacement programme. D40 was accorded running No. 12 and worked on the main lines to the fields and also the harbour branch with the refined sugar and molasses for export.

The sugar industry in St Kitts latterly became uncompetitive and was closed down completely in July 2005. It is planned to open a sugar industry museum on the island and it hoped that it will contain D40, plus an armoured Motor Rail locomotive from WWI and the last steam locomotive to work on the railway. A visitor in April 2010 reported that D40 was safely locked up under cover in a shed.

No. 12 was confined to working the harbour branch only when this picture was taken, in May 1983 at Basseterre. *Colin Churcher*

LONDON MIDLAND & SCOTTISH RAILWAY UK ARMSTRONG WHITWORTH NO. D20
STANDARD GAUGE 250HP 0-6-0 DIESEL ELECTRIC SHUNTER

Brian Webb's records clearly identify WD 883 as D58, ex-LMS 7063. The background to the picture and the tall chimneys suggests that it was taken shortly after the locomotive arrived at the CEGB Hams Hall power station in 1966.

We had hoped to be able to conclude with a picture of D20, LMS No. 7408 (later renumbered 7059) but its withdrawal in 1949 did not offer much opportunity for colour photography. We are lucky to have two rather poor unidentified colour prints of the later batch of ten 350/400HP locomotives D54 to D63 supplied to the LMS in 1936.

Note: Colour prints 40-50 years old do not hold their original colour well but as these locomotivee were the precursors of the largest design of diesel electric 0-6-0 shunters built for the British railway system in the 20th century it was felt these very rare colour photographs, possibly taken by Brian Webb, were worthy of inclusion.

The number at the bottom of the cab side appears to be 882. From Brian's records this would be D57 ex-LMS 7062. The track and locomotive indicate this is in continental Europe and the broken cab window suggests that the locomotive is standing disused somewhere in West Germany. It was reported as still extant in 1976 when it was offered for sale at 20,000 DM.

PROPOSED DESIGNS AND THE END

Locomotive and rolling stock manufacturers prepare many design proposals to meet enquiries, and for submission as competitive tendering. In some cases these design proposals are unsuccessful, getting no further than the drawing board, and Armstrong Whitworth were no exception in this respect.

Study of the works number list used for the diesel electric rail vehicles built by Armstrong Whitworth reveals some gaps, these being due to allocating numbers to proposed designs and cancelled orders.

Only a few of the actual designs of the design proposals of the Diesel Traction Dept have so far come to light, some of these are reproduced here. The diesel locomotive drawing register does still survive, but it only gives the briefest of details, a selection from this can be found in Table 8.

South American work included Bo-Bo 450 bhp Sulzer/English Electric equipped branch line locomotives weighing 54 1/4 tons for the Buenos Aires Great Southern Railway. These were to employ bogies of Saccaggio type, as fitted to the 1,700 bhp units of orders DT3 and DT4.

The Sao Paulo Railway had proposals for diesel electric train sets and mobile powerhouses. Drawing LD901 (E181) was for a twin-bogie unit powerhouse, fitted with two Sulzer LTD25 engines and Crompton Parkinson generators and Laurence, Scott & Electromotors frame-mounted traction motors, which drove by cardan shaft to the axles of the bogies. This was to weigh about 53 tons.

Armstrong Whitworth never built diesels for South Africa, but a number of designs were prepared for South African Railways. These ranged from a 65 ton Bo-Bo shunting locomotive with the Sulzer 6LD25 engine and four axle-hung traction motors, to an interesting articulated train set under drawing LD861. This three-car articulated train, seating 150 passengers, weighed 105 1/2 tons and was to be powered by two Sulzer LD25 engines. Electrical equipment was to be by Laurence, Scott & Electromotors, which meant frame-mounted traction motors and cardan shaft drives to the axles.

The Eastern Bengal Railway, India, considered a design of suburban railcar for Calcutta suburban duties with the Sulzer 6LTD19 engine and Laurence, Scott & Electromotors transmission. This vehicle, design LD1005, was to seat 88 passengers, with a service weight of 46 tons.

The incidence of mechanical transmissions among Armstrong Whitworth's work is low. One such design was for a 32 1/2 tons twin-bogie, power-bogie railcar with a Saurer BXD engine and SLM transmissions, for the North Western Railway of India. This was design LD1071 (E1030).

Design LD1078 (E1048) of October 1936 was for a Bo-Bo Sulzer/English Electric equipped shunter for Victorian Government Railways, Australia, weighing 59 tons.

The London Underground considered a Bo-Bo diesel electric of 46 tons weight, powered by a Sulzer 6LTD22 engine. This was design LD1055.

With British requirements under consideration, we come to what was perhaps the most interesting of Armstrong Whitworth's proposals: Great Western Railway investigations into alternatives to steam traction during the late 1920s and early 1930s. The study considered forms of diesel traction with mechanical, hydraulic, electric, and compressed-air transmissions, together with battery and geared steam systems. The resulting document brought together a wide selection of data covering the products of manufacturers world wide. The GWR motive power committee was able to select designs for direct comparison to their standard steam locomotive classes.

Armstrong Whitworth proposals included locomotives of existing designs, either already built or under construction. These were the DT1 railcar; DT3 1,700 bhp mobile powerhouses; DT4 1,700 bhp main line locomotive; DT7 250 bhp shunter; DT8 1-Co-1 880 bhp 'Universal' main line locomotive; and the DT16 railbus. In addition, Armstrong Whitworth supplied drawings, specifications, and design performance profiles for a variety of diesel electrics. These, however, did not include further main line units, although similar submissions by other manufacturers did.

Considering railcars first: there were three variants of the DT1 type which used the same mechanical design, but had a driving cab at the engine room end only. This indicated that the vehicles were intended as haulage units, corroborated by the high engine power installed. All were quoted for supply without the coach body portions.

Design LD322 was of 250 bhp, was similar to DT1, and described as comparable to the GWR steam railcars. The 350 bhp example (drawing LD270) had the same six-cylinder Sulzer engine and axle-hung traction motors on both axles of the bogie at the cab end. With an estimated weight of 53 1/2 tons, they were priced at £8,225 or, if twelve were purchased, £7,445 each.

With the eight-cylinder 450 bhp Sulzer engineered version, an auxiliary Saurer powered generating set was fitted and the two traction motors were fitted on the remote bogie. Apart from the bogie wheelbase of 8ft 9in. and wheels of 3ft 6in. diameter, this design (LD275) was similar to its compatriots with the following dimensions:

Length over headstocks	59ft 9in.
Bogie centres	42ft 0in.
Bogie wheelbase	8ft 0in.
Wheel diameter	3ft 3in.

Notes for table opposite:
1. Total train length 174 feet. Total train weight 109 tons. Driving cabs in power and trailing vehicle. Max speed 60 mph.
2. Total train length 192ft 8 4/12 in. Total train weight lost. Driving cabs in power and in trailing vehicles. Max speed 60 mph.
3. Total train length over headstocks 89ft 10in. Total train weight 74 tons. Driving cabs in power and trailer. Max speed 72 mph.

Lightweight railcars involved two simple Armstrong-Saurer powered vehicles. The smaller one was inspired by the Baroda cars of order DT12. This was design LD373, with a 2-A axle layout. The engine/generator set was mounted transversely at the cab and over the carrying bogie. The single Laurence, Scott & Electromotors traction motor was frame-mounted, and drove via cardan shaft to the fixed single axle. With a weight of 19½ tons it seated 40 passengers.

LD238 was a twin-bogie vehicle with the same type of engine, but with a pair of axle-hung traction motors on the bogie under the engine compartment. With a weight of 30 tons it seated 48 passengers.

Multiple-unit train sets were prominent in the GWR proposals, and Armstrong Whitworth put forward their designs for the Paddington suburban duties.

LD268 was a design for an articulated twin-unit, formed of a short power vehicle articulated to a coach portion. This was to have a 600 bhp Sulzer eight-cylinder engine, Laurence, Scott & Electromotors generator, and four axle-hung Crompton Parkinson traction motors carried on the outer bogies. With a weight of 79 tons it had the following main details:

Length over headstocks	77ft 7in.
Bogie centres	21ft 3in. and 40ft 7in.
Bogie wheelbase	8ft 0in.
Wheel diameter	3ft 3in.
Tractive effort	16,000 lbs
Top speed	65 mph
Seating capacity (coach portion)	70
Cost, chassis only, one	£12,835
Cost, chassis only, twelve	£12,155 each

The 800 bhp version of the above was specifically for a high-speed Paddington-Slough surburban service. In common with the 600 bhp unit, it was intended to operate with four intermediate coaches between two articulated units. A 1,600 bhp train, seating 470 passengers would result. Comparison with GWR 2-6-2Ts of '51xx' and '61xx' classes and their performance indicated the superiority of diesel electric traction. Although similar to the 600 bhp units, the 800 bhp example weighed 84 tons in working order, 76½ tons empty:

Length over headstocks	78ft 7in.
Bogie centres	21ft 3in. and 40ft 7in.
Bogie wheelbase	8ft 0in.
Wheel diameter	3ft 3in.
Maximum height	12ft 11in.
Seating capacity	70
Top speed	65 mph
Cost, chassis only, one	£13,500
Cost, chassis only, twelve	£12,900 each
Cost, with body, one	£14,400

On the line-service side, only one new Armstrong Whitworth design was proposed. The origin of this unusual design must surely have come from Swindon, for it would seem strange for any other railway to require a branch line, mixed traffic locomotive of 0-4-4 layout. The design, LD351, probably suited the idiosyncratic Swindon traditions, which resulted in 0-4-2Ts being built in the 1930s and large orders for 0-6-0Ts in 1947 – long after other railways had lost interest in such items. The locomotive was to use the Armstrong Sulzer 250 bhp six-cylinder engine running at 775 rpm. The directly coupled generator supplied current to one frame-mounted traction motor, with final drive by jackshaft and siderods. It was capable of duties similar to those undertaken by GWR '56xx' Class

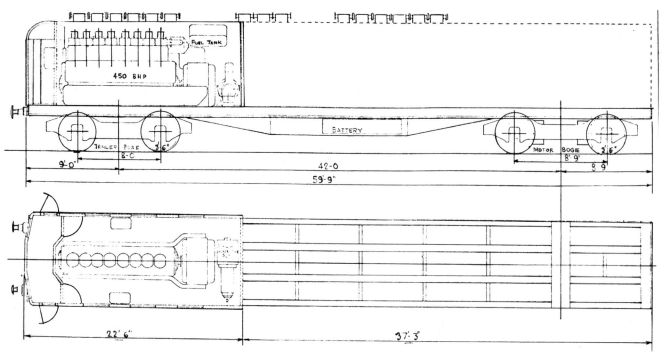

Design for a 450 bhp diesel electric power car for Great Western Railway suburban services. *Brian Webb collection*

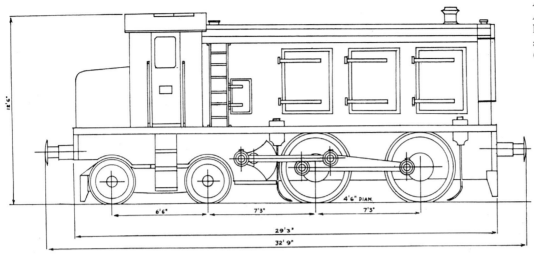

A most unusual proposal. An 0-4-4 DE branch line locomotive of 250 bhp, again intended for the GWR.
Brian Webb collection

0-6-2Ts and '54xx' Class 0-6-0Ts. A 5ft 3in. gauge version was also on offer to other railways. The main details were:

Weight	40 tons
Length over buffers	32ft 9in.
Length over headstocks	29ft 9in.
Coupled wheelbase	7ft 3in.
Bogie wheelbase	6ft 6in.
Total wheelbase	21ft 0in.
Height over cab	12ft 6in.
Driving wheel diameter	4ft 6in.
Maximum tractive effort	13,300 lbs
Cost, one	£7,094
Cost, twelve	£6,420 each

Diesel electric shunting designs from Armstrong Whitworth totalled four within the 80-350 bhp range. These designs may not have been produced specifically for GWR needs, but they were part of their submissions.

LD338 was the smaller of two 0-4-0 locomotives, powered by an Armstrong-Saurer six-cylinder engine of 80-95 bhp driving a Laurence, Scott and Electromotors generator and one frame-mounted traction motor, which was located behind the cab above a jackshaft final drive unit with side rods to the wheels.

Weight	20 tons
Length over buffers	18ft 9in.
Length over bufferbeams	15ft 9in.
Wheelbase	6ft 0in.
Wheel diameter	3ft 3in.
Height over cab	11ft 0in.
Maximum tractive effort	16,000 lbs
Cost, one	£3,429
Cost, twelve	£3,108 each

This machine was compared to the GWR '1101' Class 0-4-0T.

Two larger shunters of 0-6-0 layout were considered, and were unusual in having a rear-mounted final drive/jackshaft unit – for all 0-6-0 DE units built by Armstrong Whitworth had the jackshaft located within their rigid baseline.

The smaller unit, LD303, was to have the Armstrong-Sulzer six-cylinder 250 bhp engine running at 775 rpm. The generator and traction motor were to be of Laurence, Scott & Electromotors make.

Weight	40 tons
Length over bufferbeams	24ft 0in.
Wheelbase	12ft 0in.
Wheel diameter	3ft 6in.
Height over cab	12ft 3in.
Maximum tractive effort	24,000 lbs
Cost, one	£6,440
Cost, twelve	£5,685 each

LD316 was similar to the above design generally, but had a 350 bhp engine.

Weight	50 tons
Length over bufferbeams	25ft 0in.
Wheelbase	12ft 0in.
Wheel diameter	3ft 6in.
Weight over cab	12ft 3in.
Maximum tractive effort	30,000 lbs
Cost, one	£8,591
Cost, twelve	£7,836 each

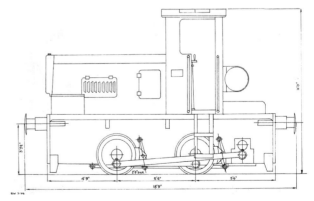

Intended to replace the GWR '1361' Class 0-6-0ST locomotives was this 80-95 bhp 0-4-0 DE.
Brian Webb collection

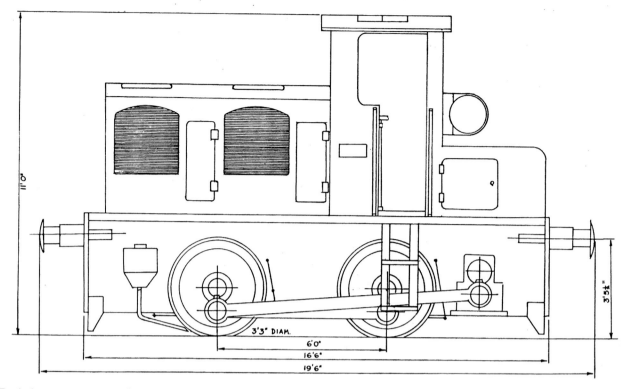

Above: With a pair of transversely mounted diesel/generator sets this 0-4-0 DE design was of 160-195 bhp and said to be equivalent to the GWR '1101' Class 0-4-0T. *Brian Webb collection*

Both locomotives were fitted with chimneys incorporating silencers. LD303 was compared to the GWR 0-6-0T of the '57xx' Class.

It is unfortunate that the GWR Locomotive Committee saw fit to reject dieselisation, as it did the Merz and McLellan electrification scheme.

The following table demonstrated the scope of diesel motive power proposed by UK manufacturers to the GWR:

Manufacturer	Shunters (bhp)	Main line locomotive (bhp)	Railcars (bhp)	Train sets (bhp)
Armstrong Whitworth	80-350	880-1700	80-450	600-800
William Beardmore & Co.	300	360-1300	200	---
Harland & Wolff Ltd	120-300	900-2200	200	900
Beyer Peacock & Co. Ltd and GEC Ltd	450	---	---	---
Metropolitan Vickers Ltd	500	---	---	---
Birmingham Railway Carriage & Wagon Co. Ltd	---	---	70-175	---
Clayton Equipment Co. Ltd	---	---	65-250	---
Ransomes & Rapier Ltd	60-90	---	---	---
John Fowler & Co. Ltd	70-300	---	---	---
W. G. Bagnall Ltd	106/128	---	---	---

Armstrong Whitworth made a brave start with its 1,700 bhp main line locomotives for the BAGSR, but it was no doubt due to Saccaggio that bogie locomotives and powerhouses were built rather than plate-framed locomotives. They did not learn this lesson, for all their subsequent main line units had rigid plate-frames – due possibly to the steam 'bias' held by the mechanical design staff – and the performance of these locomotives fell very short. To be fair, the locomotive manufacturers in many other countries fell into the same trap, some indeed trying jackshaft and siderod drive for main line diesels, an affectation *not* indulged in by Scotswood.

The work of Armstrong Whitworth in diesel traction did not prove at all successful financially, due to the lack of a home market for diesel vehicles on our steam-bound railways. Much of the earlier work completed was in demonstration units, which it was hoped would stimulate interest, but failed, with the result that prototypes were sold at low prices to dispose of them, or put into store awaiting a buyer.

Many small orders involved high development costs with low return. Larger orders came too late: for when the Diesel Traction Department was 'just rounding the corner' and receiving its first bulk orders, such as ten 0-6-0 shunters for the LMS and six

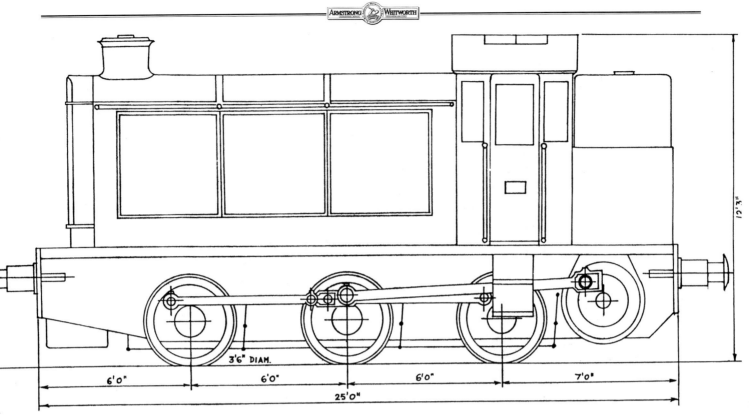

A 350 bhp 0-6-0 DE design for the GWR to replace their ubiquitous '57xx' Class 0-6-0PT design. *Brian Webb collection*

railcars for Australia, financial considerations came to the fore. The origin of the financial problems went back to the division of the armament work to Vickers-Armstrongs Ltd after the end of the 1914-18 war, leaving Armstrong Whitworth to carry on with general engineering. In 1937, with clouds on the horizon due to German militarism and little future prospect of profitability in railway work, Armstrong Whitworth decided to close down just when the Australian railcars were on test.

All railway work was to be completed, but any enquiries in progress were stopped immediately and the Scotswood erecting shop and associated buildings taken over by the government, who promptly leased them to Vickers-Armstrongs and the task of converting the works to armament work was begun. The larger order for LMS Class 5 4-6-0s was finished in 1937 and, as the last locomotives were leaving the erecting shop pits, Vickers were filling them in with concrete.

News of closure broke on 12th January 1937, and was partly due to an agreement between the Locomotive Manufacturers' Association of Great Britain to limit capacity for locomotive work – three works closing down due to this: Armstrong Whitworth; Kitson & Co. Ltd of Leeds; and Nasmyth, Wilson & Co. Ltd of Patricroft. So, a firm 'twenty years ahead of its time' regrettably closed down. Once again the lack of money, interest, and the hostilities of war had combined to set back British pioneers into the oil-engined locomotive and railcar. Inevitably one must ask – how different would be the position of the UK railway industry have been if this work had continued?

In 1931 the Armstrong Whitworth group consisted of the parent,

Armstrong Whitworth Securities Co. Ltd, controlling:

- Sir W. G. Armstrong, Whitworth and Co. (engineers) Ltd.
  Scotswood Works, Newcastle-upon-Tyne.
  Locomotives, Marine engines, General engineering.

- Controlling: Spencer-Hopwood Boilers Ltd.
  Dry back return tube boilers and spares.

- Associated company: British Isothermos Co. Ltd.
  Isothermos railway axleboxes.

- Sir W. G. Armstrong, Whitworth and Co. (Shipbuilders) Ltd.
  Walker and Willington Quay Shipyards.
  Builders of mercantile vessels of every type.

- Sir W. G. Armstrong, Whitworth and Co. (Iron founders) Ltd.
  Close Foundry, Gateshead.
  Iron castings up to 32 tons and refined pig irons.

- Craven Brothers (Manchester) Ltd.
  Reddish, near Stockport.
  Railway and general machine tools, cranes, etc.

Table 8: **Selected list of design proposals for diesel and electric vehicles carried out by the Diesel Traction Department of Armstrong Whitworth**

DRG No.	Date	Description	Gauge	Enquiry
LD147	07.07.30	DE trains, power units both ends	Std	LNER
LD169	14.10.30	850HP articulated passenger unit	Std	SR
LD170	14.10.30	900HP twin engine bogie locomotive	Std	SR
LD184	27.11.30	0-Eo-0 DE locomotive	-	Broken Hill Proprietary, Australia
LD190	04.12.30	850HP DE conversion of Newport-Shildon electric locomotive	Std	LNER
LD194	09.12.30	250HP Bo-Bo DE locomotive	-	Chilean State Rlys
LD199	16.12.30	160HP 0-4-0 + 0-4-0 locomotive	3ft 0in.	Clogher Valley Rly
LD252	18.12.30	350HP DE shunter	Std	LMS
LD260	15.01.31	850HP Bo-Bo DE mixed-traffic locomotive	Std	LNER
LD261	15.01.31	850HP 1-Co-1 DE mixed-traffic locomotive	Std	LNER
LD262	15.01.31	850HP 1-Co-1 DE mixed-traffic locomotive	Std	LNER
LD269	30.01.31	1-Co DE shunter		Broken Hill Proprietary, Australia
LD361	17.07.31	600HP Bo-Bo DE mixed-traffic locomotive	3ft 6in.	New Zealand Govt Rlys
LD366	11.08.31	180HP 0-6-0 DE	Std	Ford Motor Co. Ltd
LD373	31.08.31	80HP 6 wheel railcar	3ft 0in.	Londonderry & Lough Swilly Rly
LD376	10.09.31	750HP 1-C-1 DE locomotive	5ft 6in.	Haifa-Baghdad Rly
LD377	14.09.31	750HP Bo-Bo DE locomotive	5ft 6in.	Haifa-Baghdad Rly
LD378	17.09.31	750HP 2 Bo-1 DE locomotive	5ft 6in.	Haifa-Baghdad Rly
LD389	14.10.31	450HP 0-6-2 DE shunter	5ft 6in.	Tata Iron Co., India
LD390	23.10.31	850HP 1A-A-A1 DE locomotive	5ft 6in.	Indian State Rlys
LD446	10.02.32	250HP Bo-Bo DE mixed traffic locomotive	Std	Bermuda Rly
LD458	31.03.32	2 x 80 HP 0-4-2 DE locomotive	2ft 6in.	Eastern Bengal Rly
LD465	20.04.32	80HP 4 wheel railcar	5ft 3in.	Belfast & County Down Rly
LD470	22.04.32	600HP 2-Co-1 DE passenger locomotive	M	Mysore Rly
LD471	22.04.32	450HP 1-Co-1 DE locomotive	M	Mysore Rly
LD472	22.04.32	2 x 130HP DE locomotive	M	Mysore Rly
LD491	31.05.32	1,200HP 1-Do-1 DE locomotive	Std	GWR
LD493	07.06.32	800HP 1-Do-1 DE locomotive	M	Iraq Rlys
LD503	17.06.32	600HP 1-Co-1 DE locomotive	M	Malaya Railways
LD505	23.06.32	2 x 450HP 2-Do-2 DE locomotive	M	Malaya Railways
LD509	28.06.32	1,200HP 1-Do-1 DE passenger locomotive	Std	GWR
LD510	28.06.32	1,200HP 2-Do-1 DE passenger locomotive	Std	GWR
LD517	20.07.32	2 x 6BLD engine 1-Bo DE mixed traffic	5ft 3in.	Belfast & County Down Rly
LD523	22.07.32	6BLD two axle rail car	Std	SR
LD537	20.09.32	50HP DE railbus. 26 seats.	2ft 6in.	Great Indian Peninsula Rly
LD538	08.09.32	Worm drive twin bogie battery locomotive	2ft 6in.	Upnor-Lodge Hill Rly
LD541	15.09.32	DE and battery 0-4-0 locomotive	2ft 6in.	Upnor-Lodge Hill Rly
LD543	20.09.32	8DHP railcar	2ft 6in.	Sierra Leone
LD546	28.09.32	2 x 6BLD 0-4-0 DE freight locomotive	3ft 0in.	British Phosphates Co.
LD550	07.10.32	DE worm drive bogie locomotive	2ft 0in.	Ashanti Goldfields Corp
LD556	03.11.32	2 x B x D 0-4-0 + 0-4-0 DE locomotive	1ft 11½in.	Festiniog Rly
LD566	24.11.32	2 x B x D 0-4-0 + 0-4-0 DE locomotive	2ft 6in.	Upnor-Lodge Hill Rly
LD569	29.11.32	2 x 800HP 1-Co-1+1-Co-1 DE locomotive	5ft 6in.	South America
LD580	20.12.32	B x D DE+battery locomotive 43 ton shunter	Std	Exide Battery Co. for GWR
LD587	11.01.33	1,600HP 2-Do-2 DE mixed traffic locomotive	5ft 6in.	Indian State Rly
LD588	13.01.33	1,600HP 2-Co-2 DE passenger locomotive	5ft 6in.	Indian State Rly
LD599	27.01.33	DM 4 wheel inspection car	2ft 6in.	Baroda State Rly
LD604	06.02.33	2 x BLD 25 ton shunting locomotive	Std	Steel Peech and Tozer
LD608	17.02.33	330HP 2-4-0+0-4-2 DE Garratt Type Locomotive	2ft 6in.	Kalka Simla Rly
LD610	20.02.33	450HP 2-6-0+0-6-2 DE Garratt Type Locomotive	2ft 6in.	Kalka Simla Rly
LD613	02.03.33	8LDA28 2-Bo DE powerhouse	Std	LNER (Newcastle-South Shields)
LD618	17.03.33	250HP twin car railcar	Std	LMSR
LD619	17.03.33	330HP three car railcar	Std	LMSR
LD620	20.03.33	4 x BXD 1-Co-1 DE mixed traffic locomotive	3ft 6in.	Nigerian Rlys
LD621	27.03.33	8LD31 2-Bo-1 DE powerhouse	Std	LNER (Newcastle-South Shields)
LD624	04.04.33	900HP DE train set	Std	LNER (Newcastle-South Shields)
LD625	06.04.33	1,000HP 2-Co-1 DE suburban locomotive	Std	LNER (Newcastle-South Shields)
LD634	06.05.33	BXD DM railbus	Std	Egyptian State Rly

LD635	10.05.33	BXD rack and adhesion railcar 30 seats	Std	Transandine Rly
LD645	02.06.33	6LD25 2-4-0+0-4-2 DE locomotive	2ft 6in.	Kalka-Simla Rly
LD646	08.06.33	rebuild of battery locomotive to DE locomotive	Std	Newcastle Electric Supply
LD647	09.06.33	BLD railbus	3ft 0in.	County Donegal Rly
LD665	13.07.33	B-B DE shunting locomotive 10 tons	1ft 6in.	Royal Arsenal Rly, Woolwich
LD667	19.07.33	250HP 0-6-0 DE shunter	Std	Hong Kong
LD668	19.07.33	250HP Bo-Bo DE shunter 40 tons	Std	Hong Kong
LD669	21.07.33	450HP 0-6-0+0-6-0 DE hump shunter	5ft 6in.	Madras & Southern Mahratta Rly
LD670	21.07.33	450HP 0-8-0 DE 70 ton hump shunter	5ft 6in.	Madras & Southern Mahratta Rly
LD679	13.08.33	600HP 6LD28 2-Co-2 DE locomotive	M	Malayan Rly
LD687	29.08.33	1,000HP bogie DE locomotive	Std	Haifa-Baghdad Rly
LD709	16.10.33	4 wheel electric trolley/cable mining locomotive	2ft 6in.	Northern India Salt Sources
LD712	18.10.33	Electric and DE mining locomotive	2ft 6in.	Northern India Salt Sources
LD717	06.11.33	BXD 0-4-0 DE locomotive	2ft 0in.	Great Boulder Gold Mine
LD727	20.11.33	250HP 6LV22 railcar	Std	Entre Rios Rly
LD728	21.11.33	450HP Bo-Bo DE shunting + branch locomotive alternative	Std	SR
LD739	11.12.33	1,000HP 2-Co-2 DE locomotive to DT51	5ft 6in.	North Western Rly India
LD747	20.12.33	BXD DE railbus	2ft 0in.	Darjeeling-Himalayan Rly
LD761	15.02.34	BXD DE railbus	3ft 6in.	Tasmanian Govt Rlys
LD764	21.02.34	BLD DE railbus 72 seats	M	Malayan Rly
LD765	22.03.34	LTD19 DE railbus 40 seats	3ft 6in.	Tasmanian Govt Rlys
LD770	02.03.34	Bo-Bo battery shunting locomotive	Std	Exide Battery Co.
LD773	09.03.34	600HP 6LD28 Co-Co DE locomotive	M	Malayan Rlys
LD781	29.03.34	BoD 0-4-0 DE worm drive locomotive	3ft 0in.	Manchester Corporation
LD782	04.04.34	BLD bogie worm drive railbus 47 seats	Std	SR
LD787	13.04.34	BXD 0-4-0 DE 15 ton shunter	3ft 0in.	Singapore Aerodrome
LD789	13.04.34	Thornycroft engined DM inspection car	2ft 6in.	Baroda State Rly
LD790	19.04.34	2-Co-2+2-Co-2 DE passenger locomotive	Std	Roumanian State Rlys
LD798	03.05.34	2 x BLD 0-6-0 DE shunter	M	Gondal Rly
LD801	16.05.34	600HP Bo-Bo DE 6LD28 shunting locomotive	5ft 6in.	Tata Iron Co., India
LD824	01.06.34	2 x BXD B-B DE locomotive	M	Bombay Baroda + Central India Rly
LD835	19.06.34	800HP 8LD28 1-Co-1 DE locomotive DT23 type	5ft 3in.	Central Rly of Brazil
LD839	29.06.34	6LD25 DE power unit and four-coach semi-articulated train set	M	Leopoldina Rly
LD844	05.07.34	450HP Bo-Bo DE locomotive	5ft 3in.	Sao Paulo Rly
LD845	10.07.34	twin bogie battery shunting locomotive	Std	Exide Battery Co.
LD857	28.08.34	1,200HP 2-Do-1 DE		Sulzer Bros
LD896	05.02.35	600HP A1A-A1A DE mixed traffic locomotive	M	Malayan Rly
LD899	21.02.35	2 x BLD 25 ton 0-4-0 DE shunter	Std	Stock Order DT56
LD936	06.35	15-20 tons 0-4-0 DE shunter	5ft 6in.	Indian State Rly
LD944	02.07.35	6LTD22 DE three-coach train set	5ft 6in.	Ceylon Govt Rly
LD946	18.07.35	BoD 0-4-0 DE shunter DT61 type	3ft 6in.	New Zealand
LD948	20.07.35	LTD22 bogie DE branch line locomotive	Std	Egyptian State Rly
LD949	22.07.35	6LTD22 Bo-Bo DE shunter	M	Sorocabana Rly
LD950	23.07.35	6LTD22 Bo-Bo DE shunter	M	Sorocabana Rly for English Electric Co.
LD951	23.07.35	6LF19 0-6-0 DE locomotive	2ft 0in.	Darjeeling-Himalayan Rly
LD956	16.08.35	600HP A1A-A1A DE locomotive	Std	Central Uruguay Rly
LD960	22.08.35	Mechanical Parts 2-Do-1 electric locomotive	3ft 6in.	New Zealand Rlys
LD962	02.09.35	6LTD22 four car articulated train	5ft 6in.	Ceylon Govt Rly
LD1006	20.12.35	6LD25 DE three car train set	5ft 3in.	South Australian Rlys
LD1007	19.03.35	LTD19 DE railcar	M	Leopoldina Rly
LD1014	28.01.36	450HP 2-4-2 DE 6LD25 locomotive	5ft 6in.	Argentine Rlys
LD1018	01.02.36	450HP 0-4-4 DE branch line locomotive	5ft 6in.	Argentine Rlys
LD1020	17.02.36	LTD22 three car articulated train	Std	LMSR
LD1021	02.12.38	six wheel railcar bogie	3ft 6in.	Tasmanian Govt Rlys
LD1031	05.03.36	6LD25 Co-Co DE locomotive	Std	Trinidad Rlys
LD1044	20.03.34	1,700HP 2-Do-2 DE locomotive	5ft 6in.	Mechanical parts for Sulzer (Argentine Rlys)
LD1048	10.05.34	450HP bogie shunting locomotive	3ft 6in.	South African Rlys
LD1053	?	2-Bo-2 DE to BAGSR design	5ft 6in.	Buenos Aires Great Southern Rly
LD1060	?	LTD19 twin bogie locomotive	M	Iraq Rly
LD1081	05.11.36	BXD or BLD 0-4-0 DE shunter DT60 type	3ft 6in.	Table Bay Power Station
LD1082	23.11.36	6LDA28 1-Co-1 DE locomotive	5ft 6in.	Buenos Aires Great Southern Rly
LD1089	23.11.36	6LDA28 bogie DE locomotive	5ft 6in.	Buenos Aires Great Southern Rly

The Railway Correspondence & Travel Society is Britain's leading organisation for those interested in all aspects of railways past, present, and future. It is highly regarded by professional railway people and enthusiasts alike, a position it has held since its formation over 80 years ago.

A monthly journal, *The Railway Observer*, is sent to each member and, in addition, there are indoor meetings at 30 branches throughout the country as well as organized visits to installations of Railway interest. The RCTS has gained an enviable reputation for accurate and detailed railway literature. Full details about the Society, how to join as well as a list of current publications, is available at our comprehensive website – rcts.org.uk

QUALITY PUBLICATIONS FROM
BLACK DWARF LIGHTMOOR PUBLICATIONS LIMITED

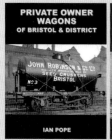

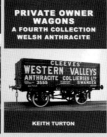
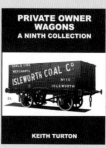

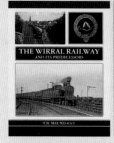

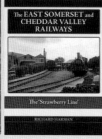
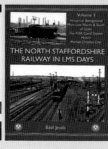
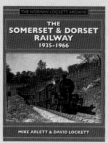

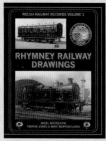

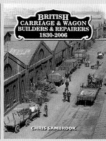

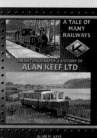

SEE ALL OUR TITLES AT: www.lightmoor.co.uk
also canal, maritime, industrial and Forest of Dean local history
120 Farmers Close, Witney, OX28 1NR
01993 773927